THE STATES AND THE NATION SERIES, of which this volume is a part, is designed to assist the American people in a serious look at the ideals they have espoused and the experiences they have undergone in the history of the nation. The content of every volume represents the scholarship, experience, and opinions of its author. The costs of writing and editing were met mainly by grants from the National Endowment for the Humanities, a federal agency. The project was administered by the American Association for State and Local History, a nonprofit learned society, working with an Editorial Board of distinguished editors, authors, and historians, whose names are listed below.

EDITORIAL ADVISORY BOARD

James Morton Smith, General Editor
Director, State Historical Society
of Wisconsin

William T. Alderson, Director
American Association for
State and Local History

Roscoe C. Born
Vice-Editor
The National Observer

Vernon Carstensen
Professor of History
University of Washington

Michael Kammen, Professor of
American History and Culture
Cornell University

Louis L. Tucker
President (1972–1974)
American Association for
State and Local History

Joan Paterson Kerr
Consulting Editor
American Heritage

Richard M. Ketchum
Editor and Author
Dorset, Vermont

A. Russell Mortensen
Assistant Director
National Park Service

Lawrence W. Towner
Director and Librarian
The Newberry Library

Richmond D. Williams
President (1974–1976)
American Association for
State and Local History

MANAGING EDITOR

Gerald George
American Association for
State and Local History

Kansas

A Bicentennial History

Kenneth S. Davis

W. W. Norton & Company, Inc.
New York

American Association for State and Local History
Nashville

Copyright © 1976
American Association for State and Local History
All rights reserved

Library of Congress Cataloging in Publication Data

Davis, Kenneth Sydney, 1912–
  Kansas : a bicentennial history.

  (The States and the Nation series)
  Bibliography: p. 219
  Includes index.
  1. Kansas—History. I. Title. II. Series.
F681.D37   978.1   76-21674
ISBN 0-393-05593-0

Published and distributed by
W. W. Norton & Co., Inc.
550 Fifth Avenue
New York, New York 10036

Printed in the United States of America

In Memory of
Lydia Ericson Davis and Charles D. Davis
My Mother and Father

Contents

Illustrations

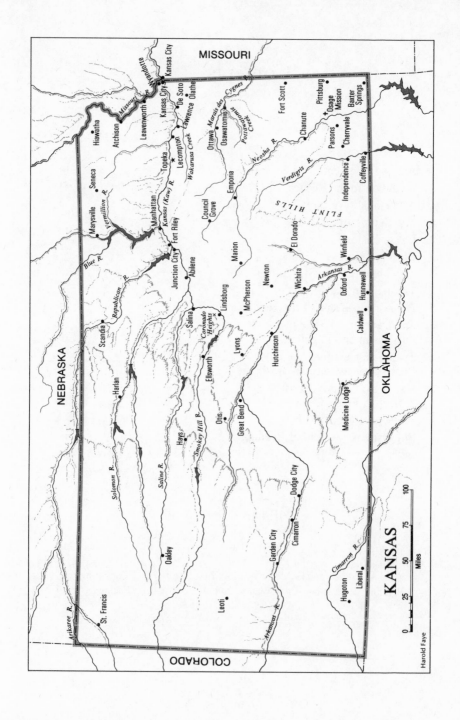

MISSOURI

NEBRASKA

COLORADO

OKLAHOMA

KANSAS

Kansas City
Wyandotte
De Soto
Olathe
Lawrence
Lecompton
Topeka
Leavenworth
Atchison
Hiawatha
Seneca
Marysville
Scandia
Harlan
Manhattan
Fort Riley
Junction City
Abilene
Salina
Coronado Heights
Ellsworth
Lindsborg
Lyons
Marion
McPherson
Newton
Wichita
El Dorado
Winfield
Oxford
Hunnewell
Caldwell
Medicine Lodge
Hutchinson
Great Bend
Otis
Hays
Oakley
Leoti
St. Francis
Garden City
Cimarron
Dodge City
Hugoton
Liberal

Council Grove
Emporia
Ottawa
Oswatomie
Fort Scott
Pittsburg
Osage Mission
Baxter Springs
Chanute
Parsons
Cherryvale
Coffeyville
Independence

FLINT HILLS

Missouri R.
Marais des Cygnes R.
Pottawatomie Creek
Neosha R.
Verdigris R.
Arkansas R.
Wakarusa Creek
Kansas (Kaw) R.
Vermillion R.
Blue R.
Republican R.
Solomon R.
Saline R.
Smokey Hill R.
Arkansas R.
Cimarron R.
Arikaree R.

Harold Faye

0   25   50   75   100
Miles

ACKNOWLEDGMENTS

Three institutions and fifteen individuals have contributed to such merit as this book may have.

At the American Antiquarian Society in Worcester, Massachusetts, was researched much of the material on Eli Thayer and the New England Emigrant Aid Company. The Kansas State Historical Society, in Topeka, not only lent me several hard-to-get books and other publications but also, through its highly professional staff, answered promptly, patiently, and with detailed accuracy my numerous specific questions. My greatest institutional debt is to Kansas State University, my alma mater, in Manhattan. Most of the actual writing was done in an Eisenhower Hall office on the KSU campus during the 1975 spring semester, when I had been named visiting professor of history.

Three KSU administrators—Dean William L. Stamey of the school of arts and sciences, Associate Dean William E. Carpenter of that school, and Joseph M. Hawes, head of the history department—are among the individuals whose help I here gratefully acknowledge. Homer E. Socolofsky, an outstanding authority on Kansas history, biographer of Arthur Capper, and currently (1976) president of the State Historical Society, actively aided my understanding of my native state as the work proceeded. So did William E. Koch of the KSU English department, an outstanding authority on Kansas folk lore and folk music.

Dr. Homer Socolofsky was among those who read the original draft of this work in manuscript and whose critiques and corrections of error have improved the work's quality. Others were of the staff of the Kansas State Historical Society: Nyle H. Miller, executive director; Edgar Langsdorf, deputy director; Robert W. Richmond, state archivist and author of *Kansas, Land of Contrasts;* Joseph W. Snell, curator, manuscript division; and Thomas A. Witty, archeologist. Two longtime personal friends, each a native Kansan who knows and loves the state well, also read and criticized: Mrs. Ellen Payne Paullin of

Newington, Connecticut, and Russell I. Thackrey of Washington, D.C.

I owe a special debt of gratitude to two other longtime personal friends, Earle Davis, professor emeritus and former head of English at KSU, and his wife, Kay. Dr. Davis (no relation of mine, as he publicly insists in self-protection) was instrumental in securing my visiting professorship; and in the Davis home I was repeatedly recreated and stimulated when the writing, which turned out to be more difficult than I expected, had worn me to a frazzle.

Finally, I wish here to thank the managing editor of this series, Gerald George, for his exercise on my behalf of an editorial competence considerably greater than I have commonly encountered in a now rather lengthy professional writing career. Mr. George, I am proud to say, is himself a native Kansan, and I like to believe that this fact has something to do with the conscientious industry and general ability he brings to his present job.

Kenneth S. Davis
Princeton, Mass.

April 1976

Invitation to the Reader

IN 1807, former President John Adams argued that a complete history of the American Revolution could not be written until the history of change in each state was known, because the principles of the Revolution were as various as the states that went through it. Two hundred years after the Declaration of Independence, the American nation has spread over a continent and beyond. The states have grown in number from thirteen to fifty. And democratic principles have been interpreted differently in every one of them.

We therefore invite you to consider that the history of your state may have more to do with the bicentennial review of the American Revolution than does the story of Bunker Hill or Valley Forge. The Revolution has continued as Americans extended liberty and democracy over a vast territory. John Adams was right: the states are part of that story, and the story is incomplete without an account of their diversity.

The Declaration of Independence stressed life, liberty, and the pursuit of happiness; accordingly, it shattered the notion of holding new territories in the subordinate status of colonies. The Northwest Ordinance of 1787 set forth a procedure for new states to enter the Union on an equal footing with the old. The Federal Constitution shortly confirmed this novel means of building a nation out of equal states. The step-by-step process through which territories have achieved self-government and national representation is among the most important of the Founding Fathers' legacies.

The method of state-making reconciled the ancient conflict between liberty and empire, resulting in what Thomas Jefferson called an empire for liberty. The system has worked and remains unaltered, despite enormous changes that have taken

xi

place in the nation. The country's extent and variety now surpass anything the patriots of '76 could likely have imagined. The United States has changed from an agrarian republic into a highly industrial and urban democracy, from a fledgling nation into a major world power. As Oliver Wendell Holmes remarked in 1920, the creators of the nation could not have seen completely how it and its constitution and its states would develop. Any meaningful review in the bicentennial era must consider what the country has become, as well as what it was.

The new nation of equal states took as its motto *E Pluribus Unum*—"out of many, one." But just as many peoples have become Americans without complete loss of ethnic and cultural identities, so have the states retained differences of character. Some have been superficial, expressed in stereotyped images—big, boastful Texas, "sophisticated" New York, "hillbilly" Arkansas. Other differences have been more real, sometimes instructively, sometimes amusingly; democracy has embraced Huey Long's Louisiana, bilingual New Mexico, unicameral Nebraska, and a Texas that once taxed fortunetellers and spawned politicians called "Woodpecker Republicans" and "Skunk Democrats." Some differences have been profound, as when South Carolina secessionists led other states out of the Union in opposition to abolitionists in Massachusetts and Ohio. The result was a bitter Civil War.

The Revolution's first shots may have sounded in Lexington and Concord; but fights over what democracy should mean and who should have independence have erupted from Pennsylvania's Gettysburg to the "Bleeding Kansas" of John Brown, from the Alamo in Texas to the Indian battles at Montana's Little Bighorn. Utah Mormons have known the strain of isolation; Hawaiians at Pearl Harbor, the terror of attack; Georgians during Sherman's march, the sadness of defeat and devastation. Each state's experience differs instructively; each adds understanding to the whole.

The purpose of this series of books is to make that kind of understanding accessible, in a way that will last in value far beyond the bicentennial fireworks. The series offers a volume on every state, plus the District of Columbia—fifty-one, in all.

Each book contains, besides the text, a view of the state through eyes other than the author's—a ''photographer's essay,'' in which a skilled photographer presents his own personal perceptions of the state's contemporary flavor.

We have asked authors not for comprehensive chronicles, nor for research monographs or new data for scholars. Bibliographies and footnotes are minimal. We have asked each author for a summing up—interpretive, sensitive, thoughtful, individual, even personal—of what seems significant about his or her state's history. What distinguishes it? What has mattered about it, to its own people and to the rest of the nation? What has it come to now?

To interpret the states in all their variety, we have sought a variety of backgrounds in authors themselves and have encouraged variety in the approaches they take. They have in common only these things: historical knowledge, writing skill, and strong personal feelings about a particular state. Each has wide latitude for the use of the short space. And if each succeeds, it will be by offering you, in your capacity as a *citizen* of a state *and* of a nation, stimulating insights to test against your own.

James Morton Smith
General Editor

Kansas

A Personal Overture:
Themes, Questions

*A*S every American historian and most literate Kansans know, Carl L. Becker opens his classic interpretative essay, "Kansas," with an account of his own first journey into the state—this in the summer of 1902. After a brief time on the faculty of Dartmouth he had accepted the post of assistant professor of history at the University of Kansas and was far from happy about it. He seems to have felt he was being exiled from green and civilized New England (he had not done well at Dartmouth) to a distant desert place: he speaks of a blankness tinged with commiseration in the expression of a New England friend when told of his imminent departure and confesses he himself "had always pictured [the state] as a land of grasshoppers, of arid drought, and barren social experimentation." [1]

Hence his puzzlement at the actions of one of the two college girls seated just ahead of him on the train that bore him up the valley of the Kaw during his first hour in the state. As the train moved west of the "dreary yards" of Kansas City, this girl abruptly broke off her theretofore "ceaseless chatter" with her companion to gaze fixedly and silently out the window for a long time. Then, turning back to her companion, she said with profound feeling, "Dear old Kansas!" Becker was astonished. The window-framed landscape seemed to him commonplace— and how could anyone regard as a beloved personality what he had always "supposed" to be "even more than Italy, only a geographical expression?" Nor could her attitude toward her home state be dismissed as a merely personal idiosyncrasy. Becker "not infrequently," in following months and years,

1. Carl L. Becker, *Everyman His Own Historian* (New York: F. S. Crofts and Co., 1935), p. 1.

3

"heard the same expression" repeated, with much the same feeling, by Kansans of widely various description. "Kansas," he finally concluded, in flat reversal of his original supposition, "is no mere geographical expression, but a 'state of mind,' a religion, and a philosophy in one."

In October 1974, the presidential address of the ninety-ninth meeting of the Kansas State Historical Society in Topeka was delivered by Dudley T. Cornish, professor of history and chairman of the history department at Kansas State College of Pittsburg. Entitled "Carl Becker's Kansas: The Power of Endurance," it was a review and critical analysis of Becker's essay in the light of Cornish's own experience of the state; and it recounted some remarkable parallels between Cornish's experience and Becker's across the half-century that separates them.

Like Becker, Cornish is no native Kansan: he was born and reared in a village in upstate New York not far from the university (Cornell) to which Becker was summoned in 1916, partly if not largely because of his "Kansas" essay. Like Becker, Cornish has encountered blank incomprehension on the part of easterners when told he is teaching in Kansas. And in the summer of 1957 he had an experience so similar to that of Becker in the summer of 1902 that it seemed almost an echo. He was homeward bound on a Greyhound bus in the company of "some thirty assorted Kansas school teachers" with whom he had made a three-week tour of "eleven Northeastern States and two Canadian provinces"—and as the southward rolling bus crossed the Kansas line into Decatur County, "suddenly, as with one mind and voice," the thirty teachers "burst into 'Home on the Range,' our very own authentic and official state song." Cornish noted "unashamed tears of joy on the singing faces." [2]

It was only a couple of weeks after Cornish delivered his presidential address, but some seventeen years after the bus ride he speaks of, that I myself rode southward from Nebraska into Kansas. It was on a bright chill morning in mid-November and I was driving down from Lincoln toward Manhattan and Topeka to begin an eight-day tour of the eastern third of the state in partial preparation for the writing of this volume.

2. Dudley T. Cornish, *Kansas Historical Quarterly* 16 (1975): 1.

Among the many differences between Becker or Cornish and me is the fact that I *am* a native Kansan, the son of native Kansans, and I grew to manhood in the state. Most of my years, however, have been lived far away from my native place. Moreover, it has been by my own free choice (or has it been by some deep necessity of the inward self?) that this is so—in view of which one might have expected only a modest measure of nostalgic emotion to invest this native's return to the scenes of his childhood. Instead, as I drove down through the northern Flint Hills into the valley of the Kaw, and as I myself more than half-expected, my sense of homecoming, of having returned to the vital center of my experience of life, became overwhelming. Nor did this tide of feeling recede as my tour continued. I could never have said "Dear old Kansas!" with a "contented sigh," as did Becker's college girl: with Kansas I have never been content, being always acutely aware of promises unfulfilled, opportunities unrealized. Neither could I ever have wept "unashamed tears of joy," as did Cornish's school teachers: my joy in the state has never been sufficiently pure, unqualified for that. But my sense of re-linkage with a particular vitally significant Space (a temporal Space) and Time (a spatial Time)—my sense of renewing acquaintance with a distinct *personality* about whom I deeply cared—was at least as strong as theirs. And as my tour continued, this sense, this generalized emotion, was increasingly permeated by those powerful ambivalences of pride-and-disgust, pleasure-and-exasperation, even passionate love-and-hate, which Kansas used to arouse or provoke in me when I lived within its borders.

All of which indicates that this state has an impact and hold upon the minds and hearts of its people that is quite remarkable, and of a quality which perhaps justified Becker's characterization of Kansas in 1910 as "a state of mind," a "philosophy," even a "religion." The native or longtime citizen of any state has for it, normally, a home feeling; and often this is emotionally ambivalent. But he does not normally have any truly vital commitment to the state *as* a state, does not look upon it as a unique cultural entity, and certainly does not personalize it and then respond to it as a personality attractive or repulsive, or both. He is generally inclined to look upon it as merely a geo-

graphic area that has been politically defined and within whose
bounds, thus defined, he happens to live. My wife, for instance,
was born and reared in northern Missouri. She confesses to a
mild nostalgia for her particular home area when we in our
travels pass nearby. But for Missouri itself she has no such
regard, pro or con, as I have for Kansas, pro *and* con—no such
regard as most born-and-bred Kansans she has met, in or out of
the state, have evinced—and she has often remarked with
puzzled wonderment upon this peculiar intensity of feeling which
Kansans have for Kansas. So have friends of ours, non-Kan-
sans, in the various places where we have lived. "I've never
met a Kansan anywhere whose heart wasn't buried in Kansas,"
said a friend of mine, a widely travelled executive of a large insurance company in Worcester, Massachusetts, when I tried to
explain to him why I am laying aside pressing work to which I
have long been committed in order to write this book. I myself
know of no other state, save Texas, whose citizens are as
strongly, intensely, personally identified with it as Kansans are
with Kansas.

Moreover, this has been true since very early in the state's
history. To the first issue of the old *Kansas Magazine,* in January 1872, John J. Ingalls contributed a sketch of Albert D.
Richardson, the newspaper correspondent who had "covered"
the Kansas territorial wars for Boston and Cincinnati papers.
Wrote Ingalls: "Kansas exercised the same fascination over him
that she does over all who have ever yielded to her spell. There
are some women whom to have loved renders it impossible ever
to love again." So with Kansas. The inhabitants of other states,
said Ingalls, "can remove and never desire to return. . . . But
no genuine Kansan can emigrate. . . . He may go elsewhere,
but no other state can claim him as a citizen. Once naturalized,
the allegiance can never be foresworn." And other Kansas
writers, down the years, have echoed and re-echoed Ingalls's
sentiments.

What *is* this hold that Kansas has over Kansans? How did it
develop? How, and *why,* has it varied in nature, in quality, over
the years?

1

The Setting of the Stage

I

*T*WO hundred years ago, this land, which would not become the physical body of the state of Kansas until four score and five more years had passed, remained pretty much the same as it had been ten thousand years before. A vast windswept slab of prairie whose size and shape were as yet undetermined, bearing upon its bosom no large body of water, no dependably navigable stream, no hill more than a few hundred feet high, it lay open and waiting (from our point of view) for event, under a sky whose horizons were almost as wide as those of the open seas. Here all landscape moods were dominated by the sky. Even where the land was heaped and rolled over lime- or sandstone undergirdings, three-fourths or more of any man's level view across it in any direction consisted of heavenly space and light with whatever cloud formations drifted over it; and even when the sky was closed off and lowering in gray glooms there remained for perceiving eyes a sense of high, far, lonely distances. There were few such eyes. This generally open prairie, this timeless land, was very sparsely inhabited in 1776 by a primitive and timeless people who, because they were few and possessed tools of limited environmental destructiveness, had left few marks upon it. Rarely had it been visited by white men. Save as an unknown quantity in the power-political calculations of distant capitals, a *terra incognita* of uncertain dimensions and a variously weighted value, it remained wholly outside history. We anticipate history, and dispense with the need to describe this land in past tense, when we ascribe to it a definite area (82,276 square miles) and the outline-shape of a parallelogram, perfect save for a bite taken out of its northeast corner by the Missouri River. Within the parallelogram are both the geographical center of the contiguous United States and, nearby, the geodetic datum of North America, the latter being the central point from which the mapping of the entire continent proceeds through radiating lines.

Such centrality, far from the moderating influence of any large body of water but directly in the line of air currents flowing north from the tropics, south from the arctic, makes for wide and swift fluctuations of temperature and an erratic temporal distribution of rainfall. Here come blazing heat and bitter cold; prolonged drouths with their dust storms, torrential rains with their floods; winds more constant and strong than prevail in most inland areas—temperamental winds that, in their irritability, utter tornadoes with notable and much noted frequency (witness the ''Kansas cyclone'' whereby Dorothy was whisked into the Land of Oz). Yet here too, paradoxically, come perfect days in greater frequency and number, year in and year out, than come to most parts of this nation, due in good part to long springs, long autumns—delightful seasons always. Even in the depth of winter, even at the height of summer, there are days springlike or autumnal, warm enough during the sunlit hours for thinly-clad people to lounge about out-of-doors but cool for easy sleep at night.

Within the general weather-pattern are regional differences resulting mostly from the fact that this immense prairie-slab, viewed horizontally, is tilted. With a width of 200 miles from north to south, during which its elevation above sea level remains about the same, it climbs a mountain's height as it reaches something over 400 miles from east to west. Its elevation is 700 feet in the southeast, 4,135 feet in the northwest—a difference of 3,435 feet. The increase in elevation coincides with a decrease in rainfall. Anyone travelling westwardly across the whole length of the land moves in steady progression from a generally well-watered country into a country where the annual rainfall, though highly variable, is of an average sufficiency for ordinary temperate zone agriculture; thence into a country where rainfall is little in any average year and becomes more so with each rising ten-mile until, at the land's western end, generally semi-arid conditions prevail. One moves, too, through three quite different kinds of landscape, regional landscapes, each coinciding with one of the three areas into which the whole may be equally divided, with rough accuracy, in climatic terms.

Of the well-watered *eastern* area, the predominant land-forms are those of stream and river floodplains, flat and fertile and varying in width from a mile or so to fifteen or twenty, bounded by lime-ridged hills rising quite steeply two to three hundred feet above the valley floor and bearing upon their crests a various width of rolling prairie. By 1776 the climactic prairie vegetation had for ages been that loveliest of grasses, bluestem (big bluestem, little bluestem), and the big bluestem then grew often tall enough in the valleys to hide a man walking upright or even, in large patches on wet years, a man on horseback. The virgin land in this eastern area also bore much timber, far more than did all the rest of the parallelogram. Indeed approximately two thousand square miles of the northeastern corner are designated on native flora maps as "oak-hickory forest," and streaks and patches of such forest are interspersed on such maps with a "mosaic of bluestem prairie and oak-hickory forest" for a hundred miles or more westward from the eastern border. Beyond this, westward, is a thirty- to forty-mile-wide band designated as pure "bluestem prairie." Here are the Flint Hills, originally so named because the natives had for eons gathered from them pieces of chert, commonly called flints, for use in all kinds of chipped stone tools, and as heads of spears and arrows. They are limestone hills whose rounded contours are periodically, rhythmically interrupted by stone ridge outcroppings forming step-terraces, and they are altogether treeless on their rolling crests save in the deepest hollows where a few cottonwoods and scrub oaks rise up in generally meager growth. They present to the traveller through them wide vistas of a surpassing wilderness beauty—a beauty that is the same now as it

was two hundred years ago, or five thousand—for those immense bluestem pastures remain virgin.

The *central* area of Kansas has, in its eastern portion, a landscape whose contours are much the same as those we have
described to the east but whose dominant summer tone is a somewhat paler green. The contours flatten out and the green grows
paler still (it becomes at last a yellow-green) as one moves
westward. The limestone undergirding of the eastern section
gives way to sandstone, some outcroppings of which have been
carved by wind erosion into fantastic monument shapes; the tall
bluestem thins out, begins to occur only in clumps here and
there, with the rest of the virgin soil being carpeted by ground-
hugging buffalo grass. Finally one enters a country where, in
1776, only short grass grew, and virtually no trees at all save on
the banks of wide and shallow streams, where were thickets of
stunted cottonwood. (Trees did not come into this area as a
common element of the landscape until the white man settled
here; they remain relatively few and small.) The traveller is then
well into the Great Plains proper and steadily climbing, with no
awareness of climbing (the land-surface is generally flat), onto
the immense tableland known as the High Plains.

The landscape of these High Plains is predominantly that of
the *western* third of our parallelogram. In 1776, before the soil
had been touched by the plow, when there were no wells sunk,
no trees planted, no farmsteads established, no towns built, no
fields irrigated, the scenic monotony and vast brooding solitudes
were greater than they are today. No visitor then from a homeland of hill and wood and lush green meadow, of deep-flowing
streams and frequent lakes, would have been likely to see here
anything but desolation, nor likely to deem remotely possible
any part of the human development that has in fact occurred.
And there are many today who, crossing this land as it now is,
in the fullest state of its development, yet see it as essentially a
desert place, an enormous windswept desolation in which there
is nothing to charm the eye, nor even any object for the eye to
rest upon. I have heard people wonder aloud how *anyone* can
bear to live amid such flatness, such monotony. "[O]n people
not born there the plains sometimes have an appalling effect,"

wrote painter John Noble, in 1927, near the end of a life he had begun on a Kansas ranch before plows had broken the plains. "You look on, on, on, out into space, out almost beyond time itself. You see nothing but the rise and swell of land and grass, and then more grass—the monotonous, endless prairie. A stranger travelling on the prairie would get his hopes up, expecting to see something different on making the next rise. To him the disappointment and monotony were terrible. 'He's got loneliness,' we would say of such a man." [1]

And this "loneliness" is somehow increased by the wind, which here blows constantly, or nearly so, and often with high velocity. Pioneer women found it hard to bear, cooped up as they commonly were in sod-walled shanties most of the time— much harder to bear than men did who labored all day long in the very teeth of it out of doors. Some would be driven literally mad by it. The constant physical pressure of the wind against their bodies whenever they went outside, rendering tangible a terror of immense empty space and harshly accentuating the solitude, the human loneliness of a plains farm; the ceaseless thrust of dust through every tiniest crack of door or window, every minuscule chink of sod-bricked wall, frustrating the most strenuous and unremitting efforts at cleanliness; above all, the endless and (for such women) nerve-rasping whispers and whines and shrieks around the edges and corners of obstacles to the flow of the wind—these fed neuroses that grew at last beyond the bounds of sanity. Such cases were rare, of course. Most of the people who settled here, women as well as men, would grow accustomed to the wind, adapting to it with no great psychological difficulty. And if fewer women than men did so—if women in general found the adjustment harder to make than men did—they also tended, once the adjustment was made, to be more defensive of their home environment when aspersions were cast upon it by "outsiders."

Like John Noble, like Kansas painter John Steuart Curry in a later year, they saw beauty here. It is an austere beauty com-

---

1. Quoted by Walter Prescott Webb, *The Great Plains* (Boston: Ginn and Co., 1931), p. 1; from an article by Noble in *American Magazine*, August, 1924, p. 44.

posed with a severely classical restraint and economy of the simplest materials. "I believe it taught me to understand the sea," said Noble, whose sea paintings brought him his greatest fame, after he had settled on the coast of France. And indeed the likening of this land to the sea—the wind-waved sea, or the sea utterly becalmed—is a simile that naturally and even inevitably occurs. A far country, high and pale and abstract, its landscapes are predominantly skyscape of which, earth or sky, the slightest defined detail assumes by its very rarity a large significance. Every variation becomes symbolic. A cloud, a rock, a slight roll of earth on the horizon rim, a solitary stunted tree standing at the edge of a shallow ravine—any of these can become the ordering principle of the whole of one's visible world, with meaningful overtones extending into the world unseen. The overwhelming sense conveyed is of distance per se, of empty space as a kind of ache of possibility—a longing for fulfillment, a yearning toward the *truly* actual and the *really* real. Gazing out across this land into the heavens, one does seem (as Noble said) to look out "beyond time itself" into the Eternal, and begins to understand why desert places with immense vistas have been the birthplace of the greatest religions.

II

In sum, though a contrary view has been widely spread abroad, this is a land of salubrious climate, bathed by an air and radiant energy that are good to the feeling, the tactile perceptions, of men's bodies. It is also a land good to see through men's eyes, and was seen as good by the few thousand primitive timeless people who inhabited it in 1776. They were a people acutely sensitive to landscape beauties—a people who in fact identified the aesthetic with the religious by making shrines (sacred springs, sacred hills, sacred woods) of places having particular natural beauty. They believed that the Great Spirit dwelt in such places more intensely, or camped there more often, than elsewhere.

They were divided among five principal tribes. Near and north of the confluence of the Kansas and Missouri rivers were the Indians who gave the former river its name (it had been named the "Great River of Canzes" on a famous French map [Delisle's] in 1718)—the Kansa, or Kaw. They were a small tribe; only 1,606 of them would be counted when a census was made in 1835. Due south of them was the far more extensive country of the far more numerous Osage. Both tribes were newcomers here in 1776, having moved from the east, and they were much alike in language and custom (both were of the Siouan linguistic stock). They lived in permanent villages surrounded by fields or, more precisely, gardens worked by women with tools too crude to permit any wide or deep cultivation— and the vegetable diet supplied by these was supplemented by nuts and fruits and berries gathered in woods and thickets. Meat was supplied by the immediately surrounding woods and grassland, for these abounded in game, most of it edible, including deer, elk, antelope, bear, rabbit, grouse, prairie chicken, wild turkey.

But the primary meat supply for these two tribes, as well as for all the other Indians of prairie and plain, was the buffalo. Small groups of these big lumbering "hump-backed cattle" (so they were dubbed by the first white men to see them) roamed the grassy portions of the Kansa-Osage homeland. The really huge herds, however, numbering often in the tens of thousands, grazed several days' journey to the west. Each of the two tribes therefore organized extended buffalo-hunting expeditions into the west every year to obtain not only meat but also hides and bone wherewith to fashion clothing, sleeping robes, tools, cooking utensils, sheltering walls. Their westward hunting was a chief provocation of hostilities between them and their (by 1776) long-traditional enemies, the Pawnee, who could and did regard the Kansa-Osage expeditions as invasions of *their* hunting ground.

For the Pawnee home country ranged southward from what was already known in 1776 as the Platte (La Platte) River into the valleys of the Republican, the Solomon, the Smoky Hill (none yet so named) and on down toward the Great Bend of the Arkansas—which is to say that the Pawnee claimed as their own all the north central position, and more, of the Kansas parallelo-

gram. Their language was wholly unlike that of the Kansa-
Osage, and they were a far more numerous and powerful tribe,
numbering some twenty-five thousand in a "nation" of wide
boundaries only a small part of which lay that year in what was
to become the state of Kansas. South of the Pawnee—east and
south of the Great Bend, in the Arkansas River Basin—were the
Wichita, a smaller and weaker tribe whose center of tribal government in 1776 may well have been a village in what is now
Oklahoma. For like the Kansa and Osage, the Pawnee and Wichita were a farming as well as a hunting people, living in fixed
villages. Like the Kansa-Osage, their languages were similar,
stemming from a common stock (the Caddoan). And like the
Kansa-Osage they were on generally friendly terms with each
other, though so much land seems to have intervened between
them that they had little intercourse.

Into this intervening land had come, by 1776, mobile groups
of the tribe that dominated the plains to the west—the nomadic
tepee-dwelling Comanche. A century before they had been a
mountain tribe, their home area the eastern Rockies in what is
now Wyoming. The perpetual buffalo-hunt whereby they lived
(their staple diet was buffalo meat, supplemented by such nuts,
berries, fruits as could be gathered; they planted no garden-
fields) had seldom if ever brought them across the plains as far
as what is now western Kansas. For they then travelled afoot,
with their loaded travois drawn by dogs. But by the early eighteenth century the Comanche had developed a horse culture par
excellence. The men were mounted warriors and hunters who
spent nearly all their waking hours on horseback. Their women
now drove horses between the shafts of travois as they moved
from one campsite of a few weeks to another. And their
marches were now far longer than before: having abandoned
their former mountain homeland, they roamed and claimed as
their own hunting ground the whole of the southern High Plains,
including what would become western Kansas and Oklahoma,
northern Texas, and eastern Colorado, displacing from the
Kansas area Apache groups who had been there, probably, since
1500.

The Comanche were a much more savage tribe, of greater ferocity, cruelty, and implacability—and they would become a much more formidable obstacle to the white man's penetration of their territory, hence of greater importance to Kansas history—than any of the tribes to the east of them. Compared with them, even the warlike Pawnee would come to seem relatively civilized and accommodating.

In 1776, when all of what is now Kansas was nominally a Spanish possession, integral to New Spain, the Comanche were a principal reason why the Spaniards' claim remained merely nominal and the country little better known to them than it had been two-and-a-quarter centuries before. To reach any part of our parallelogram by any direct route from the farthest advanced of Spanish settlements to the southwest, it was necessary to cross the Great Plains—the country of the fiercely hostile Comanche. To subdue the Comanche, if not altogether beyond the power of the Spaniards at a distance so great from their power centers, would have cost far more in blood and treasure than they were prepared to spend.

And there was, in this, a historical irony insofar as it was the horse that made the Comanche formidable. For though the horse originally evolved on the North American plains, whence it migrated to Asia across the northern land bridge that once joined the two continents, no horse had been seen here for some sixty-five hundred years before a Spanish expedition rode out of the southwest across the Great Plains in 1541.

III

The captain-general of this expedition was a young man named Francisco Vasquez de Coronado. In 1540 he led northward out of the western Mexico province of Nuevo Galicia more than three hundred Spanish soldiers, of whom two hundred and fifty were mounted, accompanied by several hundred Indians. In quest of the fabulously wealthy Seven Cities of Cibola, the expedition travelled through what is now Arizona and eastward into what is now New Mexico. By summer's end, disappointed and angry, the treasure-seekers knew the Seven Cities to be a myth. The reality was a scattering of

Zuni pueblos, none of which possessed any treasure more valuable than a few pieces of turquoise. But as the expedition wintered (1540–1541) in a pueblo of the Tigua Indians on the upper
reaches of the Rio Grande, they encountered another tale of fab-
ulous wealth, spun for their gullible ears by a myth-maker of
rare genius. Dubbed "The Turk" (El Turco) by the Spaniards
because to them he looked like one, he was the slave captive of
a Tigua warrior. His native land was a country called Harahay,
probably lying in what is now Nebraska, beyond a distant land
called Quivira, which we know to have been in what is now
Kansas. He had a natural desire to escape captivity and return to
his homeland. And so he told in great circumstantial detail of
the great cities of Quivira, far across the pastures of the buffalo
(of these Coronado had already heard; one of his exploring parties had actually seen some of them), where immense treasures
of gold and silver and precious stones could be had for the taking. He offered himself as guide. His offer was accepted.

And so, in the spring of 1541, Coronado set out for Quivira,
moving eastward to the border of what is now the Texas Pan-
handle. There he was deliberately misled to the southeast by
The Turk, who later confessed his intention to lose the Spaniards forever in a timberless, waterless land; and he might well
have done so had there not been taken along as a second guide
one Ypsopete, a Quivira native who had also become a slave-
captive of the Tigua and who, hating The Turk, now passionately denounced him as a liar. The Turk was clamped in irons.
Coronado then sent back most of his party and, with forty men
travelling "by the needle" (his magnetic compass), moved due
north, entering the Kansas parallelogram near, if not precisely,
where the town of Liberal now stands. He continued generally
north until, as one of his chroniclers wrote, "on Saint Peter and
Paul's Day [June 29, 1541] we reached the river [the Arkan-
sas]. . . . We crossed it there and went up the other side on the
north, the direction being toward the northeast, and after marching three days we found [July 2] some Indians who were going
hunting." They were Quivira [Wichita] Indians to whom Ypsopete spoke in his and their tongue. The expedition went on to
the northeast, having passed the Great Bend of the Arkansas,
into Quivira country where The Turk was strangled and Yp-

sopete set free and where Coronado spent twenty-five days in exploration. It was now obvious that the tales of Quiviran wealth were also fabrications: in none of the several villages they visited, some with as many as two hundred grass houses, were there any precious metals or stones; but Coronado was greatly impressed by the country's agricultural possibilities. It is highly probable that, one day in July or early August 1541, he looked out over this fertile land from a hill that now bears his name, Coronado Heights, a couple of miles north of what is now the town of Lindsborg. In August he began his return journey. He reached Mexico in 1542.

Not all of his expeditionary force went back with him. From the Rio Grande, where Coronado again wintered, Fray Juan de Padilla, a Franciscan priest, outfitted by Coronado and accompanied by a small party, returned to Quivira as a Christian missionary. Legend has it that he was much loved by the Quivirans, whom he Christianized, but that when he attempted to move farther on, in the country of the Guas (Kaw? Kansa?), whom the Quivirans hated, he was "slain with many arrows" by Quivirans who would thus deny to their enemies the blessing of Christianity. Certain it is that he was slain somewhere in what is now central or east-central Kansas, and probably in 1542, though it may have been a year or two later—the first Christian martyr in all mid-America.

But of this earliest exploration there was scarcely a memory within our parallelogram in 1776. There was even less of a second Spanish expedition, that of Juan de Onate in 1601. He, like Coronado, was immensely impressed by the fertility of the Quiviran soil, but he made no new explorations and established neither colonies nor trading posts. The chief effect of his journey would seem to have been the confirmation of Coronado's view that this distant land had potential value for Spain, and to encourage the founding of the town of Santa Fe a few years afterward, to serve as capital and trading center for Spain's northernmost possessions in the American interior. Thereafter, for more than a century and a half, there was no contact between the Spaniards and the village Indians whom Coronado had discovered.

But the Spaniards had left horses, strayed or stolen, which

swiftly multiplied in so favorable a habitat and revolutionized
the Indian way of life. Two generations and more of Indians on
prairie and plain, including village tribes well to the east and
north of the farthest Spanish penetration, had possessed horses
by 1776.

Considerably greater than the human impact of the Spaniards
upon the Kansas land, though still slight, had been (by 1776)
the impact of French explorers and fur traders. They began to
come down from Canada along the Mississippi in the late seventeenth century; they came up the Missouri in the first years of
the eighteenth. They made friends and allies of the Kansa and
Osage, established transient trading posts, took (several of the
traders did) Indian wives and had families of half-breed children. In 1724, a French officer, Etienne Veniard de Bourgmont,
organized expeditions which went far up the Kansas and Smoky
Hill rivers, and some distance up the Saline (his report mentions
that river's brackish waters). Fifteen years later, the brothers
Paul and Pierre Mallet, bent on opening trade with the Spanish
settlements, became the first white men (so far as is known) to
travel overland from trading posts on the Missouri to Santa Fe.
They went by a circuitous route. They had reached the Platte (it
was they who named this river) before they realized that they
had gone much too far up the Missouri. They then turned
sharply to the south and west, striking down across the Kansas
River basin to the Arkansas.

Quite possibly the Mallets crossed the latter river at the ford
where Coronado had crossed two centuries before, for they
found on the riverbank stones bearing Spanish inscriptions. The
event is, at any rate, symbolic of the conflicting claims made by
European sovereigns, through most of the eighteenth century, to
this virtually unknown land.

Spain claimed it by right of discovery. France claimed it as
part of Louisiana, by right of much more extensive explorations
than the Spaniards had made. The French might also claim possession of the river-nibbled northeast portion by right of actual
occupation for twenty years after 1744, when a small log fort,
Fort de Cavagnial, was established as a fur-trading post on the
west bank of the Missouri near the main Kansa village. The fort

was abandoned in 1764, a couple of years after France by secret treaty had ceded all of Louisiana Territory west of the Mississippi to Spain, her ally in the Seven Years' (French and Indian) War. This cession was confirmed by the Treaty of Paris, February 10, 1763, whereby all other French possessions on the continent were transferred to the British. Canada became British; the huge Missouri valley became Spanish. And none of this had had the slightest real practical effect in what yet remained, in 1776, an open land of Indians and buffalo and sweeps of virgin pasture reaching for hundreds of miles in every direction under the enormous sky.

2

Enter, History

I

*T*HE historic circumstances of Kansas's initial definition as a political entity may be traced back to two symbolic events occurring within fifteen months and six hundred miles of one another early in the seventeenth century. One was the landing of the first Negro slaves on the American mainland, at Jamestown in August 1619; the other, the landing of the Pilgrims at Plymouth Rock in December 1620.

The two events have long been linked with ironic significance in my mind by the fact that this first slave ship to Virginia happened to be a *Dutch* privateer. For Holland was then the mother of freedom in Europe. At the very moment this slave-trading Dutchman turned his ship into the James estuary, the band of Separatists who had fled England in order to worship as they chose, in Leyden, prepared a voyage of their own to Virginia— the voyage that ended instead, next year, with the signing of the Mayflower Compact and the establishment of Plymouth Plantation. It was to Holland that John Locke fled from England some sixty years later, when threatened with political persecution, there to complete during his years of exile an *Essay Concerning Human Understanding,* a *Letter Concerning Toleration,* and *Two Treatises on Government.* All three books were published within two years after he was welcomed back to England, following the Glorious Revolution of 1688—and from the second of the two *Treatises* Thomas Jefferson drew that doctrine of natural rights to which he gave such fervent expression in the Declaration of Independence. By 1776, of course, Voltaire had hurled a hundred flaming lances of mind against the twin tyrannies of Church and Crown; Rousseau had issued his *Social Contract* and, with *La Nouvelle Heloise,* had initiated the Romantic Movement which yet sweeps (now weak, now strong) across the Western world toward incalculable ends. To the logic of freedom had been added a passion for liberty.

Here, then, are two major strands of history—a dark strand of brutal economics, sustained by the social attitudes of Medieval feudalism; a light strand of democratic ideas, sustained by the moral logic of the Golden Rule. We who look back upon the woven pattern of accomplished Time can see how the two strands meet, converge in 1787 at the Constitutional Convention in Philadelphia, and we see this convergence as a moment of crucial decision. Surely the black strand must here come to an end, or to the beginning of its end in America; surely the strand of light will run on broader and stronger than before! The essential "logic of the situation," the whole tendency of the age, demands that this happen. But, alas, it doesn't. Instead the two strands are intertwined, each weakening the other, and a fatal flaw is woven into the fabric of the Republic.

This flaw is tragically clear to hindsight. To the foresight of the men who wove the fabric, however, and were themselves woven into it—to the foresight of the very *best* of these men—little or nothing of the sort appeared. Nearly all of them were men of high social and financial standing (no dirt farmers, no artisans or mechanics, were seated in Independence Hall)—men of conservative mind and temper. To most of them slavery was morally repugnant, if less so than it was to the more liberal minds (Tom Paine's, for instance) of their time. But they anticipated its disappearance, for reasons of economy, before long. They saw slaves as fixed charges upon a land that every year yielded less tobacco as soil fertility declined: slavery was becoming unprofitable in Virginia. Farther south, where the climate opposed tobacco culture, rice and indigo were grown with but indifferent success, and only on the sea islands could the easily cleaned, long-staple cotton be grown successfully: in the Deep South, also, slavery showed itself increasingly unprofitable. Thus slavery appeared in process of extinction by the "natural course of event," and in a meeting necessarily presided over by compromise it was therefore dealt with as if it were but another problem of opposing economic pressures, soluble through shrewd arrangements for a balance of power. It was written into those portions of the Constitution having to do with the apportionment of congressional representation, the assessment of direct taxes, and the recovery of slaves escaped into free states.

But the "natural course of event" included unforeseen technological developments. Within a half-dozen years after the Constitutional Convention, Eli Whitney invented the cotton gin, wherewith fibers could be efficiently cleaned from the only cotton variety (the short staple) that could be widely grown in the South. Abruptly, cotton became King. Simultaneously and consequently, there was an immense strengthening of the slave system which, if not profitable to the South as a whole, certainly became profitable for that class of southerner who wielded political power. Cotton culture required a steady supply of primitive hand-labor; only the Negro slave could provide it on a sufficient scale, according to southern planters; and the breeding of slaves as well as the illegal importation of them became steadily more profitable as the price of field hands steadily rose. Inevitably there was a growing pressure for legalized reopening of the African slave trade.

Nor was this the only contribution Whitney made to the frustration of that "natural progress" envisaged by the practical compromisers of 1787. In 1798 he contracted to supply ten thousand muskets to the United States Government within the unheard-of period of two years. He proposed to do so by substituting correct and effective operations of machinery for that "skill of the artist which is acquired only by long experience," and this is what he did in the armory he established, in Whitneyville, adjacent New Haven. By 1801, he had made, taken all-in-all, his greatest invention, namely the system of manufacturing standardized interchangeable parts through a division of labor and the use of precision tools. The consequences were quite as revolutionary as those produced by the cotton gin; they were of even greater permanent importance.

For one thing, Whitney's mass production technique served to widen the social and cultural gulf between North and South, for it was only in the North that his system of manufacture was widely adopted; it was only there, too, that antislavery sentiments grew and coalesced into a major political force. In the South, thanks largely to Whitney's earlier invention, the whole economy centered on King Cotton, and there antislavery, once a growing movement, was ruthlessly, totally suppressed by.censorship and violence. On millions of acres of wasting soil the one crop was grown by unskilled and unrequited labor while an elite class of arrogant indolent men—men afraid to face the ugly realities of their "Peculiar Institution," with its flat contradictions of the main ideas of Declaration and Constitution—cultivated elaborate social manners, an almost hysterical love of dangerous sport, an emptily formal intellectual life, a genius for endlessly quibbling legal sophistry, a rhetoric whose lush density was designed to obscure rather than reveal facts or truths, and, above all, the "habit of command." These planter rulers of the Old South also cultivated politics with a far greater assiduity than did the northern elite in general. Virtually every one of them had politics as a major preoccupation or avocation. They therefore exerted over Congress and the executive a power increasingly disproportionate to their number or economic weight, being aided in this by the inequities that compromise had written into the Constitution.

II

And practical compromise continued to preside over the slavery issue as the nation expanded. The land that would become Kansas began to be involved when the Louisiana Purchase was made in 1803.

Jefferson ordered an exploring expedition to assess the value and extent of the enormous real estate (it abruptly doubled the physical size of the United States) that was being acquired. Meriwether Lewis and William Clark, with forty-three men, left

Saint Louis on May 14, 1804, under orders to explore the Missouri River to its source and go on into the Pacific Northwest. They arrived at the confluence of the Kansas and the Missouri on June 26. They camped now on one side of the Missouri, now on the other, for several days thereafter while gathering mapping data and considerable information about the fur trade between the French and the Kansa Indians.

A second major exploring expedition, that of Lt. Zebulon M. Pike of the U.S. Army, was sent out from Saint Louis in 1806 by the ineffable Gen. James Wilkinson, governor of the Louisiana Territory, who is remembered in history chiefly for his double-dealing involvement in the western empire schemes of Aaron Burr. The Pike expedition may well have been intended by Wilkinson to implement the Burr conspiracy or even more dubious schemes of his own. Its one notable contribution to political history, at any rate, was its forceful assertion, against Spain, of United States sovereignty over the country of the Pawnee, the southwestern boundaries of Louisiana being as yet a matter of dispute between the two powers.

A third major exploring expedition, commanded by Maj. Stephen H. Long, in 1819 and 1820, included trained scientific observers. Its principal explorations of the Kansas land were made, not by Long himself, but by detachments from the expedition's main body—notably a party headed by Thomas Say, a zoologist, in 1819.

Neither Pike nor Long saw much economic value in the land extending west from the one hundredth meridian to the Rockies. "In that vast country . . . we find the soil generally dry and sandy, with gravel . . . ," wrote Pike, with an inaccuracy that suggests he may have travelled much of the time during the driest months of a drouth year in the wide shallow beds of streams that had disappeared. He went on to predict that "these vast plains . . . may become in time as celebrated as the sandy deserts of Africa," and for the same reason. Only slightly less favorable was Long's conclusion regarding the area including what would become western Kansas. "In regard to this extensive section of the country," said he, "I do not hesitate in giving the opinion, that it is almost wholly unfit for cultivation, and of course uninhabitable by a people depending on agricul-

ture for their subsistence. Although tracts of fertile land considerably extensive are occasionally to be met with, yet the scarcity
of wood and water, almost uniformly prevalent, will prove an
insuperable obstacle in the way of settling the country. . . ."
Long later published a map of the area he had explored: on it,
the bulk of the Great Plains, including what is now western
Kansas, bore the damning label, "Great American Desert." But
Long, like Pike, believed this geographic circumstance to be
fortunate for the Republic. "[F]rom these immense [desert]
prairies may arise one great advantage to the United States,"
Pike had written, "viz: the restriction of our population to some
certain limits and thereby a continuation of the Union. Our citizens being so prone to rambling and extending themselves on
the frontiers will, through necessity, be constrained to limit their
extent on the west to the borders of the Missouri and Mississippi, while they leave the prairies . . . to the wandering and
uncivilized aborigines of the country." Long wrote, in echo:
"This region [though desolate] . . . may prove of infinite importance to the United States, inasmuch as it is calculated to
serve as a barrier to prevent too great an extension of our population westward. . . ." [1]

And, indeed, by the time Long wrote the above-quoted
words, westward expansion *was* beginning to strain the bonds of
Union. The prospect of unlimited further expansion was dismaying, even terrifying, to those who, like Daniel Webster,
were passionately committed to the Union's preservation.
(Some of Webster's most sonorous rhetoric was devoted to a denial that the prospect existed: the West, said he, must forever
remain a howling wilderness.) But the cause of this strain and
fear was not the one suggested by Long and Pike—was not that
the scattering of a "rambling" people across great distances
was rendering impossible a unifying communication among
them. The cause, instead, was of the essence of the historic process of contradiction which began when the first slave ship ar-

1. Zebulon M. Pike, *The Journals of Zebulon Montgomery Pike With Letters and Related Documents,* ed. Donald Jackson, 2 vols. (Norman, Okla.: University of Oklahoma Press, 1966). Edwin James, *An Account of an Expedition From Pittsburgh to the Rocky Mountains Performed in the Years 1819 and 1820.* 2 vols. Facsimile of 1823 edition (Westport, Conn.: Greenwood Press, Inc., 1968).

rived at Jamestown and the *Mayflower* arrived at Plymouth.

For within a decade and a half after the Louisiana Purchase, the real estate thus acquired was providing the stuff of dangerous quarrel between the slave South and the free North. The territory of Orleans was admitted to the Union as Louisiana, a slave state, in 1812. Alabama was admitted as a slave state in December 1819. There were then in the union eleven free states and eleven slave—a precise balance of representation between North and South in the U.S. Senate. There was also a balance of sectional power, if a more precarious one, elsewhere in the government: the North's decisive majority in the lower house was offset by the South's greater influence over the executive. But Missouri's application for statehood was then pending, and its admission either slave or free would upset the balance: one side or the other of the slavery issue, which meant one section of the nation or the other, North or South, must gain a decisive political advantage. Hence the quarrel. Acrimonious debate interrupted the "Era of Good Feelings" for many months—until politicians whose primary aim was to preserve the Union, and who subordinated to this aim the stated purposes for forming the Union in the first place, exerted the kind of practical wisdom which had operated during the Constitutional Convention. The result was the Compromise of 1820, which admitted Missouri as a slave state and implied the future admission of Arkansas as a slave state but prohibited *forever* (this was expressly stated) the extension of slavery into any other portion of the Louisiana Purchase north of 36°30′.

This Missouri Compromise was generally regarded throughout the North as a sacred compact, virtually an extension of the Constitution itself. Three new slave states had been carved out of the purchase, but into none of the rest of that vast area, save the relatively small portion due west of Arkansas, could slavery ever penetrate. When this area, shown on maps as "unorganized Indian Territory," was settled and divided into states, as Manifest Destiny decreed, the North was assured (in Lincoln's phrase) of the political power necessary to place slavery "in the course of ultimate extinction."

But then came the Texas Annexation (1845), the Oregon Treaty (1846), the Mexican War (1846–1848), whereby a greater area than that of the purchase was acquired by the United States. The Republic now reached from sea to shining sea; and annexation of Texas meant of course its admission as a slave state. On the other hand, California, where American settlers had for years been agitating for independence from Mexico and for a union with the United States, adopted an antislavery constitution and petitioned for admission in 1849, the year in which the Gold Rush vastly accelerated California's settlement. Oregon, into whose Willamette Valley immigrants from the Mississippi Valley frontier had begun to pour by the thousands over the Oregon Trail in 1843, was designated a legal territory in 1848. It must soon enter the Union as a free state.

By now a great and ominous change had come over the mind and temper of both North and South. Formerly the generally prevailing Southern attitude had been that slavery was a regrettable necessity; now leading spokesmen for the South, or for the great planters who ruled the South, proclaimed slavery a positive good whose blessings should be limitlessly extended, and threatened secession if the territories were not opened to slavery. Formerly the generally prevailing attitude in the North had been that the evils inherent in the slave system would so weaken it that it would ultimately collapse of its own weight, provided it were confined to the areas where it already existed; now leading abolitionists loudly questioned the value of Union with slaveholders while even moderate and conservative Northerners hardened themselves against a Cotton Kingdom that steadily and swiftly expanded, a slave power increasingly powerful, arrogant, and ruthless in its aggressions. (Had not the Mexican War been a war of conquest, utterly devoid of moral justification, fomented by Southerners? Antislavery Northerners believed so.)

And so the soothing plaster applied in 1820 to sore differences between the sections began to crack badly while the sandy foundations of the Missouri Compromise began to shift and crumble.

Whereupon there rose up again the Great Pacificator, Henry Clay of Kentucky, chief architect of the Compromise of 1820. He managed now to shape a much more complicated, dubious, and flimsy an accommodation in a five-part Omnibus Bill and to gain support enough for it to achieve its passage as the Compromise of 1850. California was admitted as a free state; New Mexico and Utah territories were organized, with no provision for either the exclusion or introduction of slavery; a portion of what had been Texas was transferred to New Mexico, for which Texas was compensated by the U.S. Government's assumption of its state debt; and the slave trade was excluded from the District of Columbia. None of this, though heatedly debated in Congress, provoked deep widespread passions on either side of the Mason-Dixon line. There was appended to it, however, at the South's insistence, a greatly strengthened Fugitive Slave Act which required officials and citizens of free states to aid in capturing and restoring to their owners fugitive slaves, on pain of harsh penalties; which made it a federal crime to aid the escape of a slave; which provided no adequate safeguards against the kidnapping of free blacks by slave hunters working for bounties; and which, in toto, seemed to Northerners an invasion of free soil by some of the worst features of the slave system. It aroused passionate protest. It provoked violent resistance when efforts were made to enforce it in Pennsylvania, New York, Massachusetts. And it stimulated Harriet Beecher Stowe's writing of *Uncle Tom's Cabin,* whose immediate enormous readership on both sides of the Atlantic, following its publication in 1853, doomed any further attempt to deal with American slavery, politically, as if it were an issue of economic interests only and not an issue of moral right and wrong.

III

Meanwhile, the Kansas soil was being prepared for history's onslaught.

At about the time the first atlas was published containing Long's map-designation of the Great American Desert—that is, in the early 1820s—the Reverend Isaac McCoy, Baptist minister and teacher, who had worked among the Miami in Indiana and among the Pottawatomie in Michigan, and whose concern for Indian welfare was deep and genuine, conceived the idea of removing the tribes from east of the Mississippi into the open West where they could become Christian farmers of their own land (missionaries would Christianize them, civilize them) and eventually establish a state of their own. Only thus, as he saw it, could the red man, in his present stage of development, be protected against the white man's cupidity and generally demoralizing, disintegrative influences. The idea quickly caught on, for various obvious reasons, with men of power whose concern for the Indian's well-being was minimal. In June 1825, the necessary treaties were negotiated between the federal government and the Kansa and Osage tribes for a cession of Kansa-Osage land onto which eastern Indians could be moved. In May 1830, an "Act to provide for an exchange of lands with the Indians residing within any of the states or territories, and for their removal west of the river Mississippi" was passed by Congress and signed by President Andrew Jackson. The Indians who were to be removed were assured by the most solemn of treaty oaths that the land to which they journeyed, having been surveyed and its boundaries precisely established, was reserved to them and their posterity in perpetuity. The removal began.

Among the emigrant Indians who thus came into what is now eastern Kansas, and placed their names upon the Kansas land, were the Shawnee, the Delaware, the Chippewa, the Wyandot, the Pottawatomie, the Miami, the Kickapoo, the Ottawa, and a small number of Fox, Sac, and Iowa. With them, or to them in their new homes, came the missionaries.

Isaac McCoy was instrumental in founding the Shawnee Baptist Mission opened by Johnston Lykins in July 1831. It was located a few miles south and west of the Kansas River mouth in what is now Johnson County, and to it in 1833 came Jotham Meeker, bringing with him the first printing press to be set up on Kansas soil. Meeker printed on his press the Scriptures, hymnals, even a newspaper, the *Shawnee Sun* (*Siwinowe Kesibwi*), in the language of the Shawnee—a language that had been phonetically transcribed into alphabetical terms and taught the Indians. Other missions to other tribes were opened by the Baptists, the Friends (Quakers), the Presbyterians, the Jesuit order of the Roman Catholics.

But the largest and historically most important of all the Kansas missions was the Shawnee Methodist, opened as a school by the Reverend Thomas Johnson and his wife in 1829, on the site of present-day Turner (part of Greater Kansas City), and relocated in 1839 on a 2,240-acre grant some two miles southwest of Westport, Missouri (also now smothered by Kansas City), in what became Kansas's Johnson County. Here was established a large diversified farming enterprise, including a twelve-acre apple orchard, the first on Kansas soil. Here labored black men and women in bondage, also the first on Kansas soil (and illegally there by the terms of the Missouri Compromise), for the Reverend Mr. Johnson was a slaveholder, a strong political supporter of the Peculiar Institution, whose Negroes performed the mission's menial tasks. And here, during the following decade and a half, hundreds of Indian boys and girls from ten tribes were taught English, religion, farming, and various manual and household skills.

It cannot be said with truth, however, that this mission or the missionaries in general contributed as greatly to the Indian's temporary elevation as they did to his ultimate downfall in Kansas. Many of the missionary families who came to Kansas stayed. They conveyed to those who remained "back home" information about the fertility and overall attractiveness of this new country as a land for living and so became as magnets drawing white settlers toward what was legally Indian country. Several of them engaged in land speculations of their own, having obtained title to reserved lands through transactions that accorded far more closely with business ethics than with the Golden Rule. Thus, here as elsewhere, the agents of Christianity were also the agents of empire, exploitation, and the destruction of native cultures.

In some part they operated toward this end through services to travellers on the great westward trails that opened up when the earliest missions were established. The Shawnee Methodist Mission, for instance, became a famous stopping place for travellers on both the Oregon and Santa Fe trails, for the two trails shared the same route passing within a few yards of the main buildings. The Saint Mary's Mission, at what is now the town of Saint Marys, similarly served travellers over the Oregon Trail. Other missions on these and other increasingly well-travelled roads performed the same function, helping to facilitate a westward movement of white man that clearly threatened the Indian's continued possession of the Kansas prairie and plain.

Though fur traders returning from the Pacific Northwest had used the route as early as 1813—had originally blazed the trail, so to speak, from west to east—the first wagons to roll over what became the famous Oregon Trail were those of fur-trader William Sublette in 1830, and he began his journey to the Rockies at the Missouri River. In later years, the great bulk of the enormous traffic over it moved to the West without return. Hence the trail must be said to have had its principal starting point in Independence, Missouri, for it was there that most of the wagon trains were organized. Several alternative routes were followed up the Kansas River Valley. A main one crossed the Kaw northward at the site of present-day Topeka, then briefly followed the north bank of the river, then slanted northwestward to a place just west of present-day Marysville. There all the trail's branches in Kansas converged to form a single road up the Little Blue into the valley of the Platte. By 1840 the main trail had become a well-worn wagon road. But it was when the "Oregon Fever" began to rage in 1843, and then had added to it as travel stimulus the news of the 1848 gold strike in California, that the trail, now known as the Oregon-California Trail, became a main artery of a westward-flowing migration unprecedented in history. Only a small portion of the long road, and this relatively safe and easy, lay within the bounds of our Kansas parallelogram. Nevertheless, even here there was realized again and again the dark as well as bright meaning of "going West" (said Horace Greeley, "Go West, young man, and grow up with the country," but in frontier parlance to "Go West" meant "to die") as cholera, typhoid, smallpox and other diseases, fatal accidents at dangerous crossings of stream and hill, and attacks upon stragglers by hostile Indians left bodies buried in rudely marked and now long-forgotten graves beside the Kaw, the Vermillion, the Blue.

Independence, Missouri, was also the principal eastern terminus of the Santa Fe Trail, which had nearly two-thirds of its total length within our parallelogram and was much more a two-way street than was the road to the Northwest, having been originally a freight-trading route and remaining one after it also became a major road for westwarding emigrants. It was opened in 1821, immediately after Mexico won independence from Spain. A daring Missouri trader, Captain William Becknell, then took a pack train from the Missouri town of Franklin to the Great Bend of the Arkansas River, followed that river upstream to the Rockies, and there turned south to Santa Fe. His trip proved profitable. In the following year he made the trip with wagons and, instead of following the river all the way to the mountains, crossed it at a point a few miles west of present-day Dodge City. He moved south across the treeless, waterless Cimarron country (this was then in Mexico), where he and his party narrowly escaped death by thirst, then turned west to Santa Fe. This second journey was more profitable than the first. Thus Becknell pioneered both of the westerly branching routes (the right angles were soon taken out of them) along which rolled, in immediately following years, a swelling tide of commerce. By the early 1850s the monetary value of the Santa Fe trade was approaching a million dollars annually.

And by that time the trail was, in effect, a federal highway. One of President James Monroe's last acts in office was to sign into law a bill authorizing a survey of the road to Santa Fe, this in 1825. The three-man road commission then appointed began its work at once, completing the survey two years later.

In the summer of 1825 the commissioners signed with the Osage at Council Grove (it was named for this council) a treaty providing for the unmolested passage of trail travellers across Osage land. A similar treaty was signed a little later with the Kansa in what is now McPherson County. But with the fierce Comanche, who resented with fatal violence the white man's incursion of their hunting ground, no viable treaty was or could be made. Across the High Plains, the trail became a line of running intermittent battle, utterly savage on both sides, between Comanche warriors now generally recognized as the best light cavalry in the world and wagon trains which were always heavily armed and organized for swift defense, with mounted men reconnoitering for miles around during the day and with lookouts posted around the campsite every night. Legendary scouts, Indian fighters, mountain men had performed many a legendary deed along the trail by 1853. Kit Carson was one of them. Jedediah Smith was another. (It was near Wagon Body Springs, one of the famous map-named places on the trail, that Jed Smith, the greatest mountain man of them all, was killed by Comanche in 1831.)

The westward push required, of course, increased military protection, and near the forts would soon be clusters of white civilian settlers, the seed of future towns when nourished by population flow from the east. So it had been with Fort Leavenworth, established as a cantonment on the Missouri River in 1827, and Fort Scott, established just west of the Missouri line some eighty miles south of the mouth of the Kansas in 1842. So it would be with Fort Riley, upon which construction was begun in 1853 near the junction of the Republican and Smoky Hill. Men engaged in the Santa Fe trade were convinced that towns would eventually (must inevitably) come into being along the trail even on the western plains, though this was a country too far, too high and dry and Comanche-dominated, to be as yet thought of by anyone else as a possible permanent home for white men. One spot indicated to the freighters as a possible townsite was the one where Fort Dodge would be built a decade later and where, or near where, a small army post, Fort Atkinson, established in 1850, was being dismantled, to the dismay of travellers on the trail, in 1853.

By all this—the surveys that contradicted earlier denigrations of the country, the practical demonstration of the country's agricultural productivity by the farming success of some of the Indians, the widely reported experience of missionaries who grew to love the country, and the swelling traffic on trails west dribbling small forts and travel-service stations (notably at Council Grove) along the way—by all this, plus the growing pressure of railroads building from the east, the formerly timeless Kansas land had been dragged into Time by 1853, and become eventful. There were fewer than a thousand permanent white inhabitants, in that year, in all of vast Nebraska (it then included all of the original Louisiana Purchase that had not yet been organized), but this very emptiness had become by reverse effect an attractive force, a kind of gravitational pull, drawing toward it human plenitude.

The fullness would blot out or erase from the Kansas land all but a few traces of the Indian's life here. In the summer of 1853, George W. Manypenny, U.S. commissioner of Indian affairs, under a directive from Congress, came into the valleys of the Kaw and Neosho to negotiate treaties with Indians to recede to the U.S. Government all but a fraction of the land that, a quarter-century before, had been assigned them "forever." Manypenny was reluctant to do so. Like Isaac McCoy, he was among the tiny minority of white men who truly cared about the Indians as people and were disposed to see things, or at least try to see them, through the Indian's eyes. Nevertheless he performed his assigned task with efficiency. When he returned to Washington in early autumn he had laid the groundwork for treaties with eighteen Indian "nations" whereby some eleven and a half million acres north of the Kansas River and some two million acres south of it were unconditionally transferred to the United States. By the early 1870s all Indian land titles in the young state, save a few small reservations on which huddled remnants of four immigrant tribes, would be extinguished; by the late 1870s nearly all these original inhabitants of the Kansas land would be herded out of the state southward into the Indian Territory of Oklahoma. Thereafter the Indian would be remembered chiefly in the state as a picturesque part of the early eastern Kansas landscape and as the most hostile element of a hostile environment for settlers on the western plains. A few words of his language would remain attached to streams and hills and monumental rocks, to towns, counties, institutions, the state itself; but nothing of his traditions, outlook, or way of life would be truly integrated into the developing Kansas character.

Little more would remain, in this sense, of the missionary experience.

But the case was different with the emigrant trails. They made, I'm convinced, a deep and lasting impress upon the Kansas mind and spirit, if one impossible precisely to define, being a matter of pervasive mood and image. Especially impressive was the Santa Fe Trail, most of whose length was *Kansan* and whose mark upon the Kansas land may yet be seen, even where the soil has been long plowed, if one looks down upon it from an airplane: the soil visibly remembers through discolorations the injury done it by the myriad hooves of ox and horse, the myriads of turning wheels of white-hooded wagons, moving across the endless plain. Moving on. Always moving on. And *that* is the potent evocative image. The prairie schooners lurch, creak, sway—a long line of white sails on a sea of grass—as they beat their way slowly, inevitably, into the mystic West, bearing young men and women with dreams in their eyes; and we see this westering stream of youth as a questing stream, yearning and daring its way toward far horizons and the unknown beyond, searching for vital answers.

IV

Democratic Senator Stephen A. Douglas from Illinois, an eminently practical politician who aspired to become president of the United States, was chairman in 1853 of the powerful Senate Committee on Territories. In this capacity he had been striving for a decade to organize the territory of Nebraska. His 1853 bill for this, like its predecessors, made no specific reference to slavery, whose exclusion by the Missouri Compromise was assumed, and it passed through the House with a large majority. Even in the Senate, where proslavery strength had generally managed to overbalance antislavery strength, or at least frustrate the latter, and where the assumed exclusion of slavery from the area of course provoked stern Southern opposition, the measure came so close to passage that Abraham Lincoln, shrewdly watching from Springfield, Illinois, was convinced it *would* pass in the next session if a determined fight were made for it. For instance, Missouri's violently proslavery Senator David R. Atchison declared himself, reluctantly, in favor of it. And five Northerners voted against taking final floor action on it (two proposals to do so were defeated by just five votes) only because they deemed it premature: the territory it proposed to organize was yet legally Indian land.

This obstacle, by George Manypenny's activities, was largely removed from that portion of the proposed territory adjacent Missouri, in the summer of 1853.

But by the time the Thirty-third Congress took up the rein-
troduced Nebraska Bill in January 1854, both Atchison and
Douglas had changed their minds. Atchison now said he would
see Nebraska "sink in hell" before he would permit its organization with slavery excluded. And Douglas now claimed to have
discovered a great new "principle" whereby the slavery issue,
as it pertained to the territories, could be fairly and peaceably
resolved within the framework of Union. Or, rather, he claimed
that this discovery had been made by the Compromise of 1850,
wherein Utah and New Mexico territories had been organized
by Congress with no reference to slavery in the territorial enactment. This had been intended, said Douglas, to have the "comprehensive and enduring effect . . . [of] withdrawing the
question of slavery from the halls of Congress and the political arena, committing it to the arbitration of those . . .
immediately interested in, and alone responsible for, its consequences,"—that is, to those who actually settled in the territories. The great "principle," in other words, was that of
popular sovereignty, "Squatter Sovereignty," which clearly implied the abrogation of the Missouri Compromise, transferred to
a few thousand pioneer settlers in a wilderness the sole power to
decide what was assuredly a *national* question, and aroused fervent opposition all across the North. Opposition became unprecedentedly intense when Douglas, yielding to Southern
pressure, having agreed to divide the territory into Kansas *and*
Nebraska, inserted in his bill a clause that explicitly repealed the
Missouri Compromise.

But there was little doubt that the measure would now pass.
President Franklin Pierce made voting support of it a test of
party loyalty and threw behind it the full weight of his patronage
power, the formidable Douglas committed to the battle everything he had of combative skill and courage, and administration
Democrats were an overwhelming majority of the Senate, a
large one of the House. There was no surprise, though great dismay, when the Senate passed the bill (March 4, 1854) by 37–14.
There was little more when the House did so (May 26), 113 to
100. On May 30, the president signed the bill into law: Kansas
Territory became a legal entity.

3

Bleeding Kansas

I

$\mathcal{T}$ HE most influential of the New Englanders who came to Kansas in the 1850s did so primarily for an avowed moral purpose by which they were as much inflamed as ever were the Pilgrims and Puritans from whom most of them were descended. Passionately opposed to human slavery, passionately enamored of human freedom, they were outraged by what they saw (with Salmon Chase) as an "atrocious plot" to impose slavery upon every territory and, ultimately, every state in the Union. They were determined to frustrate this ghastly design; and to this end they were prepared to run literally vital risks—not just such gambling risks as attended any pioneering effort on the western frontier, but risks amounting to sacrificial offerings upon the alter of liberty to God the Father of all mankind. This was the *primary* motive for their emigration. Their economic motivation, though certainly present and strong, was secondary.

There was a reversal of emphasis in the motivation of the great bulk of the free-soil westerners who came here—people out of the Old Northwest, eastern Missouri, and the upper Mississippi valley—people who from the first outnumbered the New England contingent and soon did so vastly. With them, the primary motive for emigration was the desire to better themselves economically: like the earlier pioneers of the then-western frontier (their parents, their grandparents), they were driven by land-hunger, drawn by the promise of free land. The conscious purpose of making Kansas free, though present and strong in most of them, was subordinate and incidental.

In practice, however, economic self-interest and moral purpose became fused into one, as motivation, since every settler, whether from New England or the Old Northwest, was convinced (or soon became convinced) that his economic prosperity as a farmer of his own land, or as an artisan or merchant or professional man, required that the slavemaster with his slaves, especially the big plantation owner, be excluded from Kansas. And this last was a political matter. Hence the typical Kansas territorial settler was politicized—he identified with the body politic, defining himself in terms of it—to a far greater extent than were the pioneers of the earlier West or, indeed, the pioneers of any other area I can think of in the nation, save possibly the Utah of the Mormons.

Kansas, then, was born of a moral idea.

But not purely. Not simply, nor exclusively.

And if our sole purpose were to assess the relative weights of economic interest and moral concern as determinants of the original character of Kansas, we might well begin where the narrative political history of the state (particularly one written in New England) might also well begin, namely, in the mind of a young man of Massachusetts as March opened in 1854. Eli Thayer, thirty-five years old, was a member of the Massachusetts legislature that year. He represented Worcester where, in the 1840s, he had established the first four-year women's college in America, Oread Institute, on Worcester's Goat Hill. He had aimed at his ideal of higher education for women in a very practical way by establishing this institute as his highly profitable private enterprise. And he aimed at the same fusion of idealism and practicality in his proposal to end forever "the domination of slavery" by means of an "organized emigration" of free-soil men "guided and guarded by a responsible business company," as he later wrote—an inspiration that came to him while he listened to dull debates one day in the statehouse. He first broached his idea in public at a great meeting held in Worcester to protest the impending passage of the Kansas-Nebraska bill. The audience response was enthusiastically affirmative. He then drafted a charter for what he called the Massachusetts Emigrant Aid Society, pushed its passage through the legislature, and saw it signed by the governor on April 26.

This aid society was to be, not a benevolent institution, but a money-making business. A capital of not more than five million dollars was to be raised through stock subscription. With this capital, agents of the company were to be sent into Kansas Territory to prepare the way for free-soil emigrants by laying out town lots, erecting hotels, establishing mills, etc. For the use of these facilities, settlers were to be charged an amount sufficient to return "a handsome profit to the stockholders upon their investment," as Thayer wrote in his plan of organization and work. He estimated that in two or three years all the original capital, plus profit, would be recovered through the sale of "property in the Territory first occupied," enabling the company "to attempt the same adventure elsewhere."

Its author saw almost limitless possibilities in this "Plan of Freedom," as Horace Greeley soon dubbed it. When Thayer explained his proposal to the great editor of the *New York Tribune,* Greeley pointed out that two could play this game: the aid society would stimulate the South to organize an emigration of its own. Thayer agreed. He welcomed the prospect. It meant that Kansas would become a laboratory demonstration of the inferiority of slave labor to free labor, a demonstration so convincing that the South's faith in its Peculiar Institution would be severely reduced. Nor would the demonstration end in Kansas. It would operate in every new territory, under the very rules of popular sovereignty which the South now imposed on the North, and would halt forever the making of new slave states. It would even operate within the slave states already existent. These would be invaded by free labor, under the aegis of the emigrant aid company, in ways perfectly in accord with the laws and the Constitution. Thus the curse of slavery would be swiftly, peacefully, profitably, and permanently removed from the whole of the United States.

It would be removed, one must emphasize, *not* through the anguish of moral choice, *not* through any direct effortful attack upon moral wrong, *not* through political action of any kind in Washington, but through the automatic beneficence (as a kind of side-effect) of economic competition in a free market—the automatic beneficence, in other words, of an uninhibited operation of "natural" economic laws. Eli Thayer, as his published speeches and writings make clear, was very much a Natural Law and Natural Rights man in his social and economic philosophy; which is to say that his basic mind set, his way of looking at and dealing with the world, was of a piece with that which had dominated proceedings at the Constitutional Convention.

In view of this, it is instructive to look at what actually happened to his conceptions as these were worked out within the historical situation that prompted them.

At Weston, Missouri, in 1853, during the address in which he asserted he would see Nebraska "sink in hell" before he permitted its organization as a free territory, Senator Atchison had inveighed against nigger-stealing Northern vermin who threatened to invade the new land. "[Y]ou know how to protect your interests," he had cried; "your rifles will free you from such neighbors. . . . You will go there, if necessary with the *bayonet* and *blood!*" The seeds of violence thus sown on fertile soil were watered by the hugely publicized announcement that a five-million-dollar corporation had been formed to settle Kansas with free-state men—a publicity that gave many the impression that the aid society had actually in hand the five million dollars (it had in fact only twenty thousand dollars in 1854, with perhaps three times that much pledged) and had already enrolled emigrants by the thousands. There was at once aroused the greatest alarm, and vast anger, in western Missouri. Throughout the South, shouting speakers by the dozen, haranguing audiences of thousands, threatened death to all who came to Kansas under the aegis of any Northern emigrant aid organization. Associations known as Sons of the South, Social Bands, and Blue Lodges were formed to do battle for the territory. And this in turn and of course hardened the fighting determination of the free-staters. By April 1855, the principal Kansas agent of the aid company was writing Thayer for Sharps rifles with which to arm the free-staters. By early 1856, Thayer was exhorting New England audiences to buy Sharps rifles at twenty-five dollars apiece for shipment to Kansas.

So much for the notion of deciding the "destiny of Kansas"

through a peaceful competition between slave labor and free, impersonally refereed by the Natural Law of the marketplace.

Nor did a happier fate befall Thayer's notion, originally basic to his whole scheme, of making money for stockholders in the aid society.

It at once laid the society open to charges of hypocrisy hurled by both abolitionists and proslavers, and this impugning of motives was not confined to extremists.

The heaviest fire came from precisely those wealthy businessmen whom Thayer must have expected to welcome most strongly his stress on the profit motive and who in fact provided most of the new company's capital. Afraid "that people might say we were influenced by pecuniary considerations in our patriotic work," as Thayer later wrote, they forced a suspension of the original charter on the technical ground that it might impose individual liability upon stockholders. Thayer was disgusted. "I had not then, and have not now, the slightest respect for that pride in charity which excludes from great philanthropic enterprises the strength and effectiveness of money-making," said he in 1889. "There are supporters of missionary societies who make from the traffic in ardent spirits the money they contribute, who would doubtless oppose the plan of making such societies self-supporting by sharing in the property which they create. Why is it worse for a company to make money by extending Christianity than by making cotton cloth?" But such specious argument failed to move that great maker of cotton cloth, Massachusetts textile-manufacturer Amos Lawrence, who became treasurer of the aid organization and, in this capacity, insisted that its conception as a business be wholly abandoned and the necessary money raised frankly through benevolent contributions. This was done when the society was rechartered as the New England Emigrant Aid Company in February 1855.

"So we went on the charity plan," wrote Thayer with some bitterness thirty-odd years later, "and were never one-half so efficient as we would have been by the other method, and were fully twice as long in determining the destiny of Kansas." [1]

1. Eli Thayer, *A History of the Kansas Crusade*. Facsimile of 1889 edition (Freeport, N.Y.: BFL Communications, Inc.), p. 59.

II

That his organization did determine Kansas's "destiny" was the profound conviction of Eli Thayer. It was shared by a good many of his New England contemporaries. But circumstances so overwhelming favored the territory's freedom that this would probably (*not* certainly) have been achieved had there been no organized emigration whatever.

In general, free-soilers had much greater mobility and adaptability than slaveholders had. They were generally small farmers, accustomed to mixed-crop and livestock farming, for whom moving was a relatively simple matter of transporting themselves and their meager possessions to a new land. Once there, they could adjust their farming practices relatively easily to changed conditions, and they could feel approximately as secure of their property in their new homes as they had been in their old. The slaveholder, on the other hand, especially one with many slaves, generally concentrated upon the production of a single crop (cotton, tobacco, hemp) and his slaves were experienced only in the handling of that commodity. He therefore could not readily adjust his agriculture to marked changes in environmental conditions—and the Kansas climate was unfavorable to cotton or tobacco. Nor could the slaveholder easily transport his property: a considerable expense, along with risk, was required. And in Kansas Territory, with fervent free-soilers around him, no slaveholder could feel that his property was secure. There was always the threat that popular sovereignty would in the end determine a free state, rendering slave capital worthless there, and in the meantime this capital might be greatly reduced. For though slaves as property were legally defined in the same terms as cattle and pigs and horses, Negroes were unlike these animals in their susceptibility to the propaganda of freedom and were inclined to act as that propaganda directed when they could do so with any safety.

The great bulk of the Kansas free-state settlers came as individuals making their own way, or else in small parties locally organized in their former home areas, with no material help from New England. As 1854 gave way to 1855, out of a total population of more than eight thousand, only seven hundred and fifty immigrants, at most, had come into Kansas with the direct aid of Thayer's company. Nor did emigrant aid migration make up any quantitatively important segment of the flood of population into Kansas during the following months and years. All told, only three thousand names were listed as emigrants on the company's books when these were closed in late 1857 or early 1858, by which time the total population of Kansas must have approached or surpassed seventy thousand (the 1860 census enumerated 107,206).

Thayer himself claimed, of course, that the figures on the books were but a fraction of the total number (he estimated thirty thousand) who came to Kansas to ensure a free state either directly *or indirectly* as a result of his company's activities. His admiring biographer, Franklin P. Rice, whose book (never published) is in typescript among the collections of the American Antiquarian Society in Worcester, gives statistics showing that a decisive majority of Kansas immigrants holding free-state views came from states directly influenced by Thayer and his organization—from New England, New York, Pennsylvania, Ohio—and infers they came *because* of this influence. The objective validity of such inference is indeterminable.

It is certain, however, that the aid company, and those who came to Kansas under its aegis, had an impact nationally and territorially vastly disproportionate to the number of people directly involved in the enterprise. This impact not only did much to shape the main pattern of events in what came to be known the world over as "Bleeding Kansas," it also determined salient features of the personality, the mind, of the state of Kansas as it emerged from the Civil War. In part this was due to the special circumstances within which the aid emigrants made their historic migration. But even more was it due to the special quality of these emigrants themselves. They were in general people of strong character and superior intelligence and education, many of them college graduates, and they promptly, inevitably assumed leadership roles in the aborning Kansas community.

Thayer selected as his organization's principal Kansas agent a man like himself in several ways, though very different in others. Dr. Charles Robinson, thirty-six years old in 1854, was a physician with a large practice in Fitchburg, Massachusetts. He had proved his courage and leadership qualities when he adventured with a party of forty Bostonians in California during the Gold Rush. A handsome man, tall and beautifully proportioned, with a commanding presence, a generally sound judgment, much calculating shrewdness, a notable self-control, and an equally notable self-esteem (it often grated harshly on those who disagreed with him in argument; he was an argumentative man), he had also an iron if tacit commitment to Natural Law-Natural Rights doctrine joined (at least in his later years) to an otherwise notable independence of mind. It was joined also to highly developed acquisitive instincts.

The latter were even more pronounced in the man who became, in effect, Robinson's second-in-command. Samuel C. Pomeroy, a descendent of Massachusetts Puritans, was thirty-eight years old when he was chosen by Thayer and Amos Lawrence to serve as the aid company's financial agent in the territory. He managed in that capacity to serve not only the organization's, but also his own, financial interests very well. He was a far more ingratiating and politic personality than Robinson—so smooth, indeed, that his enemies took to calling him "Oily Sam"—and he was considerably less inhibited than Robinson by a concern for truth-telling and honest dealing; but he was no less hardheaded and shrewd, and he shared with Robinson a sincere and strong aversion to slavery.

The two men worked well together; they became as a team a near-perfect instrument of the aid company's purposes on the far frontier.

In July 1854, Robinson went to Kansas to prepare the way for the first party of emigrants, which was then being recruited with the greatest difficulty by the indefatigable Thayer. He chose as a settlement-place some land on the Kaw River at the mouth of Wakarusa Creek, some forty miles upstream from the mouth of the Kaw, where a few settlers from Ohio and Indiana had already arrived—land dominated by a considerable hill bearing the unlovely name of Hogback Ridge. And it was to this place, called Wakarusa, that young Charles H. Branscomb of Massachusetts led the first party (it numbered but thirty, all male) on August 1. Four weeks later, Robinson and Pomeroy arrived with a second party, numbering perhaps a hundred. Four other parties followed during the next three months, by the end of which time Wakarusa had been renamed Lawrence City in honor of Amos Lawrence (the main street was Massachusetts Avenue), and Hogback Ridge, owned and lived upon by Robinson, had been renamed Mount Oread after Thayer's Oread Institute. By then, too, Robinson and Cyrus K. Holliday had joined with others formally to found on December 5, 1854, on a site Holliday and Robinson had selected, the town of Topeka, intended by Holliday to become the capital of the state. A few months later was founded, largely through the leadership and organizational abilities of an aid company emigrant, the third principal town of the Kansas River valley, Manhattan.

Isaac T. Goodnow may be taken as representative of the kind of New Englander attracted to Thayer's "Kansas Crusade." In the fall of 1854 he had been for six years a professor of natural science in Providence Seminary, Providence, Rhode Island. He was very comfortably established there. But he was emotionally disturbed by the great political issue of that year, and when he read in the newspapers of Thayer's Plan of Freedom he was moved to correspond about it with his brother-in-law, the Reverend Joseph Denison, then preaching in Boston. It was arranged between the two that Denison would come to Providence in December of 1854, at a time when Thayer was speaking there. Thayer's powerful eloquence clinched their decision; after the meeting had ended, they both talked to him, in great excitement, until midnight. Within a few days, Goodnow had resigned his position and was writing in the newspapers and making public speeches on behalf of the aid company. In March of 1855 he led a party of some seventy emigrants to Kansas where, at the confluence of the Kansas and Blue rivers, he persuaded two groups of settlers already there to consolidate with his own to make a single town, originally named Boston but soon (after a party of eighty immigrants sponsored by the Cincinnati and Kansas Land Company had arrived) renamed Manhattan. Subsequently Goodnow was a principal founder of Bluemont Central College, which opened its doors at Manhattan on January 9, 1860, and was the forerunner of Kansas State Agricultural College, the land-grant institution of which the Reverend Joseph Denison became the first president in 1863 and which has evolved into present-day Kansas State University.

The departure of each party of Kansas emigrants became a propaganda occasion, widely and deeply impressive of public sentiment. Especially so was the departure of more than two hundred, under the leadership of Robinson himself (he had returned to Massachusetts for this purpose), from the Fitchburg railway station in Boston, on March 13, 1855, just a week after the Goodnow party had left. A great crowd gathered to see them off. Detailed reports of the farewell ceremony were printed in newspapers all across the North. Hence we know that they all sang, to the tune of "Auld Lang Syne," lines John Greenleaf Whittier had written a few months before, entitled "The Kansas Emigrant's Song," of which the first verse ran:

> We cross the prairies as of old
> The pilgrims crossed the sea,
> To make the West, as they the East,
> The homestead of the free.

Even more hugely publicized was the departure from New Haven, Connecticut, a year later, of a party of seventy organized by the fiery Reverend C. B. Lines, a young Congregational minister who had in his congregation the president and several of the faculty of Yale. These joined with the congregation of the Reverend Henry Ward Beecher's Brooklyn church to present to each adult male of the emigrant party a Bible, hymnal, and Sharps rifle, the latter becoming promptly nationally known as a "Beecher's Bible." The Lines colony founded the town of Wabaunsee, thirteen miles downstream from Manhattan on the south bank of the Kansas River, building there a church greatly publicized as the Beecher Bible and Rifle Church.

The image of the territory and its "war" that became impressed on the public mind of the North was largely made by the New England contingent on Kansas soil. The New Englanders' generally superior articulateness and sense of the importance to their cause of publicity made them favored interviewees of the correspondents of the eastern press. A high percentage of them were capable of vivid descriptive and narrative writing of their own; they could and did write articles and letters printed in eastern periodicals depicting the Kansas scene as they saw it. And two of their number, both women, wrote books that were widely read. *Six Months in Kansas,* by Mrs. Hannah H. Ropes, and *Kansas: Its Interior and Exterior Life,* by Sara T. L. Robinson (she was the wife of Charles Robinson), were best sellers in 1856.

All of which pointed, in the earliest years of the body politic, toward fulfillment of a prophecy made by Dr. Thomas H. Webb, the aid company secretary, in a letter (October 1854) from Boston to Sam Pomeroy. "It is desirable that New England principles and New England influences should pervade the whole Territory," wrote Webb; "this can only be effected by wise foresight and judicious management. Dot Kansas with New England settlements, and no matter how heterogeneous the great living mass which flows into the Territory may be, it will all eventually be moulded into a symmetrical form, and the benefits resulting therefrom will be such that generations yet to come will bless the memories of those thro' whose efforts the boon of freedom, knowledge and pure & undefiled religion were secured for them and their posterity."

To a surprising degree the relatively tiny enclaves of New England highmindedness, trader shrewdness, and "pure & undefiled religion" did leaven and mold, through the years, the great heterogeneous mass. To a surprising degree they served as mental and spiritual and genetic tissue, a tissue that operated upon and interacted with a *soma* composed of widely disparate initial materials—materials that remained widely disparate in detail. Because of this interaction the body did achieve a "symmetrical form" it could not otherwise have had and the state as a whole, body politic and cultural soul, did come to have a distinctive unitary character, a historical personality, which persists to this day. In this sense, Thayer's conviction that his New England operation decided the "destiny" of Kansas may be said to have had some validity.

But of course the smug self-satisfaction, the attitudes of intellectual and moral superiority, the unmitigated self-righteousness implicit in Webb's letter, did not go down well with Kansas immigrants from Illinois, Indiana, Ohio, or the West in general when manifested, as they all too often were, by immigrants from New England. They were manifested with particular force by the decidedly unpolitic Charles Robinson, who had little desire and no talent for personal popularity. Hence a majority of the westerners were more than prepared, they were strongly inclined, to embrace a valid alternative to Robinson's political leadership whenever one should present itself. One did in the summer of 1855. It was then that James H. Lane erupted (no other word is so accurately descriptive of his effect) upon the turbulent Kansas scene.

III

The son of a Jacksonian Democratic politician in Indiana, he had had a highly political upbringing on the Old Northwestern frontier, had been a colonel of Indiana volunteers during the Mexican War and then lieutenant governor of Indiana before being elected to Congress from Indiana's Fourth District. He remained a frontiersman in essential respects, with a special genius for self-dramatization and the hyperbolic, ejaculatory style of oratory that delighted and moved frontier audiences. His physical appearance was remarkable. Though six feet tall, he gave no impression of physical bulk, being no broader through chest and shoulders than a normally proportioned man of middle height. His face was long and narrow—hollow-cheeked, burning-eyed, dark-complexioned—and was framed by a wild halo of dark hair reaching well below his ears. His "utterly demoralized wardrobe," as someone called it, became notorious. He habitually wore cowhide boots reaching halfway up the calves of his long legs; into them were tucked the bottoms of dark trousers worn threadbare over boney knees. (He was, I might add, chronically indigent.) And even on hot summer days he ordinarily had on a coat and calfskin vest, with a black rag carelessly knotted around his thin neck to do service as a cravat. Often, indoors and out, he wore also a greasy bearskin overcoat. He seemed never to perspire—seemed, indeed, as deficient in internal heating arrangements as the snake to which

Mrs. Ropes compared him in her highly New Englandish book.
At the same time, and predominantly, he gave the impression of
hotly frictional electric energy, an energy so overwhelming that
it seemed more to possess him than he it, especially when he
was engaged in public speech.

Yet he had a sufficient control of this energy to enable him to
"play" almost any audience as a skilled musician plays an
organ. Dealing almost wholly in emotional appeal, he could
arouse his listeners to frenzied excitement or soothe them into
melancholy forbearance as the needs of the hour seemed to him
to demand. And what made his unique personality and talents
politically effective were his shrewd understanding of his particular constituency, his equally shrewd assessment of the possibilities of a situation. He was aided, too, in his pursuit of power
by his freedom from scruple and principled commitment. His
tactical and strategic flexibility was greatly increased by this:
few could straddle an issue or wholly shift their ground with
greater ease and swiftness than he, and none could do so with a
greater show of "sincerity."

For instance, representing a district with a large antislavery
majority, he had made speeches in Congress attacking the slave
power in the strongest terms, yet voted for the Kansas-Nebraska
bill, thereby destroying his chance for re-election. Why? Because, according to rumor, he and Douglas made a secret
bargain: Lane's vote for Kansas-Nebraska and his emigration to
Kansas, there to do battle for popular sovereignty doctrine, was
to be paid for by Douglas's support, and the administration's
support, of his bid to become U. S. senator from Kansas when
the new state was admitted. The rumor gained plausibility when
Lane, arriving in Lawrence in April 1855, reportedly repeated
as his own conviction Douglas's assertion that the slavery question in Kansas would and should be answered by soil and climatic conditions (could hemp be profitably grown there?), and
soon thereafter attempted to organize a Democratic party in the
territory "upon truly national [as distinct from sectional]
grounds," with "full endorsement" of the Democratic platform
of 1852. The attempt failed dismally. There was no slightest
chance that a viable National Democracy, committed in practice
as in theory to popular sovereignty, could be established in

Kansas by the summer of 1855; and Lane at once recognized that the destruction of this possibility was the work of Missourians who revelled in the title "Border Ruffian" and who, almost all of them Democrats, were led politically by Douglas's erstwhile friend, Senator Atchison.

Twice had well-armed Missourians invaded Kansas to vote illegally in territorial elections while forcibly denying the vote to bona fide settlers of free-state views—once in the fall of 1854, when a proslavery delegate to Congress was selected; again in the spring of 1855, when a unanimously proslavery territorial legislature was selected. This last violation was too much for territorial Governor Andrew H. Reeder, though he had come to Kansas holding proslavery views. By the time Lane arrived in Kansas, Reeder had gone East to warn the president personally that the "Bogus Legislature," as free-staters promptly dubbed it, was indeed the product of force and fraud and should be repudiated by the administration. Pierce *seemed* to agree. But when Reeder arrived back in Kansas, just two days before Lane's fiasco of a Democratic convention, he faced charges by Pierce's secretary of state, W. L. Marcy, that he had practiced "irregularities" in the purchase of lands belonging to Kaw half-breeds, charges, promptly denied, which provided grounds for his removal from office by Pierce on July 31.

By then the Bogus Legislature, meeting not in the designated territorial capital of Pawnee, one hundred thirty miles up the Kaw, but in Shawnee Mission, conveniently adjacent the Missouri line, had drafted and enacted over Reeder's veto an iniquitous set of "Bogus Laws." Any person who raised a "rebellion or insurrection of slaves, free negroes, or mulattoes" in the territory was to suffer death. Any person who aided or abetted such rebellion or insurrection was to suffer death. Any person who "by speaking, writing, or printing" advised or persuaded or induced slaves to rebel was to suffer death. Any person who aided the escape of a slave was to suffer death or imprisonment at hard labor for not less than ten years. Any person who knowingly introduced into the territory any printed material that, by argument or statement of opinion, might "produce a disorderly, dangerous or rebellious disaffection among the slaves" was to be imprisoned at hard labor for not less than the suspicion of his motives that initially handicapped him, and to make himself the authentic voice of the theretofore politically voiceless (or nearly so) westerners. He became chairman of the platform committee of the convention assembled at Big Springs on September 5, 1855, to organize formally the Free-State Executive Committee, the temporary governing body of free Kansas. He was elected president and dominated the proceedings of the convention assembled in Topeka on October 23 to draft the instrument, the Topeka Constitution, under which an unsuccessful attempt was made to gain the admission of Kansas to the Union as a free state. He was field commander of the free-state ''army'' during the bloodless ''Wakarusa War'' of late November and early December, 1855, which was bloodless in good part because his ostentatious preparation of men and fortifications for the defence of Lawrence against an armed mob of invading Missourians deterred attack by the latter until a thoroughly alarmed Governor Shannon arrived on the scene; Shannon, representing the proslavers, then conducted negotiations with Lane and Robinson, representing the free-staters, which resulted in the withdrawal of the invading host. (On this dangerous occasion, Lane and Robinson overcame their mutual antipathy sufficiently to work harmoniously together.) And as party executive committee chairman, Lane was in charge of an extralegal election whereby, in accordance with procedures defined by the Topeka Constitution, a ''legislature'' and ''executive'' of a ''state'' government were chosen, with Robinson (perforce) named ''governor.''

By the late spring of 1856, when opened the season of climactic decisive violence in what would soon be known the world over as ''Bleeding Kansas,'' Lane was well on the way to becoming *the* dominant figure of the now nationally famous Topeka Movement, increasingly eclipsing an increasingly resentful Robinson.

IV

No two men could have been more different in most ways of temperament, mind, and character than the darkly brilliant, dishevelled, passionate, magnetic Jim Lane and the cold-eyed,

five years. It was a felony, punishable by imprisonment o
less than two years at hard labor, to maintain "by speakii
writing . . . that persons have not the right to hold slave
the territory or to introduce into the territory "any book, p
magazine, pamphlet or circular containing any denial c
right of persons to hold slaves" there. It was further prc
that "no person who is conscientiously opposed to h
slaves, or who does not admit the right to hold slaves
Territory, shall sit as a juror on the trial of any prosecuti
violating any of the sections of this act." Nor was this fei
legislative attack upon the basic principles of democrat
ernment and justice to be curbed by the territorial executi
so it appeared. When blundering proslavery Wilson Sl
Reeder's successor as governor, arrived in Kansas on Se]
1, he at once proclaimed the Shawnee Mission legislatu
a duly elected legal body and promised rigorously to en
statutes, calling upon federal troops for aid in such enfc
if necessary.

All of which meant that there could be no overall rul
in Kansas during the months immediately ahead. Alr
free-staters had organized four militia companies. T
prepared to organize their own governmental apparatu
upon there would be, in effect, two sovereignties fac
other in hostile array on the Kansas prairie, each wit
"army," each with its own war-propagandistic pres
summer of 1855 there were four free-state newspap
territory: the *Herald of Freedom,* the *Kansas Free Sta*
Tribune, all of Lawrence, and the *Freeman* of Tope
were three proslavery papers: the *Leavenworth H*
Kickapoo Pioneer, the *Atchison Squatter Sovereign.*)
each sovereignty claimed *in toto* the same ground a
there remained in Kansas no middle ground on wl
sensus politician could take a stand.

So Jim Lane joined the free-state men, who wou
viously be a majority of the actual settlers in the te
only did he join, he became at once a dominant fi
them!

In a single passionately "sincere" speech befor
crowd possible in Lawrence he managed to overcc

coldly handsome, self-contained Doctor Robinson. But fully as great, if in other respects, was the difference between Lane and a third leading figure of the free-state movement, a figure who sprang into lurid prominence in the last week of May 1856. This third man was John Brown—Old Brown of Osawatomie, as he was often called, having celebrated his fifty-sixth birthday (May 9) in a land where four-fifths of the inhabitants were in their twenties or thirties.

Lane acquired in 1856, along with his sobriquet, the Grim Chieftain, a reputation for impetuosity, violence, and battle-lust whose intimidating effect upon Border Ruffians was valuable to embattled free-staters. It is true that, two years later, he killed a man, and suffered a leg wound himself in a dispute over a land claim, being then acquitted of the charge of "willful murder" in a trial before three justices of the peace. But in general Lane's ferocious reputation derived from his words rather than his deeds. Crimson with verbal blood were the incredible torrents of invective he poured upon his enemies in public speech; pale with prudent moderation and a calculation designed to assure a minimum of violence were most of his dealings with his enemies in the field. His was certainly a moderating, restraining influence during the Wakarusa War when many of the free-state rank and file wanted to launch an attack upon the proslavery camp. He persuaded them, as Robinson alone might not have been able to do, that the negotiated "treaty" was a triumph, not a surrender, of free-state principles. Similarly with his handling of political issues when in legislative or executive posts. Probably his most useful service to the free-state cause, overall, was his gathering together the violent passions of his followers and focussing them upon himself as their voice and instrument, then dissipating them, draining them off into harmless channels, at the times and places where (when) they might otherwise have been actually effective.

He did this, according to his admiring biographer, John Speer, in his handling of the black law issue in the Topeka constitutional convention. The free-state westerners who came to Kansas were opposed to slavery on moral grounds, but a large majority of them, perhaps three out of four, were also opposed to it on purely racist grounds. They simply wanted *no* Negroes around. They sharply differed from the New England contingent on this matter. The most heated debate at the Big Springs convention was sparked by a resolution that Lane drafted as chairman of the platform committee, asserting that "the best interests of Kansas require a population of free white men, and that in the organization we are in favor of stringent laws excluding all negroes, bond or free, from the Territory. . . ." This resolution was overwhelmingly approved, the only concession to the opposing view being the stipulation "that nevertheless such [Negro-excluding] measures shall not be regarded as a test of party orthodoxy." By the time the Topeka convention assembled, however, Lane had become persuaded that a black law provision in the constitution would destroy the chance for the admission of Kansas to the Union under it. To the opposition of the proslavers would be added that of powerful antislavery politicians—such men as Massachusetts's Senator Sumner, Ohio's Senator Chase, New York's Senator Seward—and there would be provoked also the opposition of the most influential newspapers, magazines, writers, and orators, in the North. Here, then, was a dilemma: in the time available, no rational argument or emotional appeal could overcome the passionate prejudices in which the black law proposal was rooted. Lane's solution was to present the issue to the convention, not as an integral part of the constitution, but as a mere instruction to the first legislature, following which it would be inoperative. In this innocuous form it won approval by a large majority. (The Topeka Constitution itself made no mention of the Negro but did limit the electoral franchise to "white" males and "civilized" Indian males. The proposal to strike "white" from this clause was defeated 25 to 7, with Robinson voting *yea* and Lane *nay*.) In the circumstances, Lane's strategy was "the sublimity of wisdom," according to Speer, who was himself strongly opposed to black laws.[2]

Obviously, Jim Lane was no fanatic.

John Brown, just as obviously, was. He did appear old, far older than his actual years, when he arrived on October 7, 1855,

2. John Speer, *Life of Gen. James H. Lane* (Garden City, Kan.: Speer, 1896), p. 44.

in Osawatomie, where five of his sons had settled the preceding spring. His had been a hard life, replete with failure, disappointment, frustration, ever since his earliest childhood in Torrington, Connecticut. He had fathered seven children by his first wife (she suffered mental aberrations for some years before her early death in 1832), thirteen by his second, some of whom had died in childhood and two of whom were of unsound mind; had failed as a farmer, tanner, land speculator, wool broker, and always to the accompaniment of law suits; had several times been accused of dishonesty, once of embezzlement, in his business dealings in New England, New York, and Ohio. Simultaneously, incredibly, he had impressed most who came in contact with him, including shrewd and experienced appraisers of men, as a character of exceptional strength, courage, and goodness, a dedicated man who lived by the precepts of his New England Calvinist religion. (The Old Testament was his favorite reading; "without the shedding of blood there is no remission of sins" was his favorite maxim.) The ruling passion of his life, by middle age, was a hatred of slavery and slaveholders; to this was subordinated, from it was probably derived inferentially, a love of the Negro race; and the abolitionists who met him during the year or two before his Kansas emigration recognized a fighter for freedom more brave, more tenacious, more consistent, more selfless, and far tougher than they. He bore upon him marks of the hard blows dealt him, but they were upon him as dents or cracks in an unyielding substance, not as the living scars of once-bleeding wounds. His tall form was bent, his hair grizzled. His countenance was grim, flinty, harshly grooved. His slate-blue eyes were tired. Yet there was also in those eyes a crazy glitter on occasions that became more and more frequent in the months following his arrival in Osawatomie—a glitter that would have greatly disturbed his neighbors along Pottawatomie Creek, especially those proclaiming proslavery views, had they known that his maternal line was darkly tainted by hereditary insanity. (His mother had died insane. One of his maternal aunts had died insane. Three of his maternal uncles and five of their sons, his first cousins, became insane.)

The way had been prepared for his entrance prominently into

the Kanṣas free-state movement. His son, John Brown, Jr., had been one of the vice-presidents of the first of the Lawrence conventions out of which came the decision to form a Free-State party and had served on the executive committee that prepared for the Big Springs convention where, strongly favoring the formation of a separate free Kansas government, he had as strongly opposed the black law proposal. Old Brown had hardly fully settled in his new home when, in answer to Lane's call for men to defend Lawrence against threatened destruction, he marched to that town with four of his sons and a "quantity of arms" supplied by "eastern friends" to do battle with Border Ruffians. The Wakarusa War would assuredly not have been bloodless had he had his way. Named captain of the southeast Kansas militia company, he pressed hard for an immediate attack upon the ruffian camp (he offered to lead a night attack himself, with ten men) and had to be forcibly restrained from a platform denunciation of the treaty Robinson and Lane had agreed to. He returned to Osawatomie highly dissatisfied with the outcome of events. During the winter and spring of 1856 he brooded, with growing bitterness, over the failure of free-state men to retaliate in kind for repeated killings of their own number by proslavers. He counted four free-state victims by winter's end, a fifth on May 19 when a young man returning to Lawrence was shot down on the road. He sourly noted that not one of these killers, though all were readily identifiable, was so much as indicted by grand juries composed of proslavery men.

But by the time this fifth murder had occurred, a grand jury at Lecompton, now the territorial capital, had acted with remarkable swiftness on instructions given by the man after whom the town was named, Chief Justice Samuel D. Lecompte. On May 5, Lecompte instructed the jurors to find bills for "high treason" against any persons who had actively resisted the territorial (Bogus) legislature's enactments and bills for "constructive treason" against any persons who had formed, aided, or abetted "combinations . . . for the purpose of resisting" these enactments; whereupon, without bothering to take evidence, the jury indicted Reeder (the ex-governor had now joined the free-staters), Robinson, Lane, and several other Free-State party leaders. It also recommended that the two Lawrence newspapers, the *Herald of Freedom* and the *Kansas Free State* (the *Tribune* had moved to Topeka), and the Free-State Hotel at Lawrence (newly built of stone, it was designed for possible use as a fortress), be "abated" as "nuisances."

Reeder, convinced his life was in danger, fled the territory disguised as a woodchopper. Robinson attempted flight down the Missouri but was illegally arrested by Missourians and taken to Lecompton, where he would be imprisoned for four months. Lane had gone East to present to Congress the case for the admission of Kansas to the Union under the Topeka Constitution and had not yet returned, but other free-state leaders were arrested in Lawrence, with no difficulty, on the morning of May 21, by a deputy marshal with a small posse. While these arrests were being made there were encamped on Mount Oread some eight hundred heavily armed proslavers, including Missouri militia, who had been designated a "posse" by Douglas County Sheriff Samuel J. Jones; and in the afternoon these men descended upon Lawrence flying Southern state flags (South Carolina's was conspicuous) and carrying with them five pieces of artillery. The two newspaper offices were destroyed, their presses and type broken and thrown into the river; the hotel was bombarded with cannon, then destroyed by fire; several shops were looted; and, for good measure, Robinson's Mount Oread house was looted, then burned to the ground. Against these outrages the citizens of Lawrence made not the slightest resistance, being persuaded that no effective resistance was possible in their almost leaderless condition and that this sacking of a helpless town would gain vastly increased support for the free-state cause throughout the North—as, indeed, it did.

John Brown, however, was inflamed. He learned in exaggerated terms of Lawrence's fate while marching with the Pottawatomie Rifle Company to the town's defence in the early morning of May 22. It was beyond his bearing that this final aggression should go unpunished. On the dark night of May 23, 1856, accompanied by seven men (four sons, a son-in-law, two others), armed with pistols and short swords, he crept stealthily upon the isolated cabins of proslavery men on Pottawatomie Creek near

Osawatomie to act the part God had assigned him. In the morning five dead bodies were found along creek and road. Not one of these victims had been a man conspicuously prone to violence by the standards prevailing on that violent frontier, though one was a member of the Shawnee Mission legislature; two were mere boys in their teens, slaughtered with their father. Not one had been given a chance to defend himself. And the killing had been done with ferocious brutality. Every body bore stab wounds (one had also a bullet hole through the forehead) and four had been horribly mutilated—skull split open, neck gashed, fingers and arm cut off, gaping holes torn in chest and side—by the swords that had killed them.

                              V

   This atrocity was quickly generally known throughout Kansas to be the work of Old Brown and, sad to say, was generally approved by free-staters at the time, they being convinced that it would strike terror into the hearts of proslavers who could be deterred only in this way from brutal aggressions of their own. Its predictable effect, however, was immediate retaliatory action by border Missourians. Some two dozen of them, seeking Brown, marched on Osawatomie, where they captured and turned over to U.S. Army troops two of Brown's sons (the two were imprisoned with other indicted "traitors" in the stockade at Lecompton); they also looted and burned several buildings. Early next morning, in their bivouac at Black Jack, they were surprised by Brown who, with twenty-eight men, captured them all after a brisk firefight. Thus was initiated a border war, a nasty no-holds-barred guerrilla warfare, that raged across eastern Kansas all through the summer of 1856.
   At the outset the situation of the free-staters appeared desperate. All their top political leaders save Lane were imprisoned—and Lane, under indictment for treason, remained out of the territory. They were cut off from reinforcements and supplies when the Missouri River and all Missouri overland routes were closed to free-state traffic immediately following the Pottawatomie massacre: would-be settlers were turned back; emigrant

aid and other free Kansas shipments were seized as contraband by grimly determined Missourians. They were under constant threat of military action against them by federal troops, called out to suppress "insurrection," and of assault by proslavery irregulars centered upon three strategic strongpoints (Franklin, Fort Titus, Fort Saunders) in the Kansas valley. "The prospects of freedom are gloomy," wrote the Lawrence correspondent of the *Chicago Tribune* on May 31, proclaiming a "reign of terror" in Kansas. "The Northern squatters are yielding to despair," said he. When the free-state "legislature" attempted to meet in Topeka on July 4 it was dispersed, with an awesome show of force (dragoons surrounded the meeting hall; two pieces of artillery were trained down Topeka's main street), by U.S. troops acting upon urgent pleas from the territorial executive.

But on the very day (May 31) that the *Chicago Tribune* correspondent wrote his gloomy letter, a gigantic mass meeting in Chicago heard Jim Lane—General Lane, as he was now always called—make an impassioned speech calling for aid to free Kansas. It was as effective a speech as he ever made: thousands were aroused to the highest pitch of action-breeding excitement. Some fifteen thousand dollars was pledged in aid; some one hundred and twenty-five Chicagoans declared their readiness to depart at once for settlement in Kansas; and plans were laid for flanking the Missouri blockade by opening an emigrant trail across Iowa, from the railhead at Iowa City, into Nebraska, thence southward to Topeka. In following weeks the trail was marked by stone cairns ("Lane's Chimneys") on hills, while towns along the way organized travel-aid facilities. The day that saw the Topeka legislature forcibly dispersed saw also publication of a circular announcing establishment of the "Lane Trail." And by that time dozens of great Kansas-aid meetings had been held all across the North to raise money and accumulate arms, provisions, and clothing for embattled free-staters. On July 9, in Buffalo, a national Kansas committee of seventeen prominent men from eleven states was organized. Abraham Lincoln was one of the seventeen. The committee established in Chicago an outfitting station for Kansas emigrants and, during its six months of existence, would raise approximately one hundred and twenty thousand dollars and would ship tons of supplies. In late July a separate state Kansas committee was organized in Massachusetts; it would raise in five months forty-eight thousand dollars in cash and ship westward some twenty-four thousand dollars worth of supplies.

All through July, newspapers, North and South, carried excited and exciting stories about hundreds of armed man, "General Lane's Army of the North," marching to the aid of the free-staters along the Lane Trail—stories that buoyed the theretofore sagging morale of the free-staters while arousing the greatest alarm among proslavers. Equal alarm was aroused among the sober-minded men who comprised the national Kansas committee. These feared above all else a collision between a free-state military organization and federal troops called into action by the federal executive at the behest of the territorial government. Such a collision would be in fact that "high treason" and "armed insurrection" of which the Topeka Movement had been accused by the Lecompton executive. So two representatives of the committee journeyed full-speed westward, caught up with the "army" in Nebraska, and, to their mingled dismay and relief, found that it consisted of some four hundred ill-supplied emigrants, including women and children, whose only martial quality was supplied by the warlike General Lane's attachment to it in a leadership role. With difficulty, he was persuaded to separate himself from his "command" and to permit this separation to be immediately publicized. He then, with a party of thirty armed men, entered Kansas disguised as "Joe Cook" and at once assumed command of the free-state militia along the Kaw, where invasion by an overwhelming force of Missourians was daily expected. John Brown, who had gone north to meet Lane's "army," was among the party of thirty, disguised as "Isaac Smith."

Lane's re-entry took place on August 7. Within ten days thereafter all three of the proslavery strongpoints along the Kaw had been taken by the free-staters in relatively bloodless encounters (though several men were killed), Lane making full exploitive use of the fear his name inspired among proslavers, of his talent for tactical deception, and of the fact that the Sharps rifle had greater range and accuracy than the weapons in proslavers' hands. He was also greatly aided by his friend and chief military subordinate, Capt. Samuel Walker. It was Walker, in fact, who reduced Fort Titus after Lane, for some never-explained reason, left his embattled men for a brief visit across the Nebraska border.

There ensued some two weeks of intense anxiety and mounting fatal danger.

Administratively impotent and totally demoralized, being now fully convinced of the futility of any further attempt to force slavery upon Kansas, yet with his very life threatened (as he believed) by proslavers who violently resented his feeble efforts to restrain them, Gov. Wilson Shannon on August 18 submitted his written resignation to President Pierce. A day or so later he, in effect, fled the territory. His departure was cheered by his erstwhile supporters. It meant that Secretary of State Daniel Woodson, much more militant than Shannon, became acting territorial governor. And Woodson promptly took the most extreme possible action. He announced that a state of "open rebellion" against duly constituted authority existed in the territory. He called out the territorial (proslavery) militia. He called for the aid of federal troops to crush armed insurrection. He welcomed, as augmentation of his meager local militia, a march into Kansas of a "Grand Army" of Missourians, some thousand of them, heavily armed and heavily liquored, led by Atchison. He encouraged the property-destroying harassment of free-staters in the vicinity of the territorial capital. Lane, meanwhile, breathing fire and brimstone, ostentatiously gathered his forces for an attack upon Lecompton, where, he proclaimed, "Governor" Robinson and the other treason prisoners would be freed by him and the "hell-hounds" of slavery destroyed.

A bloody encounter appeared unavoidable and imminent.

Fortunate indeed, at this juncture, was Jim Lane's penchant for indirection, his politician's aversion (for all his bombast) to headon collisions whereby the politician's compromising, negotiating art was rendered useless. Equally fortunate was the common sense and self-control, the commitment to decency and fair

play, that characterized Col. Philip St. George Cooke, commandant of Fort Leavenworth. These two measures of good fortune
fused into one in early September.

On August 29 some four hundred of Atchison's "Grand
Army" invested Osawatomie and, next day, drove out of the
village, after sharp bloody fighting (John Brown's son Frederick
was killed), Old Brown and the remnants of his original force of
thirty or forty men. Osawatomie was then looted and burned to
the ground. But the seemingly imminent (and inevitably much
bloodier) battle between Lane's free-state militia and the
proslavery forces was luckily delayed by Lane's tactically unsound division of his command into two units, one to advance
on the north side of the Kansas River, the other simultaneously
on the south side, where stood Lecompton. As generally happens in such cases, there was a failure of co-ordination: Lane,
commanding the southern advance, failed to arrive at the designated point until long after the scheduled time; and when he did,
he found that the northern unit, convinced that something must
have gone very wrong, had retired to Lawrence. By then, Colonel Cooke with his federal troops had arrived at Lecompton. He
refused to attack Lane, as Woodson urged him to do. Instead he
used his dominating military power to separate the antagonists.
He effected an exchange of prisoners captured by both sides
during the immediately preceding weeks. He encouraged a dispersal of proslavery militia, already underway out of the Mis-
sourian healthy respect for Lane's much-publicized (self-
publicized) fighting qualities. He called in person at Lane's
headquarters and persuaded him, with no great difficulty, to
abort the operation against Lecompton.

A few days later, the third territorial governor to be appointed
by Pierce arrived in Leavenworth.

Gov. John W. Geary was a stronger character, a more experienced administrator, and in general far better equipped than
either of his predecessors to respond effectively to the challenge
that Kansas presented to a political executive. Arrived at Lecompton, he moved to restore to Kansas, or impose upon it for
the first time, an evenhanded rule of law. He almost succeeded.
Robinson was released from the prison stockade on five thou-

sand dollars bond. The territorial (proslavery) militia was effectively ordered to disarm and disband. The same order was enforced upon the free-state militia. Both Lane and John Brown were persuaded (by events? by Geary personally?) to leave the territory for several months. This last action was helpful to the new governor: the mere presence of these two men was deemed an incitement to violence by the proslavery party. Peaceable farmers returned to farmsteads earlier abandoned, and by mid-autumn the towns were as quiet, the roads as safe, as they had ever been in Kansas.

Yet in the end Geary's administration suffered the same fate as Reeder's and Shannon's, and for the same reason: every attempt at evenhanded justice provoked the violent wrath of proslavers on both sides of the Missouri line, and the governor was utterly unable to master the ruffians of the Bogus Legislature. His legislative messages were without effect, his orders to law enforcement agents were increasingly ignored, his efforts at judicial reform were frustrated by proslavery judges, and, more and more seriously, his life was threatened by proslavery extremists. In mid-March of 1857 he fled the territory, travelling at night.

But by then the last remote chance that Kansas could be made into a slave state through force and terror had been lost. It was recognized even by the proslavery party to have been lost in August and September of 1856, when the events I've described secured to free-state forces the valley of the Kaw and greatly strengthened the national (Northern) support of the Kansas free-state cause. Thereafter, peace reigned almost uninterrupted in the area centered on Lawrence, where all the crucial encounters had occurred.

In southeastern Kansas, however, where proslavery strength, augmented by flights from Lecompton and centered on Fort Scott, was probably greater in 1857 than it had been along the Kaw in 1856 and where, thanks to John Brown, the ugliest, bloodiest events of the Kansas ''war'' had already occurred—in southeast Kansas, violence continued unabated, if also without effect upon the central historical issue. The policy of aggressive action initiated by Old Brown was continued by a lawless freebooting band of free-state settlers in Miami, Linn, and Bourbon counties. Led by an abolitionist fanatic from Ohio named James Montgomery—a former schoolteacher, in his late forties, who was a hero-worshipper of John Brown—these men raided across the territorial line into the neighboring Missouri counties of Cass, Bates, and Vernon, where they assaulted slaveholders, sometimes fatally; forcibly freed slaves, who were then sent northward along the Underground Railway; and returned to their Kansas homes loaded with plunder: money, jewelry, household furnishings, clothing, horses and mules. This raiding became known as "jayhawking" and those who engaged in it soon gloried in the title "jayhawker."

There was retaliation, of course.

In May of 1858 a native Georgian named Charles A. Hamelton, who had settled in Linn County and had (as proslaver) suffered from, and been embittered by, the political and physical victories of the free-staters, led a gang of Missourians across the line near the hamlet called Trading Post for the avowed purpose of wreaking fatal vengeance upon men, his erstwhile neighbors, whom he deemed particularly obnoxious. He carried a list of their names. Eleven of them were captured, one at a time, and taken as a group into a ravine beside the Marais des Cygnes. There they were lined up against a raw earthen bank. A volley was fired. All eleven fell. Five were killed outright. A sixth was killed as he lay wounded on the ground. Four, badly wounded, were left for dead, but survived. The eleventh man, miraculously, was not hit at all but fell with his companions and, splashed with their blood, feigned death successfully.

Some weeks later, John Brown, who had been absent from the territory many months as he prepared to strike a final blow against slavery, in Virginia, reappeared in Kansas. In the last month of the year he led a raiding party across the Missouri line, destroyed considerable property, killed a slaveholder and liberated eleven slaves—an act that effectively ended the "jayhawking" of the territorial years by provoking a Missouri executive and legislative response sufficiently strong to deter it. A reward of $3,000 was offered by Missouri for John Brown's arrest. The reward was never paid, of course. Old Brown per-

sonally led the eleven freed Negroes northward, then departed
for his rendezvous with destiny at Harper's Ferry. . . .

VI

None of this southeastern border violence of 1857 and 1858
had (to repeat) any historically decisive effect whatever. The
last forceful attempt of the proslavers having finally failed in
1856, popular sovereignty was given a chance to operate at the
ballot box according to the terms Douglas's bill had vaguely
defined—and insofar as this purely local sovereignty could answer the question of whether Kansas would be free, the answer,
given in the autumn of 1857, was emphatically affirmative.

The question, however, was *not* purely local. It was, as has
been stressed, a *national* question and could be finally answered
only by a total, unequivocal national decision. Every event on
Kansas soil from 1854 onward had had immense national political repercussions. Even before the Kansas-Nebraska bill was
passed, the existing two-party system was being broken up by
"the hell of a storm" Douglas had raised: Northern Whigs and
disaffected Democrats who had formed a Free-Soil party in
1848 merged, in 1854, with other outraged free-state citizens to
form a new Republican party that was at once strong enough to
win a majority of the lower house of Congress in the mid-term
elections barely eight months later. Thereafter the new party,
exclusively Northern and thus ominously implying a party exclusively Southern, fed and waxed in strength on read-and-
heard reports that vastly amplified the sound and exaggerated
the fury of every confrontation between freedom and slavery in
Kansas Territory. Terrific in any case would have been the impact upon antislavery consciousness of news that Lawrence,
K. T., had been sacked on May 21, 1856, by a proslavery mob
from Missouri that had been designated a law-enforcement
arm (!) of territorial government—a government that, in turn,
was the agent of national administration policy. Shattering of
every disposition toward moderation and compromise was the
joining of this news with that of the clubbing near to death on
the U.S. Senate floor of Sen. Charles Sumner of Massachusetts

by Rep. Preston S. Brooks of South Carolina on May 22, after Sumner had delivered an excessively long and (admittedly) intemperate speech on "The Crime Against Kansas."

The Kansas issue overshadowed all others in the 1856 presidential campaign. The young Republican party, essentially a single-issue (antislavery) party, nominated as its candidate the dashing "Pathfinder of the West," John C. Fremont, who won eleven free states, including all the northeast. The dying Whig party nominated former President Millard Fillmore, who carried but a single state, Maryland. The Democratic candidate, James Buchanan (Pierce was not even seriously considered by his party for a second term), won the election, but with a popular vote considerably less than the combined votes for his opponents, and though he won fourteen slave states by a wide margin he won only five free ones, in none of which was his victory margin impressive.

He could not have won at all within the prevailing party system had he not been, like Pierce, a "dough-face"—that is, "a Northern man with Southern principles"—which is to say that he won on such terms as made it almost impossible for him to take any action strongly opposed by the slave power, even had he been personally disposed to do so. And he was not so disposed. A strict constructionist who took the narrowest possible view of the constitutional powers of the federal executive, he was convinced that the Union could be preserved only if the political leaders of the planter South were permitted to have their way. He had not been an hour in office when his personal inclinations and governmental conceptions caused him to blunder disastrously. He said in his inaugural address that the question of slavery in the territories was in process of decision by the U.S. Supreme Court and that all good Americans must accept this decision as the definitive, the final answer. This implied that he knew what the decision would be; it suggested to many that he had had a hand in shaping it (he seems, in fact, to have used his influence as president-elect to bring one undecided justice into line with the majority); and it joined him to Chief Justice Roger B. Taney as target of the opprobrium at once attached to the Dred Scott decision when this was read by Taney for the seven-justice (Democratic) majority two days later. The decision was aggressively wrongheaded and outrageous of first principles. The Negro had no rights a white man was "bound to respect," it declared, and Congress no right to bar slavery from territories—the latter clearly implying that no territorial legislature could do so either since territories were creatures of Congress. Even popular sovereignty appeared doomed.

And the bitter anger this provoked among Kansas free-staters was not reduced by the announcement, four days after Dred Scott, that Robert J. Walker had been appointed by Buchanan to succeed Geary as governor of Kansas Territory. A native of Pennsylvania, Walker had profited as a young man from speculations in Mississippi land and slaves, had been Polk's secretary of the treasury during the Mexican War, and was naturally assumed by Kansans to be as fervently proslavery as Wilson Shannon or Daniel Woodson. Actually Walker was a free-soiler in his private views, having been soured upon the Peculiar Institution by his personal experience of it. He was as determined as Geary had been to make popular sovereignty work fairly in Kansas and had been persuaded to accept the governorship only after Buchanan solemnly pledged full administration support of this effort.

Delayed by personal business, Walker did not arrive in Lecompton and make there his inaugural address (it had been read and approved by the president) until May 27. His words were yet another expression of faith in Natural Law as a solver of human problems: it repeated arguments Douglas had made during the Kansas-Nebraska debate, that Lane had reportedly used when first he came to Kansas. "There is a law more powerful than the legislation of men, more potent than passion or prejudice, that must ultimately determine the location of slavery in this country," Walker proclaimed: "it is the isothermal line; it is the law of the thermometer, of latitude or altitude, regulating climate, labor, and productions, and, as a consequence, profit and loss." But Walker's faith (a touching faith, at so late a date) had limits. The "isothermal line" would not automatically solve everything. If it ruled against slavery in the territory there would remain the question of whether Kansas was to "become a

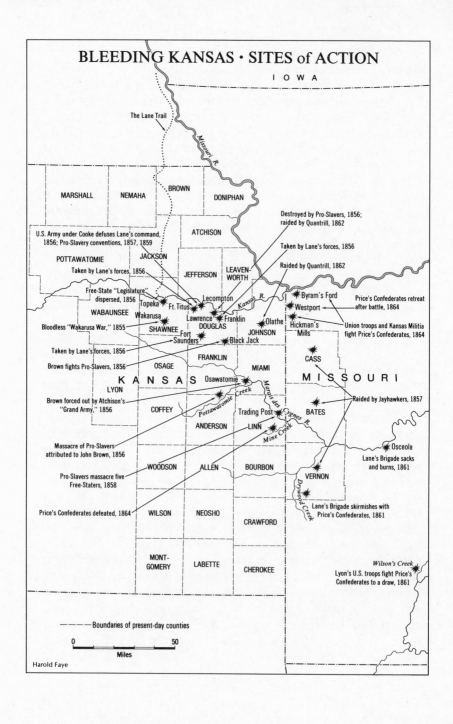

BLEEDING KANSAS · SITES of ACTION

I O W A

The Lane Trail

Missouri R.

MARSHALL NEMAHA BROWN DONIPHAN

Destroyed by Pro-Slavers, 1856;
raided by Quantrill, 1862

U.S. Army under Cooke defuses Lane's command,
1856; Pro-Slavery conventions, 1857, 1859

ATCHISON

Taken by Lane's forces, 1856

POTTAWATOMIE   JACKSON

Taken by Lane's forces, 1856

JEFFERSON   LEAVEN-
WORTH

Raided by Quantrill, 1862

Free-State "Legislature"
dispersed, 1856   Topeka ☆ Ft. Titus
Lawrence ☆

Lecompton   *Kansas R.*

Byram's Ford ☆   Price's Confederates retreat
after battle, 1864

☆ Westport ◄

WABAUNSEE   Wakarusa

Bloodless "Wakarusa War," 1855   SHAWNEE
Fort
Saunders ☆   DOUGLAS   ☆ Franklin   ☆ Olathe   Hickman's   Union troops and Kansas Militia
Mills   fight Price's Confederates, 1864

Taken by Lane's forces, 1856
☆ Black Jack   JOHNSON ☆

Brown fights Pro-Slavers, 1856   FRANKLIN

OSAGE   MIAMI   CASS

K A N S A S   Osawatomie ☆   M I S S O U R I

LYON   *Pottawatomie Creek*   *Marais des Cygnes R.*

Brown forced out by Atchison's
"Grand Army," 1856   COFFEY   Trading Post ☆   ☆ BATES   Raided by Jayhawkers, 1857

ANDERSON   LINN ☆   *Mine Creek*

Massacre of Pro-Slavers
attributed to John Brown, 1856

Osceola

Pro-Slavers massacre five
Free-Staters, 1858   WOODSON   ALLEN   BOURBON   Lane's Brigade sacks
and burns, 1861

☆ VERNON

Drywood Creek

Price's Confederates defeated, 1864   WILSON   NEOSHO   Lane's Brigade skirmishes with
Price's Confederates, 1861

CRAWFORD

MONT-
GOMERY   LABETTE   CHEROKEE   *Wilson's Creek* ☆
Lyon's U.S. troops fight Price's
Confederates to a draw, 1861

-------- Boundaries of present-day counties

0 |————|————|————|————| 50
Miles

Harold Faye

State controlled by the treason and fanaticism of Abolition" (". . . an asylum for [Missouri's] fugitive slaves, . . . a propagandist of Abolition. . . .") or, instead, a good neighbor to Missouri, fulfilling its "constitutional duties" to an adjacent slaveholding state—and this was a question Kansans themselves, as human beings, must answer. The wrong answer would be "fatal to the continuance of the American Union." [3]

He then moved promptly and vigorously to assure Kansans of fair and honest elections—or, at least, elections as fair as was permitted by the palpably unjust apportionment of representation the Bogus Legislature had decreed. He was unable to persuade free-staters to participate in the election of delegates to a constitutional convention to be held in Lecompton that fall— an election held in mid-June, too soon for the free-staters to have become convinced that the new governor really did mean fair play. Only 2,200 of 9,251 registered voters cast ballots in this election, which, of course, resulted in a unanimously proslavery convention. But after much soul-searching and heated arguments in conventions of their own, free-staters did participate in the election of a new legislature, October 6, 1857. Precinct policing by federal troops reduced illegal voting in this election. Nevertheless there was obvious fraud in two areas— enough of it to enable proslavers to retain control of the legislature if the fraudulent returns were accepted. Walker threw them out, to the intense fury of proslavers. This gave the Free-State party a decisive majority of both houses. The legislature would no more be "bogus" and the extra-legal "Topeka legislature" might now be dispensed with.

But two weeks later the proslavery constitutional convention assembled in Lecompton. When it adjourned on November 3 it reported a draft constitution, which said that the "right of property is before and higher than any constitutional sanction, and the right of the owner of a slave and its increase is the same and as inviolable as the right of the owner of any property whatever." It also provided for a manner of submitting this document to the vote of the people that would, in effect, deny them

3. The address is excerpted by Daniel W. Wilder, *Annals of Kansas* (Topeka: Kansas Publishing House, 1875), p. 125.

any real choice with regard to slavery, since obviously this constitution would be emphatically rejected if the Kansas electorate were permitted to vote freely and fairly upon it. The "Schedule" called upon the electorate to choose, in a vote to be taken December 21, between the "Constitution with Slavery" and the "Constitution with no Slavery"—but this "Schedule" also said that, no matter how the vote came out, "the right of property in slaves now in this Territory shall in no manner be interfered with."

Events thereafter moved swiftly.

Facing the same Missouri-based proslavery wrath that had driven his predecessors from office, abandoned by Buchanan, who was hardly less wrathful than the local proslavers over the governor's rejection of the fraudulent October ballots, Walker resigned his office on December 17 and was succeeded, reluctantly, by James W. Denver. The free-staters boycotted the December 21 balloting wherein there was again massive fraud and whose announced result was 6,226 for the "Constitution with Slavery," 539 for the "Constitution with no Slavery." The free-staters then, through their control of the legislature, forced a popular vote on the Lecompton Constitution as a whole—balloting (January 4, 1858) in which the proslavers refused to participate but wherein, with *no* measurable fraud, 10,226 votes were cast *against* the constitution.

Thus was demonstrated unmistakably to the whole of the nation, South as well as North, the determination of Kansas to be free—and several leading proslavery Democrats announced their conviction that national administration policy must now be based upon this obvious fact. For instance, no spokesman for the Kansas proslavery cause had been more vehement than J. H. Stringfellow of Atchison, yet he addressed to the *Washington Union* on January 7, 1858, a letter strongly opposing the admission of Kansas under the Lecompton Constitution. The slavery question in Kansas "is settled against the South by immigration," said he. But Buchanan refused (perhaps he was unable) to see or hear. Already he had expressed his desire that Kansas be at once admitted as a slave state—this in his December message to Congress—and he stubbornly persisted in this folly. On

February 2 he submitted the Lecompton Constitution to Congress with a special message asserting that it represented the freely expressed will of the people. He urged the prompt admission of Kansas under it.

And so the last faint chance of preventing the ultimate catastrophe was destroyed.

There followed Douglas's declaration of political war upon Buchanan for having betrayed popular sovereignty; the hopeless splitting of the National Democracy into Northern and Southern factions; the Lincoln-Douglas debates of 1858 whereby the uncompromisable moral issue at the heart of the Kansas question was defined by Lincoln with luminous clarity; the spectacular growth of the Republican party registered by the elections of 1858; the renewed bid of Kansas for admission as a free state under a new constitution drafted at Wyandotte in the summer of 1859; John Brown's fatal blow at Harper's Ferry, his swift trial, his execution in the last month of 1859 (on the day Old Brown was hanged, Abraham Lincoln, speaking in northeastern Kansas, referred to him as a man of surpassing courage and rare selflessness whose punishment for murderous treason was, nonetheless, just); the Republican nomination and election of Lincoln as president of the United States; the secession of Southern states, enabling Congress, as Southern senators withdrew, to admit Kansas under the Wyandotte Constitution (January 29, 1861); the formation of the Confederacy and its organization for war; and Lincoln's sad, desperate, yet determined appeal in his inaugural address to "the better angels of our nature" whose touch upon the "mystic chords of memory" might "yet swell the chorus of Union."

All these events were as flashes of flame along the powder train initiated by practical compromise in the Convention of 1789, extended by practical compromise in 1820 and 1850, yet further extended by the eminently practical, pragmatic Douglas in 1854, and finally ignited beyond hope of dampening by Buchanan, acting as a tool of the slave power, in 1858. Through and from Kansas it led directly, inevitably to the Union-blasting explosion at Fort Sumter in April 1861.

4

The Thirty-Fourth Star
Shines Dimly Through
Smoke Clouds of War

I

*T*HE preceding chapter had to do with the early history and development of Kansas as body politic: it therefore dealt exclusively with political events and leaders. This is not as serious a distortion of the total picture as it would be in the case of most states, because of the intensely politicizing circumstances in which the typical Kansas territorial settler made his westward move, but it is a distortion, all the same.

For most of the typical settler's energies were inevitably absorbed by daily tasks and physical environmental concerns having nothing to do with politics—the harsh tasks of providing, with handtools only, a sufficiency of food and a bare adequacy of shelter for himself and dependents in a wilderness that was only too trackless (the lack of communication facilities bedeviled Kansas economically until well into the 1860s) and often bared its teeth in a slashing hostility to its invaders. Life was lived on the most primitive level. Shelter for the earliest settlers consisted often of dank dugouts that stank of the excrement of chickens, pigs, dogs that shared them with humans; or of wretched log cabins with dirt floors and walls so imperfectly chinked that the bitter winds of winter blasted through them, freezing water sometimes within a few feet of a blazing stove or fireplace. Food was of the coarsest, clothing of the rudest. During the warm seasons farm women quite generally went barefoot and wore trousers under short skirts: even New England women soon did so, women who had "dressed in style" when first they arrived. For food, there was a heavy reliance on wheat bread and corn pone, cornmeal in various forms, and various cuts of pork, with green vegetables during the garden season and root vegetables from the root cellar at other times, but almost no fruit at all, for there were few fruit trees in the territory. The days were filled with dreary, grinding toil from sunup to sundown for both men and women—the men struggling to break fields out of stubborn prairie sod and to cut the wood required for building and fuel, the women struggling constantly and often hopelessly for a minimum of household cleanliness while also performing such tasks as sewing, cooking, soapmaking, candlemaking, and the preparing of food for winter storage. When this labor, which sufficed to produce a bare subsistence, was forcibly interrupted for any extended period by political activity and irregular warfare, outside aid was required to keep the settler alive. There was a great deal of sickness. Indeed, a perusal of the published diaries and letters of frontier families leaves the impression that the average Kansas pioneer was ill to the point of incapacitation for at least a solid month out of every year. Malaria, or "the ague," was endemic. Many called it simply "Kansas fever"—and because it was linked to lowland areas, these, where the soil was immensely fertile, were often shunned in favor of upland areas whose fertility was much less. At Wabaunsee, for instance, where everyone bought his land from the colony organization, where the initial price per acre was the same for all, and where the distribution of acreages was by lot, those who drew rich bottomland along the Kaw received rebates in recognition of the extra risk they ran of illness. Fevers other than the ague were also common, along with poxes, respiratory ailments, and "itches" of various kinds.

Twice during the territorial period did the Kansas weather manifest its tendency to go on occasion to extremes; each time weather became the territory's overriding concern, severely limiting the average settler's interest in anything else for the time being. A violent sleet storm announced the arrival of winter in the Kaw valley in December of 1855, cooling the martial ardor of invading Missourians and hastening their retirement at the close of the Wakarusa War. The winter that followed was, from all accounts, as severe as any Kansas has ever experienced, with deep snows, high winds, and subzero temperatures for days on end. Ill-housed and ill-provisioned, Kansas settlers suffered bitterly: several died from hunger and freezing, and hostilities between free-staters and proslavers, which would certainly have raged through an ordinary mild winter, were for the most part suspended until spring. The opposite weather-curse, an extreme of drouth and heat, befell the territory in 1859–1860. It is recorded that from mid-June of 1859 until November of 1860 not a single rain fell heavy enough to soak two inches into the ground and that, during the intervening winter, there were but two light snows, neither of them heavy enough to hide the ground from view. Both winter and spring wheat failed almost totally (fewer than five hundred bushels were harvested from four thousand acres of good soil in Shawnee County), as did corn, every other crop, and every vegetable garden. Thousands fled the territory, and there would have been wholesale starvation had not Northern states, long accustomed to donating to the Kansas cause, come again to the settler's aid. Upwards of twenty thousand people became wholly or partly dependent upon charitable contributions, which were forthcoming in generous amount from state governments—the New York legislature appropriated fifty thousand dollars, the Wisconsin legislature a somewhat smaller amount—as well as from private donors. (Indeed, in the drouth's aftermath there were charges, never effectively investigated, that relief contributions had been generous beyond minimum needs and that Samuel C. Pomeroy, who managed their distribution as executive of the Kansas Territorial Relief Commission, had quietly assigned the excess to his private pocketbook. Certain it is that he, who aspired to become U.S. senator, made a great deal of political capital out of his relief work: he saw to it that every bag of seed, every sack of flour, every package of clothing was stamped with his name. Moreover, he did become a wealthy man with quite remarkable abruptness in a time and place of general poverty.)

In late May of 1858 twenty men led by John Easter, a butcher, departed Lawrence for "the gold region in the vicinity of the Rocky Mountains in Kansas." Their incitement was a circumstantial tale told Easter by two Delaware chiefs. Three months later a returned member of the party generated excitement in Leavenworth with his report that the Delaware chiefs had spoken truth. There was placer gold on Cherry Creek, and no doubt on other creeks, near Pike's Peak, in the farthest western reaches of Kansas Territory—gold in an abundance rivalling that found at Sutter's Mill in California just ten years before. Immediately, as Daniel W. Wilder records in his *Annals of Kansas*, "Pike's Peak" became "the leading topic of the Kansas press." Within days it was a leading topic in the national press as well, and the gold fever mounted all across the country during the following months, especially among adventurous young men whose start in economic life had been adversely affected by the depression following the financial panic of 1857. In the spring and summer of 1859 there poured through Kansas and Nebraska toward the Rockies a tide of gold-seekers and those who proposed to service them at great profit to themselves—some one hundred thousand men altogether. They found little gold. The placer deposits proved to be few and poor. Virtually all of them had given out by autumn, by which time less than seven hundred and fifty thousand dollars worth of gold had been taken, not enough to offset 10 percent of the total cost of the gold-seekers' equipment and travel; whereupon many thousands who had gone west in the spring with "Pike's Peak or Bust" gaily lettered on their covered wagons returned eastward through Kansas with a wry and rueful "Busted" added to the original lettering.

But by then what had begun, for Kansans, as a wholly apolitical excitement was beginning to have, for them, important political repercussions. For by then there had been established along the western border of Kansas Territory several towns destined to be permanent, notably Denver. The latter, on Cherry

Creek, some fifteen miles from the east front of the Rockies, was named after the fifth governor of Kansas Territory, who was the first to resign his office voluntarily (Denver did so in October of 1858; he was succeeded by Samuel Medary). It had more than five thousand inhabitants by the late summer of 1859. And its survival as the commercial metropolis of a prosperous mining region was assured by the discovery in May 1859 that rich veins of silver as well as gold were buried in the nearby mountain rock. Obviously governing power over this developing area could not be effectively extended across hundreds of miles of empty plain through slender, easily broken lines of communication from a capital in eastern Kansas. So in the late summer and early autumn of 1859 there began the political procedure leading to the creation of the territory of Colorado, just one month after Kansas had become a state.

Nor was there any objection on the part of leading Kansans to this truncation of their own legal territory. At the Wyandotte Convention, the western boundary was fixed where it now is, thereby assigning to Colorado approximately half the width of the westward-climbing High Plains.

Another important effect of the gold rush, for Kansas, was an immediate improvement of east-west communications through the territory, plus further assurance of a central route for the Pacific Railroad. Construction of the transcontinental railroad was delayed all through the 1850s by sectional rivalries and jealousies, North versus South, with the latter insisting upon an extreme southern route. This last was the route chosen by Buchanan's postmaster-general, an ardent proslavery expansionist named A. V. Brown, when a government contract for the carrying of semiweekly mails overland to California was signed in the fall of 1857 with the Butterfield Overland Mail Company. But the leading founder of the Denver Town Company persuaded W. H. Russell of the great freighting and stageline firm of Russell, Majors & Waddell to make Denver the western terminus of a stage line, the Leavenworth & Pike's Peak Express Company, which Russell organized in early 1859. It carried a heavy passenger traffic and much mail and freight from Missouri across the length of Kansas for a few months, again demonstrating the feasibility of the central route as an all-purpose highway and future railway line. Traffic fell off sharply, however, after Colorado's surface mines had given out, and in the end this subsidiary cost Russell, Majors & Waddell a great deal of money.

The same fate befell another Russell enterprise of which the Pike's Peak gold rush was a partial stimulus. This was the Pony Express. The announcement in late January 1860 that it was being organized and would begin operation on April 3 caused much excitement in Kansas. Cried the *Leavenworth Daily Times:* "GREAT EXPRESS ENTERPRISE! FROM LEAVEN-WORTH TO SACRAMENTO IN TEN DAYS! CLEAR THE TRACK AND LET THE PONY COME THROUGH!" Actually no pony of the express passed within forty miles of Leavenworth. The route stretched from Saint Joseph, Missouri, across two thousand miles of prairie and plain, mountain and desert, with the Kansas portion of it running through Doniphan, Brown, Nemaha, and Marshall counties, then northwestward across the northeastern corner of Washington County toward the Platte River. Along this route were stations spaced nine to fifteen miles apart—there were a dozen of them in Kansas—at each of which the rider was mounted on a fresh pony. A bare two minutes was allowed for the transfer to a new horse, or new horse and rider. A normal day's ride for each expressman (or night's ride; the express operated day and night, in every kind of weather) was through three stations, using two remounts—some thirty to fifty miles covered, wherever terrain permitted, at full gallop. The service began at the promised time, the schedule was maintained from the first, was often shortened thereafter, and the Pony Express rider became a national hero. He deserved the role. Invariably a young man of light weight, wiry, strong, with immense stamina and courage, he daily (nightly) performed feats of superb horsemanship, risking his life in wilderness country that was also often hostile Indian country; and invariably he brought the mail through.

The venture, however, was a commercial disaster, despite the high rates charged (initially five dollars per letter) in addition to regular postage. It continued for only eighteen months, until the transcontinental telegraph was completed in the fall of 1861, and in that time its total receipts failed to pay one-tenth of its total costs. The Pony Express ruined the great firm of Russell, Majors & Waddell, which had played a major role in the opening of the West; the business was forced to close several years before the westward-building railroads had rendered obsolete its stage and wagon-freighting operations.

II

For Kansans, the outbreak of the Civil War was not the shock that it was to most Americans and meant no totally new departure from familiar ways of life. Nearly all the men in the new state were of military age, nearly all had been to some extent involved in local militia activities, and the women of Kansas had become inured to hardship and danger, and used to thinking of themselves as the companions of warriors for freedom. The national war, for these people, but continued and elevated to the level of tragic drama the melodrama, always crude, often absurd, of Bleeding Kansas. Such fighting as occurred on or adjacent to the Kansas soil was for the most part an enlarged repetition of the violence that had raged a few years before down the valley of the Kaw, was an amplified prolongation of the violence that had never entirely ceased in southeast Kansas.

As for Kansas political events during the Civil War period, they proceeded strictly according to the dramatic plot or pattern that had begun to take shape in the late summer of 1855 and was finally determined by the dissolution of the Free-State party and the organization of the Kansas Republican party (or by the manner in which this happened), in 1859. In other words, politics and war were fused as they had been—as personal economic motive and ideological commitment had been—in territorial days. There was now even the same cast of characters in the starring roles as there had been before—Robinson, Lane, Pomeroy, et al—with the salient personal features of each character magnified and intensified in proportion to the increased scale of event.

Kansas, a one-party territory from 1856 onward, was a one-party state, a Republican state, when admitted to the Union. As would be generally true throughout the first century of its existence, its important political oppositions were not between Democrats and Republicans but between factions of the latter. "Governor" Robinson of the territorial period became Republican Governor Robinson of the new state; Republicans Jim Lane and Sam Pomeroy, having made a secret deal in which they pooled their support in the legislature (senators were then elected by the legislature), became the state's first two U.S. senators; the central conflict of Kansas politics, supplying frictional heat aplenty for the first two years of statehood, continued to be the feud between Lane and Robinson; and Lane, who had won most of his battles with Robinson during the territorial period, continued to win victories, finally scoring one so complete that Robinson, though he tried, was never again able to win important elective office.

This final victory came from a full and ruthless exploitation of the Robinson administration's vulnerability, and culpability, in the illegal sale of state bonds—a sale pressed by the new state's desperate financial condition. The transaction was too complicated to be explained in the space available here. Suffice it to say that a state law was most certainly broken, that the breaking of it netted substantial profits to close associates of Robinson if not to Robinson himself (there is no conclusive evidence regarding this last allegation), and that Lane was instrumental in the initiation of proceedings in the legislature that resulted in the impeachment of Kansas's governor, auditor, and secretary of state for "high misdemeanors in office." In the subsequent trial, the auditor and secretary of state were convicted. Robinson was acquitted. His political effectiveness, however, was destroyed. He was not renominated for a second term when the state Republican convention, dominated by Lane, met in September of 1862. The nomination went to Thomas Carney, who was inaugurated governor in 1863. But the split in Kansas Republicanism between Lane and anti-Lane factions continued, and Carney's political doom was sealed when, tempted by a typically oily piece of deceit on the part of Sam Pomeroy, who was among the leaders of the anti-Lane faction, he joined the latter and attempted by trickery to obtain for himself the Senate seat Lane held. He went down, then, under Lane's adroitly powerful assaults.

The main source of Lane's political preponderance, aside from his native skill and indefatigable local "politicking," was his friendship, personal as well as political, with Abraham Lincoln: from this came his control over federal patronage in Kansas, used by him with great shrewdness and utter ruthlessness, in the Jacksonian spoilsman tradition in which he had been reared, to gain and consolidate power. The mutual attraction of president and senator puzzled contemporary observers and has confounded several historians. "Lane's singular influence over Mr. Lincoln and the secretary of war, Mr. Stanton, is one of the most inexplicable and disastrous facts that concern Kansas in 1861–65," says Leverett W. Spring in his *Kansas,* a beautifully written little book having a strong pro-Robinson New England bias.[1] Lane first met Lincoln during the latter's speaking tour of northeast Kansas in December 1859. But their friendship had its beginnings in April 1861, when Senator Lane, newly arrived in a Washington highly fearful of capture by Confederates exulting over Sumter, raised a company of 120 volunteers, with himself as captain, and was assigned by the regular military to guard the White House. For a couple of nights, until other arrangements could be made, he and his "Frontier Guard" bivouacked on the velvet carpet of the East Room. For the whole of a tense crowded week he was in daily intimate contact with the president. And for the rest of Lincoln's life Lane's "singular influence" over him continued, and was reciprocated (Lincoln's "singular influence" over Lane seems actually to have increased after Lincoln's death), affecting national and Kansas history in ways that, I think, were more subtle, more complex, more important, and less wicked overall than Spring suggests.

In the summer of 1861, without having resigned his Senate seat, Lane appeared in Kansas armed with presidential authority to raise two regiments of volunteers and, as brigadier general,

1. Leverett W. Spring, *Kansas: The Prelude to the War for the Union* (Boston: Houghton, Mifflin and Co., 1885), pp. 273–274.

command a Kansas brigade (it was at once known as the "Lane Brigade") in action against Confederate forces in Missouri. Robinson promptly declared Lane's Senate seat vacant and appointed to it Frederick Stanton, who, as a member of the Robinson faction, had been a candidate for it in the March election. Lane hurried back to Washington to defend his seat in hearings before the Senate judiciary hearings, argued on purely technical grounds that he had not yet *really* accepted the brigadier general's commission, managed to postpone a final decision until Congress had adjourned its special session, then returned to Kansas where, on August 17, he assumed command of the Third, Fourth, and Fifth Kansas regiments at Fort Scott. He named as his second-in-command the notorious Jayhawker Montgomery, now a colonel in command of the Third Kansas, and had also under him the most cruel, rapacious, unscrupulous Jayhawker of them all, Charles R. Jennison. Of this brigade of twelve hundred men some units were virtually criminal gangs, and no unit was adequately disciplined.

By that time two Kansas regiments, the First and Second infantry, had distinguished themselves in battle. On August 10, at Wilson's Creek in southwestern Missouri, they had been among the forward units in action under Gen. Nathanial Lyon against Confederate troops under Gen. Sterling Price—an action in which the Union troops were forced to retreat following Lyon's death on the field but which was in effect a stalemate. No battle of the whole war had a higher percentage of casualties among those engaged than this one (more than 23 percent of the approximately eleven thousand on both sides were killed or wounded), and no Union regiment there suffered more than the First Kansas, which lost 284 out of 644 men. The Second Kansas lost only somewhat less. Company E of the First, commanded by young Capt. Samuel J. Crawford, a political friend of Lane's, went into battle with 76 and came out with 26. Company F of the Second Kansas, commanded by Lane's fighting friend of '56, Capt. Samuel Walker, went into battle with 64 and came out with 24. Throughout the war, as a matter of fact, Kansas supplied more fighting men to the Union cause, in proportion to the total male population of fighting age, than any other state in the Union and had, of all states, the highest battle mortality rate. Among the main actions in which Kansas troops participated were Corinth in Mississippi; Pine Bluff, Pea Ridge, Cane Hill, Pilot Knob, and Prairie Grove in Arkansas; Chickamauga in Georgia; and Lookout Mountain in Tennessee. Kansas troops fought with Grant throughout the valley campaign that ended with the fall of Vicksburg, and with Sherman in the campaign climaxed by the fall of Atlanta. Of heroic sacrificial blood, and of such glories as a battlefield may yield, Kansas had sown and harvested its full measure by April of 1865.

But no glory came from the operations of Lane's Brigade in the fall of 1861. At Drywood Creek in Missouri on September 2, a detachment of this brigade skirmished for a short hour with a small advance guard of Price's force, then retreated precipitously, causing panic in Fort Scott (evacuated by its residents, the town was plundered by Jennison's men, who were supposed to defend it)—and this was the nearest approach to a set battle the brigade as a whole had made when Lane, after three months of command, resumed his Senate seat in Washington. His most notable achievement was the sacking and burning of the defenceless town of Osceola on September 23 (Lane's personal share of the loot is said to have included a thousand dollars in gold, a number of silk dresses, and a piano)—an achievement that greatly augmented the flaming hatred of Lane and Kansans throughout western Missouri.

Further fuel was piled upon this fire of hatred by Lane's recruitment of Negro soldiers. He was the first Union commander to enlist Negroes for combat service, and many if not most of his First Regiment of Kansas Colored Volunteers were Missouri slaves forcibly freed from their owners by his brigade. Lincoln, whose overriding concern in 1861 was to secure Missouri and other border slave states to the Union, publicly officially opposed the recruitment of Negroes as fighting men. But he personally loathed slavery and was increasingly impressed by the logic of such public statements as the one Governor Robinson made in his March 1861 message to the first Kansas legislature. At a time when Lincoln, anxious to prevent Virginia's secession, had not made up his mind to supply Fort Sumter,

Robinson declared: "If it is true that the continued existence of slavery requires the destruction of the Union, it is time to ask if the existence of the Union does not require the destruction of slavery." Lincoln now asked himself that question and did nothing effectively to halt Lane's black recruitment. The fact that Lane's Negroes actually engaged in combat against Missouri bushwhackers on at least one greatly publicized occasion, acquitting themselves well, gave impetus to the process leading toward the Emancipation Proclamation of January 1, 1863, wherein Lincoln proposed the use of Negro troops in the Union armies. (Subsequently, the First and Second Kansas Colored, the latter commanded by the aforementioned Samuel J. Crawford, distinguished themselves in regular combat.)

As for Lane's sacking of Osceola, it gave a decided impetus to the process leading toward Quantrill's murderous assault upon a defenceless Lawrence in 1863.

William C. Quantrill became the most feared as he was the most ferocious of all the Missouri guerrilla commanders within a few months after he organized his band of irregulars in December of 1861. In raids across the Kansas line, in 1862, he shot down scores of unarmed civilians and plundered and destroyed much property. Particularly bloody and destructive was his raid of Olathe in August of 1862. But Lawrence, where he had lived in the 1850s under the assumed name of Charley Hart and where he was under indictment for crimes of burglary, horse-thievery, and Negro-kidnapping (he'd fled town to avoid arrest)—Lawrence, capital of Kansas abolitionism and home of the hated Jim Lane, whom he purposed to capture and (literally) burn alive—Lawrence was the special object of his vengeful wrath. With three hundred horsemen he crossed the line near Aubrey in the early evening of August 20, 1863. His passage was witnessed but unprotested by a company of Union soldiers whose captain, incredibly, despatched no warning courier westward; so that it was a wholly unsuspecting and unprotected Lawrence that, at five o'clock in the morning of Friday, August 21, was awakened from sleep by the sound of galloping hooves, revolver shots, bloodcurdling yells, and the screams of wounded and dying men. Four hours later, the marauders, bloodstained and loaded with loot, formed column and rode eastward, leaving behind them a scene of horror. All the business district and two hundred houses of the town were either destroyed or aflame. Dead men by the dozen, some one hundred and eighty in all, shot down with no chance for self-defence, lay sprawled upon sidewalks and streets, in yards and gardens, and amid flaming ruins: the nauseating stench of burning human flesh was everywhere, under the heavy pall of smoke.

It is remarkable that, of Lawrence's most prominent citizens, only the mayor was killed in this massacre. Charles Robinson and Jim Lane were both in town. Both escaped. Lane, clad in his nightshirt, fled his newly built brick house a few minutes before Quantrill's men reached it (the house was promptly looted and burned), hid in a cornfield until the raiders departed, then organized and led a vigorous pursuit of them that, though ineffectual, did him more credit than his field operations as brigade commander. Four days later, on August 25, Brig. Gen. Thomas Ewing, Jr., who commanded the District of the Border (Kansas and Missouri), issued his famous General Order No. 11 whereby all residents of three Missouri border counties and a portion of a fourth, save those living within a mile of five named towns, including Independence and Kansas City, were required to move or to be forcibly removed from their homes. The carrying out of this harsh order caused great hardship for thousands of people, who had had nothing whatever to do with guerrilla activities but was perhaps justified on military security grounds. After the execution of Order No. 11 there were no bushwhacker raids on Kansas towns.

Only once during the war was Kansas threatened with large-scale invasion by regular Confederate forces. In the fall of 1864 forces under Gen. Sterling Price struck through Missouri toward Leavenworth and Kansas City. The Kansas militia was called out, somewhat tardily, by Governor Carney to support the regular Union troops in the area, and fought bravely in battles at Byram's Ford and Hickman's Mills on the Blue River, near Kansas City, Missouri, on October 22; at Westport (now a part of Kansas City) the following day; and at Mine Creek in Linn County, Kansas, on October 25. Price then retreated into Arkansas.

His raid affected the outcome of that year's elections in Kansas.

Lane had played a leading role in the nomination of Lincoln for a second term. This last was by no means a foregone conclusion in early 1864, when the war was going badly and seemed interminable. Secretary of the Treasury Salmon P. Chase, supported by powerful financial and commercial interests, aspired to (and conspired for) the presidency. His chief manager was Lane's Kansas colleague, Senator Pomeroy; and in February 1864, Pomeroy issued a "strictly private" circular letter that went to a select but extensive list of editors, bankers, and other influential people and, inevitably, was soon published in full by the press. It disparaged Lincoln's personal qualities and executive record, asserted his re-election was neither desirable nor possible, and found "united in . . . [Chase] the qualities needed in a President during the next four years." Lane was disgusted. It has been said that Lincoln personally selected him to open the 1864 nomination campaign with an address to the Union League Campaign Club in New York City's Cooper Union. He made there a (for him) remarkably logical and temperate presentation and defense of the administration's record. At a meeting of the grand council of the Union League on the eve of the Republican (National Union) party's national convention the following June, in Baltimore, he made an impassioned, highly effective plea for the second Lincoln term. Hence Lane's personal standing with the president, and with his party nationally, was high in the summer of 1864.

But in Kansas he was in serious political trouble. The state Republican convention, again dominated by Lane, nominated young (twenty-nine), politically inexperienced Colonel Crawford as gubernatorial candidate, and a slate of candidates for the legislature favorable to Lane's re-election to the Senate. Whereupon anti-Lane Republicans broke away to form what they called the Union Republican party, nominating for governor Judge Solon O. Thacher of Lawrence, who was much better known than Crawford. Both conventions adopted resolutions supporting Lincoln's re-election. (The embittered Robinson, equating Lincoln with Lane, refused to act with even anti-Lane Republicans. He headed a small group of so-called "Radical

Democrats" who denounced Lincoln as a tyrant and presumably pledged themselves to the Democratic nominee, Gen. George B. McClellan.) The anti-Lane campaign gained momentum as the summer passed; by mid-October it seemed virtually certain of success. Lane himself was despondent.

Then Price's raid.

Lane's early warning that it impended was publicly derided by his opponents (they deemed it a cheap election trick), while he at once attached himself to the Union commander's head-quarters. When the action began, a steady stream of despatches slugged "With General Lane at the Front" appeared in the Kansas press. Lane's gubernatorial candidate broke off his political campaigning, assumed a Kansas militia command, and distinguished himself on the Blue, at Westport, and especially at Mine Creek. When Kansans went to the polls eleven days later they cast 13,387 votes for Crawford, only 8,448 for Thacher, and sent to the legislature a large majority committed to Lane's re-election. They also gave Abraham Lincoln the strongest support proportionately (seventeen thousand to four thousand) that he received in any state in that election.

III

On January 12, 1865, when the Kansas legislature in joint session elected him on the first ballot, 82 to 16, to a full six-year term in the U.S. Senate, Jim Lane stood joyously at the apex of his career. For ten years, "gaunt, starry-eyed, magnetic, exuding the force of a cyclonic personality," he had "swept over Kansas like a spirit from the dark ages," as William Allen White once said. Now he was all but crowned as the Sun King of Kansas politics, "the central figure around which all the others revolved," as the *Leavenworth Daily Conservative* editorialized.[2] Political enemies tacitly confessed the futility of further efforts against him: several of them joined that night in a great celebration in the Topeka House of his immense and intensely personal victory.

2. William Allen White, *Kansas Magazine* (1934): 87, *Leavenworth Daily Conservative*, July 14, 1866.

Eighteen months later Jim Lane was a broken man, repudiated by his constituency, denounced from one end of the state to the other, publicly accused of accepting bribes in the awarding of Indian contracts, deserted and snubbed by former friends. On July 1, 1866, he put a pistol in his mouth and fired a bullet through his brain. (He lingered for eleven days before succumbing to a wound that would have been instantaneously fatal to most men; he even recognized and spoke to a visitor on one of those days.)

Between Lane's final triumph and tragedy occurred mighty national events. Lee surrendered to Grant. Lincoln was assassinated. The Thirteenth Amendment was adopted. And President Andrew Johnson's effort to carry out Lincoln's Reconstruction policy ("with malice toward none, with charity for all") embroiled him in a Constitution-testing struggle with congressional Radicals (i.e., men determined, often for highly selfish reasons, to impose a harshly punitive peace upon the South).

Lane's downfall resulted from his support of the Lincoln-Johnson policy in opposition to the Radicals, of whom he had been notoriously the Kansas leader. Particularly outrageous of his constituency had been his vote to sustain Johnson's veto of the Civil Rights Bill ("I think I can show that . . . [it] is mischievous and injurious to the best interests of the black man," said he) [3]—a veto that was nonetheless overridden.

Kansas had suffered more directly, more extensively from slave power aggressions than had any other Northern state: in the breasts of Kansans the spirit of vengeance flamed higher, therefore, than it did, perhaps, in any other state. Moreover, not a few Kansans, westerners as well as New Englanders, had sincere regard for the Negro and believed he should be clothed with a sufficient political and economic power to protect him against the lash of exploitation that would certainly be swung over him, to the extent that this was possible, by his former masters.

Jim Lane had fanned the spirit of vengeance in the past, and garnered votes by so doing. Jim Lane had again and again

3. J. H. Lane to John Speer, April 11, 1866, in Lane Papers, Kansas State Historical Society.

evinced concern, in public word and deed, for the Negro's welfare. And now Jim Lane betrayed the principles he had stood
for, betrayed the voters he was morally bound to represent.

Why did he do it?

His contemporary enemies asserted, and historians have
agreed, that Lane's personal motive was, as always, a simple
lust for political power. "In return for a continued monopoly of
Federal patronage in Kansas he supported Johnson's Reconstruction policy," says historian Albert Castel, flatly. And there
can be no doubt that patronage was a factor in Lane's calculations. But to assume that this was his sole or even chief motive
is to assume that his shrewd instinct for power and acute sense
of political wind-direction, abundantly demonstrated at every
earlier crisis-point in his career, were suddenly blunted into im-
becility in late 1865 and early 1866. I find more plausible the
explanation that Lane, during these months, grew a historical
conscience as he developed an awareness of fundamental issues—this in consequence of his experience, his profound
admiration of Abraham Lincoln—and became convinced the
Radicals were wrong, the president right on the issues of
Reconstruction and congressional power that divided them. By
this explanation the story of the closing months of his life becomes genuinely tragic, as he himself becomes symbolic and
symptomatic of a change of phase in Kansas history. Formerly a
pure energy, as innocent of ideology and a knowledge of good
and evil as wind or flowing water, or (a more apt metaphor) the
electricity that wind and flowing water generate, he now became
mind-burdened, conscience-burdened in heavier weight than his
strength of character could bear. By this explanation it was conscience, *not* a frustrated power-lust, that killed Jim Lane. "His
suicide was his own verdict on his life and actions," as Spring
says.

At any rate, as Castel writes, "Lane's macabre death fittingly
marks the end of the Civil War era in Kansas history." Theretofore this history had been essentially national and ideologi-
cally political; it now became "more local," to quote Spring
again, as politics became dominated by economic interests.

Yet there was of Lane's death an ironic aftermath that

belongs as much to national political history, and as importantly so, as it does to the history of Kansas.

The man whom Governor Crawford appointed senator in Lane's place, and who was soon thereafter elected by the legislature to serve until the term expired, was Edmund G. Ross. An Ohio native, a printer by trade, he had come to Kansas from Milwaukee as one of Lane's "Army of the North" in the summer of 1856, had been a leading member of the Wyandotte Convention, had fought as captain and major in the Eleventh Kansas Infantry (later cavalry) in the war. When named senator, he was assumed to be as radical as Lane had been until 1865. In Washington, however, he refused to join Pomeroy and the other Radicals in their relentless attacks upon the president. When Johnson was impeached in February of 1868, Ross announced that his vote in the Senate impeachment trial (it began March 13) would be determined by the evidence and his sense of duty, *not* by the loud "guilty" demands of his Kansas constituency. When the Senate acted on the crucial eleventh article of impeachment, on May 16, 1868, the vote was just one short of the two-thirds needed to convict—and Ross voted for acquittal. He did the same, and conviction again failed by a single vote, when action was taken on articles two and three, some ten days later. Whereupon the Radicals, in a frenzy of rage, vowing vengeance upon those who had frustrated their design, conceded defeat: Johnson was acquitted of all charges.

Upon Ross was poured from press, pulpit, public platform, and through private letter such a torrent of vituperation as no Kansas politician has since suffered. He was accused of having accepted a bribe for his vote. Cried the *Oskaloosa Independent:* "On Saturday last Edmund G. Ross . . . sold himself, and . . . to the utmost of his poor ability signed the death warrant of his country's liberty. This act was done deliberately, because the traitor . . . loved money better than he did principle. . . ." Cried D. R. Anthony of the *Daily Conservative:* "Kansas repudiates you as she does all perjurers and skunks." One editorialist reminded Ross that "the pistol with which Jim Lane committed suicide" yet existed and "is at your service." His once-promising Kansas political career was dead; its body

was buried beyond the possibility of exhumation from Kansas
soil by the time his Senate term expired in 1871, though he himself did not realize that fact until some years later.

IV

It is perhaps not amiss—certainly it ties up loose ends of the
Bleeding Kansas–Civil War story and indicates the nature of the
political period that immediately followed—to forecast here the
respective fates in their personal lives, and in historical reputation, of the two men who represented Kansas as U.S. senators
at the opening of the Gilded Age.

Edmund Ross returned from Washington thoroughly disen-
chanted with the Grant administration, and with that extensive
portion of the garden of Kansas Republicanism whose most perfect flower at the time was Sam Pomeroy. Railroad building was
a vital concern of Kansans in those years. Jim Lane had devoted
much energy during his first year in the Senate to passage of the
Pacific Railroad bill and the assurance under it of large federal
grants and loans in aid of Kansas railroad construction. He had
even enlisted Lincoln's support of his successful effort to force
the Union Pacific, Eastern Division, to build through Lawrence
and Topeka after Samuel Hallett, heading the company, surveyed a line by-passing these towns by several miles. In
December 1862, Lane had introduced a bill "to promote the
construction of railroads and telegraphs in the state of Kansas"
that, with some special interest amendments by Pomeroy, became law in March 1863. (Pomeroy was a highly effective
agent of the Atchison, Topeka, and Santa Fe Railroad he had
helped Cyrus K. Holiday and others to organize in 1859; his
chief amendment of Lane's bill provided the Santa Fe with federal land grants of more than two million Kansas acres, provided the company's constructed road had reached the western
Kansas border by March 3, 1873.) Ross himself had done what
he could to get railroads built through Kansas. But no reason-
ably astute U.S. senator in the late 1860s could remain wholly
unaware of the wholesale graft, corruption, and outright thievery that accompanied the westward thrust of rails. There was

Crédit Mobilier, for instance. Ostensibly the construction company for the Union Pacific, a corporation distinct and separate from the U.P., its major stockholders just happened to be also the major stockholders of the U.P.; and its real purpose, so thinly disguised as to be readily discerned by even inexperienced eyes, was to rob the public treasury by making exorbitant charges for its "services" to Union Pacific. The organizing genius of this enterprise was Republican Representative Oakes Ames of Massachusetts. During Ross's senatorial years, Ames busily distributed share of Crédit Mobilier stock among congressmen and senators, and to Schuyler Colfax, vice-president of the United States—"wherever they would do the most good" in securing special favors for Union Pacific and heading off any investigation of its financing. Such slimy chicanery, and there was much more of it in what would soon become known as "Grantism," nauseated Ross.

Nor could his disgust with the prevailing brand of Republican politics, national and state, have been in the slightest reduced by the manner in which the Kansas legislature, in January 1871, went about choosing his successor. Alexander Caldwell, a wealthy Leavenworth banker, contractor, railroad man who had lived in Kansas less than ten years and was virtually unknown to the general citizenry, bought the election for $60,000, including a $15,000 payment to his chief rival ex-Governor Carney just before Carney withdrew from the race. This bribe was exposed when popular revulsion against a seemingly endless series of sordid political scandals, national and state, forced the 1872 legislature to investigate not only the senatorial election of 1871 but also that of 1867, in which Pomeroy won a second term. The latter investigation was inconclusive, but Caldwell was forced to resign his senate seat.

By then Ross had broken with the regular Republican party. He soon became a regular Democrat, which was tantamount to renouncing all hope of a successful political career in the Kansas of those (and later) years. His attempt to publish a Coffeyville newspaper came to a ruinous end when a tornado destroyed his office (1872); he then published, with little monetary success, a Lawrence paper, the *Standard;* and when he accepted the Democratic nomination for governor in 1880 he suffered a defeat of humiliating (nearly two to one) proportions. Two years later he moved to New Mexico where, as a Democrat, his brave stand against the Radicals of 1868 was belatedly recognized and rewarded by President Grover Cleveland: he was appointed territorial governor for four years (1885–1889). In our time his name is probably known to the general public chiefly because he is one of the heroes of John F. Kennedy's *Profiles in Courage*.

A single widely read book is also chiefly responsible for such memory of Sam Pomeroy as yet remains in the popular mind: his portrait is drawn as the corrupt "Senator Dilworthy" of the "Happy-Land-of-Canaan," and the climactic episode of his political career is narrated, acidly but with essential accuracy, in the novel that named the time, Mark Twain's (and Charles Dudley Warner's) *Gilded Age*.

On January 29 (Kansas Day), 1873, when the legislature in joint session was voting, by individual voice, for U.S. senator, State Senator (Col.) A. M. York of Montgomery County (the "Noble" of the novel), having been called upon to vote, made his way dramatically to the speaker's desk and cast upon it two packages containing $7,000 in bills. "I visited Mr. Pomeroy's room in the dark and secret recess of the Teft House [in Topeka] on Monday night," said he, "and at that interview my vote was bargained for. . . . I promised in consideration of $8,000 in hand to vote for Samuel C. Pomeroy (he was to receive the final $1,000 when his ballot was delivered) and I now redeem that pledge by voting for him to serve a term in the penitentiary not to exceed twenty years." [4]

Pomeroy never went to the penitentiary, of course.

When brought to trial in Kansas on the charge of attempting to corrupt a public official, he was discharged by the court on a granted motion of *nolle prosequi*. When investigated by a committee of the U.S. Senate, the charge against him was dismissed because (a) "the whole transaction . . . is the result of a concerted plot to defeat Mr. Pomeroy," (b) the "burden of proof is on the party making the accusation," and (c) York had not

4. *Topeka Daily Commonwealth*, January 30, 1874.

"sustained his charge by sufficient proof, contradicted as it is by the evidence of . . . Mr. Pomeroy"—an amazing conclusion, which even in that year could not have been reached, much less accepted by the Senate as a whole, if Pomeroy, in consequence of the York disclosure, had not been defeated in his bid for re-election. His term expired on March 4, 1873, only one day after the investigating committee's report was made. His place was taken by John J. Ingalls, whom the Kansas legislature had elected within an hour or so after York had spoken— this, too, being an amazing and suspicious action, since simple justice would have postponed the voting, as Pomeroy's supporters desperately requested, until Pomeroy had a chance to prepare a defence.

And that was the end of Pomeroy's Kansas career.

He subsequently retired without honor, but with a considerable fortune, to Washington, D.C., then to his native Massachusetts, where he died in 1891.

5

Per Aspera: Kansas Emergent

I

KANSAS is free," exulted newly inaugurated Governor Samuel J. Crawford in his message to the legislature, January 10, 1865, "and now offers to the immigrant a home unsurpassed in beauty, richness, and fertility." Thus did he announce the shift from political to economic developments as the main foci of the new state's attention, the main channel of its energies. The "richness" he proclaimed, however, as he advertised for immigrants, did not pertain to the state government itself at that moment. "As a matter of fact," he remembered years later, "we had nothing with which to set up housekeeping except the State Seal, a lease on some leaky buildings, and quite an assortment of bills payable." [1]

A close look at this Great Seal of the State, adopted in 1861 by the first state legislature, is rewarding for one who seeks to understand the spirit, the character of the Kansas that emerged from the Civil War. Its central design is a symbolic landscape. A rising sun peeps over the rim of a hill on the far side of a broad river upon whose bosom rides a two-stacked paddlewheel steamboat. On the river's near bank stands a plain log cabin, with a curl of smoke rising from its fireplace chimney; before the cabin runs a trail on which are two oxen-drawn covered

1. Samuel J. Crawford, *Kansas in the Sixties* (Chicago: A. C. McClurg, 1911), p. 226.

94

wagons, moving west. Beyond the trail rises a low hill up whose gentle slope two horsemen chase five buffalo, and in the immediate foreground, as the central figure of the whole, is a farmer grasping the handles of a horse-drawn plow. Crudely drawn, in whimsical perspective, the scene is primitive, bleak, masculine. No woman is in it nor a single tree, no garden or cultivated field. But above it, as an arch of triumph and a promise shining in the morning sky, are thirty-four stars arranged in three semicircular rows, one star for each state in the Union, topped by a banner inscribed *Ad astra per aspera*. The phrase is generally translated, "To the stars through difficulties"; it is typically referred to in children's Kansas history texts as "peculiarly descriptive" of the state's beginnings.

All of which tells us something about the view Kansans have historically had of themselves.

It also indicates a partial fulfillment of Doctor Webb's 1854 prophecy that New England enclaves would give symmetry and a unitary personality to whatever initially "heterogeneous . . . great mass" might pour into the state. It is, in fact, *direct* evidence of the deep and lasting impress that New England made upon the mind and basic institutions of a state that was at its birth emphatically western and became increasingly so, became indeed the very prototype of "Wild West" in its own western reaches, during the two decades following the war. For both motto and essential seal design were the handiwork of John J. Ingalls than whom, of all the New England contingent in the Kansas of 1861, none was more New Englandish. . . .

Let me pause here to introduce him properly. He was destined to be for two decades Kansas's leading political and literary figure (the combination is rare in American history) and had in both respects an important shaping influence upon the Kansas psyche.

Born of Puritan stock in Middleton, Massachusetts; reared in Haverhill, Massachusetts; educated at Williams College; he had read law in a Haverhill office and had been admitted to the Essex County bar before emigrating to Kansas in 1858. He was then twenty-four, physically small and frail, but of a combative disposition, assertively masculine (he seems to have had a deep dread of being deemed a "sissy"), which is to say he was by nature an extreme partisan. Of his considerable intellectual gifts, the greatest was his gift for language. Molded by a classical education, this talent for language had already enabled him to write prose and verse distinguished enough, sensitive enough, to suggest that he might become a great writer. In the event it enabled him to employ sarcasm, irony, and hyperbolic invective with an elegance and wounding effectiveness seldom matched in public life. In social philosophy, or philosophical attitude, he was already well on the way to becoming what would later be called a Social Darwinist. Politics, in his view, was a species of war. Indeed, all life was strife—an adversary proceeding in which death was the inevitable final victor. He was much addicted to "survival-of-the-fittest" themes, was privately (seldom publicly) inclined to equate strength of character and self-honesty with ruthless selfishness and a lust for power—an equation having as its counterpart a belief that no idealistic social reformer could be other than a hypocrite, a fool, a cowardly weakling, or a sex-deviate ("she-man" or "he-woman") unfit for survival in the real world. Yet this belief was neither total nor universal: he greatly admired Charles Sumner, for instance—had done so ever since, aged twenty-one, he heard Sumner speak in Boston against the Kansas-Nebraska bill.

His motives for emigration were mingled in typically New Englandish ways.

His hatred of slavery was profound, as was his later commitment to Negro civil rights. He saw Bleeding Kansas as a land for heroes, a battleground between Good and Evil. But by 1858 the question of whether Kansas would be free or slave had been settled, insofar as it could be settled on Kansas soil, and it seems to have played little part in Ingalls's decision to go there. More important, and representative of the manner in which myriads of easterners were enticed westward, was a certain beautifully colored lithograph, allegedly depicting with photographic accuracy the flourishing Missouri River town of Sumner, K. T. (it was named for Charles Sumner)—a lithograph placed in Ingalls's hands by a Sumner town company agent who also gave him copies of a weekly newspaper, the *Sumner*

Kansas Gazette, wherein the town's "Rise and Progress" and future greatness were glowingly described. Upon that distant Kansas ground stood Opportunity (his most famous poem, written long afterward and still anthologized, was a sonnet entitled "Opportunity") surrounded by "the fascination of the frontier; the temptation of unknown and mysterious solitudes." She beckoned with seductive smile, promising "the exultation of helping to build a State . . . forming its institutions, and giving direction to its career." [2]

It was this last challenge that kept Ingalls in Kansas despite the shock of disillusionment that came with his first sight of Sumner—this and the kind of Puritanism expressed in the letter he wrote his father two days after his arrival in the territory. "[T]he discipline is what I need to develop that part of my character which has not hitherto been called into exercise," he wrote in typical Kansas–New England fashion, "and it remains to be seen whether there is any heroic stuff in my mould." [3] For the town turned out to be a collection of miserable hovels. No church was there nor any other of the public institutions the lithograph had depicted. The shock could not but encourage a further growth of the cynicism, the contemptuous distrust of "human nature," which was already well-grown in his character. Two years later, after a tornado sweeping through Sumner had drastically reduced its already meager chance for survival, Ingalls moved to nearby Atchison. By then he had firmly committed himself to a political career—had been a member of the Republican Central Executive Committee, a member of the territorial legislature, a delegate to the Wyandotte Constitutional Convention. In the latter he had been chairman of the drafting committee and was, by his own testimony, responsible for the "language, expression and arrangement" of the document under which Kansas was admitted as a state. [4]

It was while a state senator that he submitted the Great Seal

2. Article contributed by J. J. Ingalls in 1896 to booklet entitled *A Kansas Souvenir,* issued that year by Kansas Immigration and Information Association.

3. J. J. Ingalls to his father, Oct. 6, 1858, Ingalls Papers, Kansas State Historical Society.

4. J. J. Ingalls to his father, Aug. 14, 1859, Ingalls Papers, Kansas State Historical Society.

design and proposed the motto adopted by the first state legislature.

II

Both motto and seal design continued apt for the state that,
emerging from the Civil War, now marched westward (through
with its New Englandish head and face toward the East) into the
1870s.

Individual Kansans suffered tragically during the war, but the
state as a whole made marked economic progress—especially
during the war's last year. After the drouth of 1860 was broken
in April 1861 by heavy rains, the rains continued in sufficient
quantity and frequency to assure excellent crops for four years,
livestock raising flourished, and railroads that had reached the
eastern Kansas border when the war began and crept slowly
westward as the war was fought (there were forty miles of laid
track in the state in 1864) opened new market outlets for Kansas
farm products. The Kansas State Census of 1865, taken in May
of that year, showed an increase in farm acreage from
1,778,400 in 1860 to 3,500,000 in 1865, an increase in farm
value from $12,258,239 in 1860 to $24,796,535 in 1865, an
increase in total property value from $21,327,890 in 1860 to
$72,252,180 in 1865. Overland freight trade with West and
Southwest had grown apace, fed by railroad connections to the
east, and so had the Kansas towns most concerned with it:
Leavenworth, Atchison, Wyandotte. Lawrence's growth had
been slowed by Quantrill's Raid, but its recovery from that tragedy was remarkably swift. Fort Scott, boomed by the military
establishment there, also multiplied its population.

There was progress, too, in the making of educational institutions, building on foundations laid during the territorial period.
Leverett W. Spring tells us in his *Kansas* that the territorial
legislature, between 1855 and 1860, incorporated no fewer than
eighteen universities and ten colleges, twenty-eight institutions
of higher education in all, of which twenty-five "perished—a
mortality unparalleled in the history of education." One of these
institutions was Baker University, a Methodist school, which

yet survives in Baldwin. Another was Bluemont, in Manhattan, whose principal founder, Isaac T. Goodnow, elected state superintendent of public instruction in 1862, re-elected in 1864, gave initial shape to a state public school system generally acknowledged to be, by the late nineteenth century, one of the nation's best. When Bluemont's building and facilities were given the state as nucleus of the Kansas State Agricultural College in 1863, endowed with ninety thousand acres of Kansas land under terms of the Morrill Land-grant Act, Goodnow and his fellow townsmen strove to make the land-grant institution also the state university. They were frustrated (mostly) by Governor Robinson's ambitions for Lawrence: it was in the latter town, on Mount Oread, that the University of Kansas was established in 1864, opening its doors two years later. Operating by then was a State Normal School (now Emporia Kansas State College), established in 1863. Also established during the war were Leavenworth College, Lane University at Lecompton, and Lincoln at Topeka. Of these, only one survives: Lincoln, originally a Congregational institution, flourishes as Washburn University.

In September 1863, the Union Pacific, Eastern Division, began building the line that reached Lawrence in November of 1864, Topeka a year later, Junction City a year after that, and then moved across the Great Plains with increasing rapidity and steadily lowering per-mile construction costs until, having been renamed the Kansas Pacific, it reached Denver, its western terminus, in August 1870. By then the Union Pacific, Southern Branch, having begun construction in 1867 and renamed the Missouri, Kansas, and Texas ("Katy"), had reached the state's southern boundary and passed on into Indian Territory on its way to Texas, its line running southeastward from Junction City through Council Grove, Emporia, Parsons. By then, too, the Atchison, Topeka, and Santa Fe had rails laid from Kansas City to Emporia and Newton, thence westward over (almost precisely) the old Santa Fe Trail to the state's western border. Some ten other railroad companies had completed shorter lines. This construction activity continued unabated, knitting together with threads of steel all the principal Kansas towns, until 1873, when the preceding decade of wild speculation in railroad financing resulted in the collapse of the great New York banking firm of Jay Cooke and Co. (Cooke had been financial agent for the Northern Pacific) and initiated a financial panic followed by a national economic depression lasting nearly five years. Few miles of new track were laid in Kansas during these five years. But by 1878 the state, which had had a mere forty miles of rail line in 1864, had nearly three thousand miles and the outline of a railroad system that would ultimately (by 1917) have approximately ninety-four hundred miles.

Seldom has economic enterprise been the central theme of a gaudier history than railroad-building was in Kansas.

The construction process was itself colorful; it tingled with competitive excitements. There were, for instance, the ephemeral "end-of-track" towns, which were instantaneously born on wild prairie or plain, lived vivid violent lives for a few weeks or months, then suffered instantaneous death as a new rail terminus was established farther on. Actually, on the same line, they were the same town, a mobile one bearing different names in succession (Coyote, Monument, Sheridan were three names along the Eastern Division of the Union Pacific). The population consisted of the workers, engineers, supervisors who built the road, and the tradesmen, gamblers, saloonkeepers, and prostitutes who provided them with their rough necessities and pleasures; the structures were for the most part tents and flimsy prefab wooden structures that could be easily knocked down, loaded on flatcars for movement by rail (hence the term "hell-on-wheel" often applied to such towns), and easily put up again in the new location farther west. The rapidity with which these new locations succeeded one another was a measure of the competition for very tangible prizes in land-grants (to qualify for the grants, generally, certain specified points had to be reached by a certain specified time) and for the honor of a new daily or weekly track-laying record, such records being communicated from one building line to another throughout the West. On the High Plains, where the terrain presented few problems of grade or bridge construction, several miles of track could sometimes be laid in a single day by crews that had learned to work together in rhythmic co-ordination.

But where the terrain most favored swift and easy rail construction were Indians who most fiercely and desperately protested that construction: there were not a few occasions in the late 1860s and early seventies when construction crews, with or without accompanying soldiers, were forced to lay down picks and shovels, pick up rifles and revolvers, and fight for their lives against attacking war parties of Comanche or Cheyenne, Kiowa or Arapaho, these being four of the five plains tribes (the fifth was the Apache) who became most closely allied in violent opposition to the white man's invasion of their homelands.

III

For what the white man anticipated with pleasure in the midst of Civil War—the opening to white settlement of the Great Plains—was anticipated by the red man with well-justified dread. Already the white man's wanton slaughter of buffalo had vastly alarmed and angered him. David Dary in his remarkably fine *Buffalo Book* tells of a report by the Indian agent for the upper Arkansas (that country was reserved to the Cheyenne and Arapaho by an 1861 treaty) saying that, in the spring of 1863, no buffalo could be found within two hundred miles of his station and that "[t]housands and thousands of buffalo are killed by [white] hunters during the summer and fall [each year] merely for their hides and tallow, to the . . . injury of the Indians." Later in that same year, 1863, a special Indian agent, sent into western Kansas to vaccinate Indians against smallpox, a disease unknown to them before the white man came, reported them to be extremely "bitter against the white hunters and traders." In the summer of the following year a full-scale Indian war broke out, to continue with considerable interruptions but also with great ferocity for more than a decade.

Each side committed atrocities.

White settlers by the score—men, women, children—were slaughtered, often with the greatest cruelty, by warrior bands in Washington, Clay, Mitchell, Saline, Republic, Cloud, and Lincoln counties in the late 1860s. The capture of a wagon train at Cimarron Crossing on the Santa Fe Trail gave into Indian warrior hands seventeen white men who were tortured to death by fire. Indeed, it seldom happened that a plains Indian's captive was permitted a swift, painless death. Often he died through hours or even days of excruciating pain inflicted by past masters of torture (flaying alive was common). And this of course encouraged the land-hungry, profit-seeking white man in his self-justifying belief that the Indians were not really human but, instead, vicious animals that must be exterminated.

When Cheyenne under Chief Black Kettle were persuaded to move their village from the Solomon Valley in Kansas to Sand Creek just north of the upper Arkansas in Colorado, being most solemnly assured of peace and safety there by Maj. E. W. Wynkoop of the U.S. Army, this in the autumn of 1864, they were promptly set upon by an ambitious, egotistical, brutal, and incredibly stupid young officer named John Chivington, the colonel commander of the Third Colorado Volunteers. A U.S. flag waved over the Cheyenne village, and villagers were standing unarmed under it. Clearly they had no expectation of trouble and were wholly unprepared to meet it. Nevertheless, Chivington ordered his all-too-willing men to fire into the helpless crowd, and scores of men, women, and children fell dead or dying. The warriors who survived the initial slaughter retreated to the cover of the creek bank and there fought back with bows and arrows and a few old muskets against Chivington's high-powered rifles: they managed to inflict casualties, enough of them to cause Chivington to desist before he had massacred the whole village. But more than two hundred Cheyenne were killed (Chivington claimed to have killed five hundred), and when the troopers returned to Denver they rode through the streets flaunting in triumph some one hundred Cheyenne scalps.

This senseless butchery led predictably, inevitably, directly to the death by violence of many hundreds of white people all along the plains frontier during the months and years that followed, for the Cheyenne and Arapaho now raged across the land in retaliatory action, joining with other tribes, and would never again trust the white man to keep his pledged word if he might gain personal advantage from the violation of it. The U.S. Government was forced greatly to expand its military presence in Kansas. To the earlier forts of Leavenworth, Riley, Zarah, and Larned were added in the 1860s Forts Dodge, Harker, Hays, Wallace. Yet the Indian raids continued. There was a peace conference attended by government officials and hundreds of representative Indians in 1865, on the Little Arkansas just north of where Wichita was founded soon afterward. There was an even larger conference at Medicine Lodge in 1867. Treaties were formally negotiated and signed. But these did nothing to diminish the white man's land-hunger, his determination to transform into farm and ranch the pasture of the buffalo, and since this was the basic issue the war continued. Some two hundred Kansans were killed by Indians in the interval between the Little Arkansas and Medicine Lodge treaty-signings. Two hundred more would be killed by the end of 1868. There was in fact an Indian raid along the Solomon at the very time the Medicine Lodge conference was being held—and in the following year (1868), Kansas volunteers engaged in one of the three or four most famous Indian fights in western history.

At Fort Harker in Ellsworth County, in September of 1868, Col. George A. Forsyth, on orders from Gen. Phil Sheridan, departmental commander, recruited a mounted company of fifty experienced Kansas frontiersmen (one or two more were later added to Fort Wallace), including Civil War veterans, scouts, and professional buffalo hunters, to pursue a reportedly "small band" of Indians camped near the western Kansas border. By nightfall of September 16, Forsyth and his command were on Arikaree Creek, a fork of the Republican River, five miles due west of Kansas's northwest corner. They were apprehensive. Trail signs indicated they were in the vicinity of a much larger body of "hostiles" than the report to Sheridan had estimated. They posted pickets in every direction around their bivouac, and Forsyth himself kept an all-night vigil. Nevertheless, next morning they were surprised, not by the fact of attack upon them but by the strength of it; for the dawn's early light revealed them to be surrounded by nearly a thousand Cheyenne, Arapaho, and Sioux, an almost unprecedentedly large Indian force. Hastily they retreated to an "island" in the Arikaree—actually a shrub-covered sandbar one hundred and twenty-five yards long and fifty yards wide, rising less than three feet above the dusty caked-mud streambed (virtually every natural waterway is dry in that country at that time of year). Hastily they distributed themselves at strategic points, scooped out shallow individual pits in the sand, heaped up low breastworks, huddled behind the carcasses of horses. And in this precarious position, fighting with superb coolness and skill, they beat off several heavy assaults before night closed down the action. They suffered heavy losses. Five of them lay dead or dying in the darkness, including the company's surgeon and its second-in-command, Lt. Fred H. Beecher (he was a nephew of Henry Ward Beecher, of Harriet Beecher Stowe). Fifteen others, including Forsyth, were seriously wounded. Their situation seemed utterly hopeless. They were near the end of food, water, ammunition. But that midnight two of their number, both experienced scouts, miraculously slipped through the encircling lines and, travelling only at night until near the end of their journey, made their way to Fort Wallace. Meanwhile, subsisting on rotting horseflesh, muddy water drawn from shallow wells sunk in the sand, and an almost incredible fortitude, the men surrounded in the Arikaree managed to survive and defend themselves against sporadic probing attacks until, on the ninth day, the rescue party arrived from Fort Wallace. Those rescued were very near the last gasp of their lives: the men not wounded were incapacitated by sickness, famine, and exhaustion.

The Indian losses in this encounter have never been precisely ascertained. Some historians assert that several hundred braves were killed; others place the number killed at around seventy-five, with perhaps one hundred fifty wounded. But among the slain was Roman Nose, the great Cheyenne chief, whose genius for intertribal organization had made him a particularly formidable foe.

In early November 1868, a little over a month after the Battle of Beecher's Island (so the U.S. Army officially named it, in honor of Lieutenant Beecher) and only two months before his term expired, Governor Crawford, who had been re-elected in 1866, resigned his office to assume command of the Nineteenth Kansas Volunteers, newly recruited for the first winter campaign ever conducted against plains Indians. General Sheridan had decreed it, being persuaded that wintering Indians, immobilized by lack of forage, would be unable to defend themselves against a determined assault. It proved a difficult campaign: winter was unusually severe on the southern plains that year; Crawford's Nineteenth Kansas became lost in a sudden blizzard and suffered greatly. The most memorable event was Lt. Col. George A. Custer's murderous attack upon a sleeping Cheyenne village on the Washita, in present-day Oklahoma, where more than a hundred Indians were slaughtered, including Black Kettle, the chief who had escaped Chivington's rifles. But there followed a peace of sorts (there was occasional marauding by small groups of Indians) lasting five years on the Kansas plains.

Then, in the summer of 1874, when most of the army troops headquartered in western Kansas forts were withdrawn for an expedition against the Cheyenne beyond the state's boundaries, a series of bloody raids by Indians down the Arkansas, the Smoky Hill, the Saline, left a reported twenty-six Kansas citizens dead, some of them after horrible tortures. Thousands fled their homes in terror. Not until state militia had been called out by the governor to reinforce, in plains patrol, such army units as remained in the state was the bloodshed halted.

The last Indian raid in Kansas came four years later.

In September of 1878 two Northern Cheyenne chiefs named Dull Knife and Little Wolf, rebelling against confinement upon a reservation in the Indian Territory far from their beloved native home, led a small band of nearly starving braves toward that home. Had they been assured safe passage across western Kansas they would have made it as swiftly as possible, but of course regular army troops, augmented by local militia, sought to intercept and capture them. The Indians then used elusive tactics, living off the sparsely settled country in ruthless fashion, killing some dozens of Kansans along the way, and escaping across the state's northern border. The chiefs were finally stopped and captured with their band, several of whom were killed during the encounter, in western Nebraska. Dull Knife and Little Wolf and their principal lieutenants were then put in jail, expecting to be hanged for murder, but it appears that none ever was.

Thereafter, the Indian *as* Indian ceased to have any part at all in Kansas history. He had always been, from the westering white man's point of view, merely a hostile element of the wilderness environment—and by 1878 this environment had been so transformed by the white man in western Kansas that the Indian could no longer have lived there, as he had in the past, even if the white man had abruptly withdrawn. For by 1878 the buffalo, upon whose abundance the plains Indian's life and culture were wholly dependent, had disappeared from Kansas and was rapidly approaching total extinction.

The story of the buffalo slaughter of the 1860s and (especially) early seventies is a melancholy one for anyone who loves nature and would have mankind live in harmony with it.

There were probably many more than thirty million of these great shaggy beasts on the Great Plains in the early 1800s and at least twenty million in 1850. Vast herds yet roamed the enormous grassland in 1860. When the railroads built west later in that decade there was at once a marked depletion of Kansas buffalo populations. Professional buffalo killers, who had to be professional Indian fighters as well, were hired by contractors to provide meat for the construction crews. William F. Cody, the famed "Buffalo Bill" of later Wild West shows, was one such professional; he reputedly killed 4,280 buffalo in eighteen months to feed builders of the Union Pacific, Eastern Division. Commercial killing for meat and, more importantly, buffalo robes was greatly increased as the rails advanced into the buffalo range and linked it to eastern markets. There was then a great increase in buffalo-killing for sport, also. Railroads, eager for passenger traffic into land not yet settled, promoted buffalo-hunting excursion trips at special reduced fares.

But the climactic, almost incredibly enormous slaughter began when European and American tanneries, plagued by a sudden shortage of cattle hides in the face of an expanding leather market, discovered in the winter of 1870–1871 that excellent leather could be made from buffalo. By the summer of 1872 an estimated two thousand men were shooting buffalo for their hides alone in that portion of Kansas west of Wichita and south of the Arkansas (by the terms of the 1867 Medicine Lodge treaty most of this area was closed to the white man's hunting), and at least as many were hunting north as south of the river in the state. It is probable that as many buffalo were destroyed in 1872 as had been during the preceding five years (literally acres of Kansas plain were completely covered by peg-spread drying hides); and the slaughter in the following year, the peak year, was some seventy percent greater! By the end of 1874 it was all over in Kansas: hardly a buffalo was left in the state. By 1880 there were but a few hundred (perhaps a thousand) in the whole of the United States, and of these at least a third grazed in fenced pastures as captives of men who sought thus to keep the species from becoming extinct.

Many Kansans were sickened by this buffalo slaughter while it was going on, and raised their voices strongly against it. Several newspapers did so, including the *Leavenworth Commercial,* the *Wichita Eagle,* the *Kansas Daily Commonwealth* of Topeka, the *Kansas State Record* of Topeka. Widely published was an 1872 statement by Col. W. B. Hazen of Fort Hays bitterly condemning "this wicked waste, both of the lives of God's creatures and the valuable food they furnish." Indeed, there was sufficient popular support of a buffalo-protection bill to secure its passage through the Kansas legislature in early 1872, though not enough to force its enactment over the governor's veto of it.

A few weeks before his veto action this governor, James M. Harvey, had been host to Grand Duke Alexis of Russia at the close of the single most famous buffalo hunt in Kansas history. Alexis, a noted sportsman who had killed big game in Asia and Africa, came by special train with a large party, under the auspices of the United States Government, to kill in the American West. His hunt through western Nebraska, eastern Colorado, and western Kansas was personally arranged by General Sheridan—and the Grand Duke and his party had just destroyed some two hundred buffalo west of Fort Wallace when they boarded their special train to ride over Kansas Pacific rails to Topeka. There, Alexis, having been formally received by the legislature, was accorded one of the few state dinners ever given in Kansas. It was served on January 22, 1872, in the Fifth Avenue Hotel, the largest and most fashionable hostelry in the state, and the guests feasted enormously upon, among other things, a dozen kinds of game: buffalo, rabbit, moose, venison, elk, bear, quail, duck, turkey, prairie chicken, antelope.

This glittering episode just *may* have had something to do with the governor's buffalo-protection veto. Harvey, a homespun type who gloried in the title "Old Honesty" and pretended to "no great erudition," must have doubted that the always superabundant buffalo could now have become, all at once, an endangered species, whereas it was certainly true that a ban on buffalo-shooting would deprive Kansas in the future of such distinguished visits as this by a son of the Czar of all the Russias.

Others found in the Grand Duke's Kansas visit no reason for joy or gratitude. The *Record* in Topeka published on June 26, 1872, an article entitled "The Murder of the Buffalo" in which the writer, after pointing out that the American bison was no "savage animal" whose killing "required any special skill or bravery or nerve," made acid comment upon the "sport" (quotation marks were placed around the word) in which Alexis had "participated . . . to the intense gratification of his royal father and . . . the profit of the special correspondents." The writer quoted from the letter of "an army officer" (probably Colonel Hazen) as follows: " 'To shoot the buffalo' seems a mania. Men come from London . . . and from all parts of the Republic, to enjoy what they call sport. Sport! . . . I see no more sport in shooting a buffalo than in shooting an ox, nor so much danger as there is in hunting Texas cattle.' "

IV

Of Texas cattle, many Kansans had had a great deal of experience, much of it unhappy, by the summer of 1872—and few who shared this experience would have denied that the fabled longhorn, descendent and cousin of the fighting bulls of Spain, was indeed more dangerous to hunt than the buffalo when running wild on the range. More alert and intelligent than the buffalo, more nervously cantankerous, quicker of movement,

far keener of sight and hearing, the longhorn was most formidably armed by the horns that gave it its name, horns thick at their
skull-base but tapering to sharp points as they grew upward and
outward to an average spread of around four-and-a-half feet,
though on occasion the spread was six feet and more. In every
respect the longhorn was tough (its meat was generally tougher,
less tasty than the buffalo meat); and this was, *in toto,* an economic asset in the circumstances that prevailed in the later
1860s and early seventies.

There was one element of this overall toughness, however,
which aroused great hostility on the part of Kansas farmers. The
longhorn was totally immune to a certain disease, the Texas
fever, carried by ticks that often or generally infested heavily its
hide and hair during the warm seasons (the ticks could not survive freezing weather). Native Kansas cattle, on the other hand,
were emphatically *not* immune.

So the first Kansas state legislature, in May of 1861, prohibited the entry at any time of *any cattle at all* from Texas and
Indian Territory save those that were the property of bona fide
immigrants.

Against this prohibition surged enormous economic pressures
as soon as the Civil War was ended. In the United States as a
whole, between 1860 and 1870, the human population greatly
increased while the cattle population markedly declined—a
trend juxtaposition that, by the law of supply and demand in a
nation of meat-eaters, should have meant high cattle prices. And
they *were* high in the North: cattle buyers paid from five to ten
dollars per hundredweight in Chicago and Cincinnati. But in
Texas, where the war had closed almost every market outlet for
cattle, and where the longhorn, flourishing on the vast range it
shared with the buffalo, had more than doubled its numbers,
cattle were virtually worthless in 1865 and 1866, bringing less
than a dollar *per head* when they could be sold at all. In the
summer of 1866 Texas cowboys attempted to drive some two
hundred and sixty thousand cattle in great herds through southeast Kansas to Baxter Springs, thence to Sedalia, Missouri, in
defiance of the quarantine. This passage was forcefully opposed
by armed and organized Kansas farmers, rendering the attempt

generally unprofitable when not actually ruinous for the Texas cattlemen who made it. As the railroads built westward across Kansas, however, creating new shipping points that were not only nearer Texas than any theretofore available but also located in as-yet-unsettled country, it became practically inevitable that these shipping points would be soon reached by trail-driven Texas cattle in enormous numbers; and the Kansas legislature acquiesced in and contributed to this inevitability, in late February of 1867, by drastically revising the quarantine statute. The new legislation lengthened the quarantine period for the area where the quarantine applied, but it removed all legal bars to the entry of Texas and Indian Territory cattle into that portion of Kansas lying west of the sixth principal meridian and south of a line drawn east-west through the center of the state (the northeast corner of the parallelogram this formed was some sixteen miles east of present-day McPherson). Elsewhere in the state, the entry of any cattle from the fever-infested areas was prohibited between March 1 and December 1.

A few weeks after this new legislation was adopted there came into Kansas an Illinois livestock dealer named Joseph G. McCoy, who was young, daring, imaginative, tenacious, and possessed of both venture capital and a genius for promotion. Having decided upon the tiny hamlet of Abilene on the Union (Kansas) Pacific as the site for a large depot from which to ship Texas cattle to eastern urban centers, he prevailed upon Governor Crawford not only to waive strict application of the new quarantine law (Abilene is some sixty miles northeast of McPherson) but also to bestow public blessings upon his enterprise. Abilene thus became the first, the prototypical western cowtown (Wild Bill Hickok was town marshal in 1871) to which, in northward extension from its original terminus at halfbreed Jesse Chisholm's trading post on the Little Arkansas, where Wichita now is, came the thousand-mile-long Chisholm Trail. Up it more than a million Texas longhorns were driven to McCoy's loading chutes between the fall of 1867 and the fall of 1871. Abilene established the general pattern of experience for the Kansas cowtowns that succeeded as the railroad terminii moved westward into as-yet-unsettled country—Ellsworth,

Newton, Caldwell, Wichita, Hunnewell, Dodge City. The last town became the major cattle market for the whole Southwest for a long and lurid decade, the archetypical Wild West town. And there is factual base for the myriad fictions that have been set here. If no Matt Dillon ever lounged at ease in the Long Branch Saloon (there was one) or walked warily the middle of a Dodge City street, gunhand hovering over holstered revolver, Bat Masterson did. Wyatt Earp did. So did Charlie Bassett, "Mysterious Dave" Mather, Doc Holliday, Luke Short, Bill Tilgham, and several other gunfighters of gaudy reputation.

V

Yet for me, as I write this book, the most interesting and significant fact about the Kansas cowtowns with their raw violence and sensuality—and, indeed, about the plains Indian wars and Great Buffalo Kill as well—is that they had so little penetrative or shaping impact upon the essential, the permanent Kansas mind or character. I suppose this is because these things happened always and only at the periphery (or beyond) of the settled area. They were no part of the direct experience of most Kansans. They were consequent upon an alien intrusion or had to do with an even more alien prior occupancy, and the attitudes, the general psychology they expressed or which accompanied them simply did not fit into the pattern of thinking and feeling already well-established in the New Englandish-Old Northwest Kansas that emerged from the "Bleeding" and Civil War years. They were, so to speak, indigestible by the Kansas spirit.

This was recognized and generally acutely felt by Kansans at the time. Despatches from the cowtowns and other towns that sprang up on the plains beside railroads and adjacent to military posts, printed in the eastern and east-central Kansas press, had often the character and tone of correspondence from a picturesque but morally reprehensible foreign land—almost as foreign to Topeka, Lawrence, or Leavenworth as to Boston. Thus the *Junction City Union* for July 8, 1871, described Hays City as "a row of saloons on the Kansas Pacific . . . . the Sodom of the plains." The *Record* of Topeka, August 5, 1871, described Abilene as really two different towns. "The north side is literary, religious and commercial . . .; the south side . . . possesses the large hotels, the saloons, and the places where the 'dealers in card board, bone and ivory' most do congregate. When you are on the north side of the track you are in Kansas, and hear sober and profitable conversation . . .; when you cross to the south side you are in Texas. . . ."

And "Texas" (using the term generically) had greater spiritual distance from the essential Kansas than did the "Europe" that began to pour into the young state in the early 1870s.

There had evidently been something more than a trickle of such immigration, proportionate to the total stream, in the 1850s. The 1860 census recorded nearly twelve thousand European-born settlers in Kansas Territory, about 11 percent of the total population. But the really big influx of Europeans coming in considerable parties, immigrants who formed their own communities where they maintained their ethnic integrity, did not begin until the Civil War had ended. The Homestead Act was then enabled to operate full force and, more importantly, the westwarding railroads, endowed with vast acreages of federal land in Kansas plus substantial land-endowments from the state and huge acreages purchased for a song from the Indians, began to make strenuous efforts to dispose of these holdings to settlers.

The Homestead Act of 1862 gave 160 acres of federal land to any citizen, or any person declaring an intent to become a citizen, who paid a filing fee of ten dollars and then lived upon and improved the given acreage for five years. It was supplemented in 1873 by a Timber Culture Act, which gave 160 acres of timberless plains land to anyone who promised to plant on it forty acres of trees, later reduced to ten acres, to maintain this planting for ten years. (The relatively few Kansas settlers who took advantage of this latter act did so to add 160 contiguous acres to prior holdings in a country where meager rainfall made a half-section too small, really, to be an economic farm unit. The tree-planting stipulation was generally ignored by settler and government alike.) From the total acreage thus opened to settlers must be subtracted, of course, the land granted to, and otherwise acquired by, the railroads. In Kansas this amount came to well over ten million acres. But the railroads did not (could not) regard this enormous real estate as of much value per se; they did not expect to profit hugely, directly, from its sale. Their big profits could come only when and because the land adjacent to their roads was settled, producing freight and passenger revenue, and they accordingly were eager, generally, to dispose of their land holdings at attractively cheap prices—often for the $1.25 to $2.50 per acre the federal government commonly charged when it sold public land, seldom for as much as the $7 which the Santa Fe charged for its richest land in the Arkansas River valley. They launched carefully planned, expensive advertising and sales promotion campaigns aimed at attracting European immigrants of "the better sort" as well as immigrants from the eastern United States. They competed intensely with one another for the land-hungry immigrant's trade: they co-operated with steamship lines in this endeavor, had their own immigration agents at every port of entry, sent agents abroad, and printed and distributed abroad, in the various European languages, promotion brochures by the tens of thousands.

A great famine in Sweden combined with the discontent bred by repressive government made the American advertisement of land and freedom particularly attractive to Swedes in 1867 and 1868, instigating a mass emigration to America that continued into the eighties. Organized in 1868 by Swedes recently arrived in this country were two land companies—the First Swedish Agricultural Company of McPherson (County), formed in Chicago; the Galesburg Land Company, formed in Galesburg, Illinois—which bought a total of 27,248 acres from the Kansas Pacific in southern Saline and northern McPerson counties and founded, near the McPherson–Saline line, the town of Lindsborg. In that same year was organized the Scandinavian Agricultural Society of Chicago, which purchased twelve sections of land along the Republican River and established the colony of New Scandinavia, whose principal town is now called Scandia, in Republic County. Both area-settlements, greatly promoted in the "Old Country," became magnets attracting an extensive immigration and thus the nucleii of Swedish farming communities occupying contiguous hundreds of square miles of fertile Kansas land. Lindsborg especially was given immense and glowing publicity in Sweden, so much so that it became among common folk there one of the most famous of American places. (My mother, née Lydia Ericson, whose immigrant parents came from Sweden to a homestead farm in the Lindsborg area in the late 1870s, was fond of the story of a Kansas-bound Swede who, landing in New York City, was overwhelmed by the hugeness and richness of the metropolis. "If this is New York," cried he in his native tongue, "what must *Lindsborg* be like!")

In 1871, the Czar (Alexander II) whose son Alexis would kill buffalo in Kansas the next year, decreed a previously announced Russian army reform whereby the former system of recruiting soldiers only from the lower classes was replaced by a system operating on the principle of universal military liability. Revoked was that total exemption from civil and military service, for themselves and their descendents in perpetuity, which, joined to the promise of free farmland and freedom from taxation for thirty years, had induced thousands of Germans to emigrate to Russia on invitation of Catherine the Great in the late eighteenth-century. Two large groups of co-religionists, one of Lutherans, the other of Roman Catholics, had initiated their eastward migration from German principalities in the 1760s and 1770s. They had established themselves along the Volga in the provinces of Samara and Saratov that, by a century later, had been rendered by them richly productive agriculturally. A third group consisted of members of the antiworldly pacifistic Christian sect (or sects; there were several, closely related) who subscribed to the teaching of Menno Simons in the sixteenth century, especially of Mennonites in the vicinity of Danzig, lately brought under militaristic Prussian rule by Frederick the Great. These people began their move in the 1780s, not as individual families or small collections of families in the way the Volga Germans had done, but as entire religious communities. They established themselves in South Russia, in the area between the Dnieper River and the Sea of Azov where they,

KANSAS

A photographer's essay by A. Y. Owen

Photos in Sequence

Hay bales near Hardtner.
Garvey grain elevator, Wichita.
Feed lot at Ingalls.
Cessna airplane plant, Wichita.
Topeka skyline.
Downtown Wichita.
Cathedral of the Plains, Victoria.
Cattle on the prairie in central Kansas.
Clothes drying in the wind near Independence.
Boys standing in raindrops after a drought, El Dorado.
Feed mixer for cattle, Garden City.
State Capitol in Topeka.
Young people in Salina.
Amish wagon on road near Yoder.
Ranch near Tipton.

too, prospered—more so, it would appear, than the Volga Germans did. They raised much or most of the wheat exported from Black Sea ports to Western Europe.

In all three groups of Russian-Germans, the Czar Alexander's reforms, especially the announced reform of the army law, aroused intense anxiety. Relief from this anxiety was offered, with every art of advertising and salesmanship, by the Sante Fe railroad, the Kansas Pacific, the state of Kansas with its highly promotional State Board of Agriculture, and a newly formed (1871) Kansas Immigration Society. In March of 1874 the Kansas legislature co-operated in the effort by amending the state militia law, enabling anyone who objected to military service on religious grounds to obtain exemption from such service by simply signing a declaration of objection in the office of the county clerk. Simultaneously, an advance agent of the Mennonite Russian-Germans acquired 100,000 acres from the Santa Fe. There at once began what soon became a massive immigration of these people into the central Kansas counties of Marion, McPherson, Harvey, and Reno. Two years later, the Volga Germans began to come into Kansas, settling on land acquired from the Kansas Pacific in Ellis and Russell counties, with Roman Catholics largely concentrated in the former and Lutherans in the latter. Russian-Germans continued to come into their respective ethnic and religious communities in Kansas all through the 1880s and into the 1890s.

Closely akin to the German-Russian Mennonites in essential respects, more so than to most native-American Kansans, were the "Pennsylvania Dutch" immigrants of the late 1870s. They, too, were Mennonites of pure German stock: most of their forebears had been originally of the Palatinate of Bavaria, had fled to Switzerland to escape religious persecution in the seventeenth-century, had then gone to Holland, and had come from Holland (hence the "Dutch" label) to Pennsylvania in the early eighteenth century. One group of them became known as River Brethren because they lived on or near the Susquehanna. They greatly prospered there. All the same, the young among them were susceptible to propaganda extolling the virtues of Kansas, economic and otherwise, with which the railroads flooded Pennsylvania in the seventies. The upshot was that, in 1878–1879, a remarkably well-organized colony of several hundred sober, pious River Brethren arrived in the erstwhile wicked cowtown of Abilene, bringing with them fifteen carloads of household and farming equipment (also more than a half-million dollars in cash) with which they at once began to establish homes and fields on virgin land acquired from the Kansas Pacific. Prominent among them were Jacob Eisenhower, his wife Rebecca (Matter) Eisenhower, and their four children, one of whom, David, was destined to become the father of a president of the United States.

There also came Germans directly from the empire, scattering over Kansas, including Baptists and Methodists as well as Lutherans and Catholics; German Hungarians into Rawlins County; German and French Swiss into Nemaha County; Austrians into Barton County; and a quite considerable number of Bohemians, most of them into Ellsworth County but some of them, later, into Rawlins. In 1890, one out of every ten Kansans was foreign-born, and perhaps one out of every four or so might have been deemed "foreign" by ancestor-proud descendents of old American stock—for the children of most of these immigrants were raised in homes where the old country language was spoken to the virtual exclusion of English (services in Lindsborg's large Bethany Lutheran Church were conducted in the Swedish language until 1928), and in communities that persisted in old country customs, institutions, cultural attitudes.

But these people in general were *not* foreign to the essential Kansas spirit—not in their basic characters, beliefs, attitudes. From the very first they fitted into the established pattern as "Texas" (again, generically) could never do, evincing none of the gambling passion and proneness to violence that only a few years before had characterized some of the principal towns (Abilene, Newton, Ellsworth) to which they came. Instead, they reinforced the strands of Puritanism that New England had firmly woven into the initial cultural and social fabric of Kansas.

They also reinforced (generally) the unyielding strands of conservatism that a business-oriented Republicanism was weav-

ing into the state's political fabric. Even the German Roman
Catholics did so, despite their liking for beer, their opposition to
the rising tide of prohibitionism, their consequent dismaying
tendency to vote the Democratic ticket. The Swedes and Mennonites were especially conservative politically, seemingly in-
stinctively so, and their communities would stand as granite
fortresses of Republicanism amid the creative political turmoil
of the late 1880s and early nineties.

"[E]very Swede is born a Republican and will remain such if
no unforseen accidents overtake him," declared the Reverend
Dr. Carl Swensson, pastor of the Bethany Lutheran of Lindsborg, in the year (1881) in which he founded the yet-flourishing
Lindsborg liberal arts school, Bethany College.[5] Similarly with
the Mennonites: in the crucial elections of the early 1890s they
voted almost unanimously Republican.

To the European immigration was added in 1878–1880 an
influx of some thirty thousand Negroes fleeing the South.

By that time the Radicals had ceased to be a dominant force
in the federal government. Withdrawn were the federal troops
who had been enforcing Reconstruction upon the former Confederate states, propping up carpetbag state governments that were
notoriously corrupt but also protective of the Negro, being in
good part made up of blacks. White supremacy, which indeed
had been quite effectively maintained at the height of Reconstruction by such terrorist organizations as the Ku Klux Klan,
was now openly reasserted, with wholesale violations of the citizen rights, the suffrage rights, guaranteed Negroes by the laws
and Constitution of the United States. At a black convention attended by delegates from fourteen states in Nashville, Tennessee, May 7, 1879, speaker after speaker exhorted black people
to emigrate "to those states and territories" that would respect
their rights—an exhortation greatly stimulating to a movement
north already underway. The movement was dubbed the "Ex-
odus." Those who made it were dubbed "Exodusters." And
Kansas received more of them than any other state. Fugitive

5. Quoted, Emory Lindquist, "The Swedish Immigrant and Life in Kansas," *Kansas Historical Quarterly*, 29 (Spring 1963): 13.

relief societies had to be organized to care for them, since
nearly all of them arrived destitute. One all-black community,
Nicodemus, had already been established (1877) in Graham
County, and among the grandchildren and great-grandchildren
of those who settled there are several (a surprisingly high percentage) who have achieved distinction. They include E. P. Mc-
Cabe, who became Kansas state auditor, believed to be the first
of his race ever to be elected to a major state office in the North;
the great University of Kansas and Chicago Bear football
player, Gale Sayers; Veryl Switzer, a great Kansas State University athlete who has achieved statewide prominence as an
educational leader in Manhattan, Kansas; and Lorenzo Fuller,
musical performer and composer.

VI

Among the Mennonites who came to Marion County in May
1874 was a fourteen-year-old boy named Ferdinand J. Funk,
whose father, upon arrival, purchased an eighty-acre farm on
which winter wheat was growing. (There was much argument
among Kansas farmers at that time over which was best suited
to Kansas conditions, wheat planted in the spring for harvest in
mid-summer or wheat planted in the fall for harvest in the following early summer.) It was dry during the 1874 winter wheat
harvest time, for which threshers and the mowers of hay fields
could be grateful. But the dry spell, alas, lengthened into
serious drouth, and by early August, the Funks like all other
Kansans were anxiously scanning the sky daily, hourly, for
some sign of rain.

There was no such sign on August 6. "There was not a hint
of a cloud . . . that day," as Ferdinand Funk recalled long afterward, "until along about four o'clock in the afternoon." At
that hour, abruptly, the sunlight was dimmed. A weird darkness
swept over the sky, swiftly rising out of the northwest, and "in
a matter of a few minutes it was so dark that" the chickens
"hastened to their roosts." Terror gripped the boy. Its grip
tightened upon him when there came out of the horrid dark a
strange, dry, whirring-rasping sound, followed immediately by
a hard dry rain or hail that pelted the boy's uncovered face and

hands and clung tenaciously to his clothing. The sky then brightened as abruptly as it had darkened. The sun shone clear again out of a cloudless sky. And what it shone upon was a world drowning in grasshoppers—millions upon millions upon millions of them—voraciously feeding upon every green thing. They covered the ground "in some spots to a depth of three or four inches." Trees along the creek were so loaded with them "that large limbs were broken off," and all trees were stripped of leaves. By nightfall "there wasn't a stalk of that field of corn over a foot high." Nor did the grasshoppers move on after this vast initial destruction was accomplished. They remained upon the increasingly devastated land, day after weary day, eating, ceaselessly eating, with their numbers imperceptibly diminished by the gorgings upon them of chickens and turkeys or by the kerosene bonfires that farmers made of them. When the spring wheat crop was devoured, along with all other crops, all other greenery, they fed on other things. "They seemed to like sweaty things. . . . They gnawed the handles of pitchforks and other farm tools that had absorbed perspiration and they ate the harness on the horses or hanging in the barn."[6]

All over Kansas—from Missouri to Colorado, from Nebraska to Indian Territory—the story was the same. A farm wife in Jefferson County told of how "the sun, dimmed like the beginning of an eclipse, glinted on silvery wings as far as eyes could pierce" while "blades of grass and weedstems" bowed down under "the weight of the clinging inch-long horrors"—how "a faint, sickening stench of their excrement" offended her nostrils—how within a few hours the "garden truck . . . disappeared, even the dry onions . . . leaving smooth molds in the ground empty as uncorked bottles."[7] It is literally true that, in this ghastly summer of 1874, trains on Kansas railroads were slowed, even halted in some instances, because the drive-wheels of locomotives could obtain no proper purchase upon rails thickly greased with crushed grasshoppers.

6. Charles C. Howes, *This Place Called Kansas* (Norman, Okla.: University of Oklahoma Press, 1952), 166–167, quoting a personal reminscence by F. J. Funk.

7. Robert W. Richmond, *Kansas, A Land of Contrasts* (Saint Charles, Mo.: Forum Press, 1974), quoting personal reminiscence of unnamed woman.

No Kansas farm escaped this plague of Rocky Mountain lo-
custs. But it was in the newly and yet sparsely settled western
counties that the suffering was most acute. Here the residents,
having staked their all upon a pioneering effort only recently
begun, when faced with dire adversity, had no reserves of any
kind to fall back upon save those of courage, resolution, stubborn persistence, endurance. Their living conditions were at
least as harshly primitive as those of the Lawrence of
1854–1855, and in a physical environment considerably less
hospitable. Having moved out upon an enormous treeless plain
where lumber was rendered prohibitively expensive by shipping
costs, if obtainable at all, they perforce lived in dugouts and
shanties of which the walls were made of strips of virgin sod
that had been sliced into bricks, after having been turned over
by breaking plows. The roofs were made of sod laid grass-side-
up over paper or tar-paper or sheets of tin sustained by the
scantiest frames of wooden poles. For cooking and heating fuel,
the settlers commonly depended upon the dried buffalo dung
(''buffalo chips'') that yet lay abundantly upon the land, a fuel
that gave considerably less heat per unit-volume than any wood,
and far less than coal. Fortunate it was, therefore, that the sod
houses, their thick walls broken by the minimum necessary
doors and windows, proved to be remarkably warm in winter,
as they were cool (but dark) in summer—though even so the
winter of 1873–1874 (it was as severe as that of 1868–1869
across the ceaselessly windswept Great Plains) had been for
every new settler a hard experience. Hence the joyous relief
with which the settler's eyes measured, in June of 1874, the
prospect of a plentiful harvest; hence his growing anxiety as
drouth set in; and hence the final profound gloom, the fear-
soaked despondency, with which he contemplated the grasshoppers' utter ruin of all his labors in the field. (Stark terror
overwhelmed women who, their husbands away for the day,
were solitary in isolated shanties, far from any neighbor, when
the insect hordes descended. The Jefferson County woman
whose story of the plague I have quoted was told by a passing
neighbor of one such—a ''young wife, awaiting her first
baby,'' who ''had gone insane from fright.'')

Some of these western pioneers abandoned their land; others would have done so had they possessed the means of moving elsewhere. Some narrowly survived the following winter only because relief supplies came to them in response to the call for help issued to all Americans by Governor Osborn, and because local relief was provided in small quantity through the sale of county bonds, as authorized by special state relief legislation. Not a few saved themselves by gathering up the buffalo bones and horns with which vast reaches of buffalo grass were littered in the wake of the great slaughter. Hauled by wagons to railroad shipping points, the bones brought from $2.50 to $3.00 a ton, the horns $6 to $8 a ton. There had been a considerable buffalo bone traffic in 1872 and 1873. But in 1874 the total shipments were treble those of the year before and six times those of 1872.

Fearfully anticipated through the winter of 1874–1875 was a repetition of the locust plague in the following summer, when the billions of grasshopper eggs deposited in Kansas soil were hatched. And in the event there was a heavy infestation in early summer. The insects soon moved elsewhere, however; the damage they did before their departure was negligible compared with that of the year before. Nor has there been during the century since any repetition of the plague of 1874 upon the Kansas land, owing in part to entomologists of the Kansas State Agricultural College who developed a poison bran method of grasshopper control and to state legislation enabling counties to help farmers obtain the poison needed for the mixture.

One development for which the grasshoppers were at least partly responsible—a development of crucial importance to the Kansas economy—was a final decision in favor of winter wheat over spring wheat, and of wheat over corn, as the major grain crop for the state. A large acreage of winter wheat had been planted by a land promoter named T. C. Henry near Abilene in the fall of 1873; considerable acreages of winter wheat were scattered elsewhere over the state at the same time; and it was only this wheat, harvested before the grasshoppers descended, which was generally profitable in 1874. Virtually every grain of spring wheat and corn was destroyed. And the decision for winter wheat was encouraged by those Russian-Germans who arrived in Kansas in late summer or early fall: they were eager to commence planting at once on their new land, it was of course winter wheat that they planted, and their profit from it proved generally greater than was obtained from spring wheat. Moreover, some of the Mennonites had brought with them from south Russia a strain of hard red winter wheat, called Turkey Red, which proved to be particularly well suited to Great Plains conditions and from which plant breeders in the state agricultural experiment stations have developed all the major wheat varieties now grown in Kansas. Of perhaps equal importance in its effect upon the state's economy is the fact that the Russian-Germans were accustomed to dryland farming. From Russian steppes they imported tillage methods designed for the kind of soil and climate that prevailed over the Great Plains—tillage methods soon adopted by their Kansas neighbors. To them was added, on the western High Plains, when these were broken by the plow, the custom of letting fields lie fallow every other year, so that two years' rains, stored in the subsoil, could be used to grow a single crop.

VII

If the greatly publicized grasshopper plague of 1874 slowed somewhat the immigration from the eastern United States and from Europe into Kansas, the fact is not evident in available population statistics. The Kansas railroads and the Kansas State Board of Agriculture continued their land-sales promotion efforts. The governor soon issued a proclamation that "Kansas is . . . rich in the ability to feed and care for every citizen" despite the setback of the plague. And the hard times following the financial panic of 1873, by dimming the prospects for financial advancement where they were, caused many eastern Americans, especially the young, to be highly susceptible to this propaganda. Immigration continued apace. In 1870, the population of Kansas, having more than doubled in the five years since the end of the Civil War, was 364,400; in 1880, it was 996,100. And the population increase continued far into the 1880s at only somewhat less than the rate of the 1870s.

Three things spurred it.

One was the initiation in 1878 of a "wet cycle" across the Great Plains—a series of years during which the rainfall was much above normal. Of course no one then knew what a "normal" amount of rainfall was in a country where accurate weather records had been kept for but a few years, yet where annual weather fluctuations are so great that decades are required to reveal their general pattern. Ignorance and interest conspired to foster delusion. It became widely believed that the boundary between the subhumid and semi-arid climatic belts was moving westward with, and because of, the plowing, tree-planting, and occasional irrigation accompanying the movement of population.

A *second* thing was the return and rapid increase of business prosperity from 1877 onward, creating among men of property in eastern states a plethora of savings. For these, profitable employment was sought, and western farmers, who perforce must operate on credit as they opened new land, would pay considerably more for the money they borrowed than would established eastern farmers or businessmen. Hence the abrupt appearance of a multitude of mortgage companies organized for the sole express purpose of funnelling eastern savings into western farmers' hands faster than the banks could do it, at relatively high interest rates and with only a perfunctory regard for the ultimate security of the loans since the local agents' incomes consisted of their commissions.

The *third* thing was technology's answer, in the late 1870s, to one of the most vexing problems the farmer faced as he moved out of an originally forest-covered country onto the open prairie and plain. Fences of rail or sawed board or stones were practical for farmers in New England, the Middle Atlantic states, the South, and the eastern and northern portions of the Old Northwest. They were generally uneconomic for the enclosure of field and pasture in eastern and central Kansas where, in lieu of them, thousands of miles of hedge, generally osage orange, were planted in the 1860s and 1870s. Wooden and rock fences were utterly impossible, and hedges probably so, on the treeless, endlessly windswept plain. Here farmers and cattlemen

were at odds with one another, in any case, over the proper use
to be made of the erstwhile buffalo range. The farmer demanded
protection for his fields against trampling herds; the cattleman,
bitterly opposed to the plowing of this land, insisted upon open
range; and in the mid- and late-1870s it looked as though the
cattleman would win his way by default. There was no efficient
and economic fencing material available for plains use. Then
came barbed wire. It met the farmer's need precisely. It soon
forced the Kansas cattleman to build fences of his own, trans-
forming his operation from ranching to stock farming. It was an
immense stimulant to plains settlement. Within a few years,
millions of acres of Kansas land that must otherwise have lain
idle and empty had become fenced field and pasture spread
around new farm homes. (Barbed wire, considered as a strand
of history, is among the several that link in special intimacy my
present home state of Massachusetts with my native state of
Kansas. The leading maker and distributor of barbed wire was
the firm of Washburn and Moen in Worcester, Massachusetts.
Founder and head of that firm was Worcester's Ichabod Washburn, a contemporary of Worcester's Eli Thayer—and some of
the huge profits barbed wire fetched out of Kansas into his cof-
fers were returned to Kansas when he, a devout churchman,
quite richly endowed the liberal arts college in Topeka that now
bears his name. To this day, Washburn University's athletic
teams are known as "The Ichabods."

Besides, or in the process of, spurring the population growth
of Kansas, these three things (the wet cycle, barbed wire, easy
credit) encouraged a rise of land values and a profiteering optimism that was perhaps justified at first but soon got wholly out
of hand. By the mid-1880s, Kansas was in the throes of a real
estate boom the likes of which it had never experienced before,
not even during the highly speculative 1850s along the Kaw and
Missouri, and has never experienced since. In town after town
across the state, the prices of town lots were lifted high above
the solid ground of reality, far into the wild blue yonder of
dreams. Wichita, extravagantly boosted by Col. Marsh M. Murdock's newspaper, the *Eagle*, led the way. Here in 1887 some
lots increased ten times in price within a couple of months, and

in just five months of that year (January through May) real estate transfers totalled $35 million. Wichita's population soared: it had been 4,911 in 1880, according to the federal census; it approximated 40,000 in 1888, according to city officials and the *Wichita Journal of Commerce*. Yet it failed to keep pace with the town additions. In those aforementioned first five months of 1887, no fewer than forty-two square miles adjacent the city were platted into lots. Elsewhere in the state the speculative fever was only slightly lower. Also inflated everywhere in the state were farm acreage prices. They were especially and vastly so in the vicinity of the booming towns, where it was by no means unusual for a farm to sell for five times the price it had brought a half-dozen years before, and where many sold for a dozen times what they had cost in the late 1870s. Meanwhile, year by year, the debt load of the Kansas farmer increased in approximate proportion to the seeming general prosperity. In 1885, the per capita mortgage debt was more than twice what it had been in 1880, in 1887 it was three times what it had been in 1880, and at decade's end the number of mortgages was half the number of people in the state (that is, there was one mortgage for every two Kansans).

Accompanying the real estate boom, being rooted in the same optimism and cupidity, were the "county-seat wars" that raged in one newly organized county after another across western Kansas in the 1880s. In three instances—the contest between Leoti and Coronado for the Wichita County seat (Leoti won); Ingalls and Cimarron for the Gray County seat (Cimarron won); Hugoton and Woodsdale for the Stevens County seat (Hugoton won)—there was fatal violence. Eight or ten men were killed, a dozen or so wounded, by gunfire.

And the bitter irony of all this sound and fury is that, in the end, it did indeed signify nothing. Those who won the competition gained from their victory no profit whatever—or certainly none that could have seemed to them, in retrospect, at all commensurate with the vital risks they had run, the blood they had shed. Their optimistic assumption had been that the tide of immigration, which in a mere two years had increased the population of western Kansas by a quarter-million, would continue into an indefinite future, enabling them to reap within a few years at least one hundred dollars for every dollar sown as a real estate investment, *provided* only that their town was designated the seat of county government. But this optimistic arithmetic of course assumed a continued swift and vast expansion of population. In the event, there was swift and drastic contraction. Moreover (adding to the bitter irony) this event was already prepared, had in fact already essentially begun, before the county-seat wars reached their bloody climax.

In January 1886 occurred the worst blizzard (actually a series of blizzards) in Kansas history—worse even than the storms of the winter of 1855–1856. The whole state suffered severely as drifting snow blocked rail transportation and fuel shortages became acute. But by far the worst suffering was in western Kansas where, day after day through most of January, a wind of gale strength howled across the High Plains, intermittently loaded with fine snow, creating a "chill factor" of one hundred below zero (and lower) in air whose temperature never rose above zero and was sometimes twenty or more below. In southwestern Kansas, where "cattle barons" (they gloried in the title) had for several years increasingly profitably overgrazed the yet-open range, fully 80 percent of all the range cattle died from frost and starvation, with the surviving animals generally so emaciated they could not be fattened enough for marketing the following season.

Thus was wiped out, abruptly, a significant segment of such ground of reality as the Kansas town boom rested upon, though the general boom continued for a time. Indeed, encouraged by plentiful rains and bountiful crops in 1886, the boom mounted swiftly through the succeeding winter to its ultimate crazy peak in the summer of 1887.

But that *was* the peak and the end of it.

The rains ceased. Crops withered in hot dry winds under a sky of brass all through the late summer of 1887, and with them withered the boom psychology, the boom "prosperity." Notably in Wichita, but also in the other boomtowns to the degree of their preceding madness, the earlier rush to buy real estate was matched or overmatched by a present rush to sell. Land prices plummeted. Scores of mortgage companies, speculating banks, real estate firms, railroad promotion companies, and various other businesses dependent upon Kansas farm prosperity were driven out of business, often into bankruptcy. And there was no recovery, there was instead a worsening of the malaise, during the immediately following years. These were quite as dry as 1887 had been. Indeed, 1887 ushered in a whole decade during which rainfall upon the Great Plains was as much below average as it had been above during the decade preceding (there were but two years of good crops out of the ten, though 1889 was the best corn year ever; there were five years of practically total crop failure)—and in the opening years of this dry cycle the Kansas population flow was reversed, was already beginning to flow back out of western and west-central Kansas toward the east at the very time that those passionately greedy partisans were fighting one another on the streets of Cimarron, Hugoton, Ingalls for profit that could come only from a continued huge immigration.

Thousands upon thousands of covered wagons bearing ill-clad, sad-faced families moved drearily eastward out of the state in the late 1880s and early 1890s, some of them proclaiming to all and sundry, through crude lettering on their canvas, "In God We Trusted, In Kansas We Busted." The total population of the state, which reached a maximum of 1,518,788 in 1888, fell to 1,334,734 in 1895—a loss of 184,054. Large areas of western Kansas were almost wholly depopulated, with at least half the people who had lived on the Kansas High Plains in 1886 having departed by the decade's end. Several towns that had been bustling and optimistic in the early 1880s were totally abandoned by the mid-1890s, leaving rows of former dwellings and business blocks, some of them very substantial structures, standing desolate on the empty plain, stark monuments to mighty dreams that had died. Many or most other plains towns barely survived. Hugoton is said to have been reduced at one point to a mere dozen occupied houses, for all that it was the county seat of Stevens County. In 1915 Hugoton's population was only 308. The county-seat town of Leoti in that same year (1915) had a population of 273. The county-seat town of Cimarron had 559.

6

The Developing State of Mind: Puritanism and Populism

*T*HE 1870s, eighties, and early nineties were not only a period of successive economic, environmental crises in Kansas; they were also a time of creative ferment, culturally and politically, such as Kansas has not known since.

It can hardly be said that pure science—that is, scientific work concerned solely with the discovery of new truth—received much encouragement in the Kansas of those years, but there was heavy emphasis upon applied science—that is, scientific work aimed at specific economic benefits. Economically valuable knowledge of the physical body of the state was obtained by the state geological survey, established in 1864. The Kansas Agricultural Experiment Station, established in 1888 at the Kansas State Agricultural College in Manhattan, with its branch stations elsewhere in the state, contributed greatly to improved crops and livestock, disease and insect control, better farming practices. In general, the *Transactions* of the Kansas Academy of Science, first issued in 1873, reflected the fact that practical science fed into pure science rather than the other way around in Kansas and so fed most creatively into the biological sciences—genetics, physiology, biochemistry, etc.

Nor did the fine arts of music and painting receive much for-

128

mal academic emphasis, or community encouragement of other kinds, in Kansas during the first fifteen or twenty years after the Civil War. The most interesting contributions in this area were direct spontaneous expressions of personal experiences of the frontier by untutored minds and sensibilities; they were literally "primitives" having more historical than aesthetic value. This judgment is true of the work of Henry Worrall, who came to live in Kansas in 1868, achieved a national reputation as pictorial journalist, and also painted Kansas landscapes and portraits of Kansans in oils. His most widely known single work, a huge oil canvas satirically entitled "Drouthy Kansas," is a pictorial rendition of a number of "tall tales" about Kansas's agricultural productivity (corn ears so huge on cornstalks so high they must be harvested from a ladder with a hatchet, etc.), expressing the unbounded optimism the long sequence of abundant crop years had bred. Far more serious an artist was George Melville Stone, a Topeka native who studied in Paris, returned to Kansas to help found an art school in Topeka which was eventually incorporated into Washburn University, and became the state's foremost portrait painter. Stone also painted Kansas scenes in a style reminiscent of Millet, becoming known as "the Millet of the Prairies," and had a part in the flurry of art-promoting activity that began with the organization of a short-lived Kansas State Art Association in 1883. Far more important than the association to Kansas painting and painters were the art courses offered by various colleges, state and private (denominational). Particularly important was the founding of Bethany College at Lindsborg in 1881, for Bethany placed its principal emphasis on art and music.

With regard to the latter, a major cultural event in Kansas was the organization at Bethany College in 1882 of the Oratorio Society of Lindsborg and the initiation soon thereafter of an annual presentation at Easter of *The Messiah* and, on other occasions, other of the classical oratorios. Most of the adult population of Lindsborg became involved in the chorus, which ultimately numbered hundreds and became nationally famous, so much so that internationally famous singers were proud to accept invitations to perform solo parts in front of it.

Of early Kansas's very meager original contributions to music, the most significant, their value not assessed on academic scales until well into the twentieth century, were folk songs of the trail and range and pioneer farm—songs first sung around cowboy campfires, or in lonely shanties of log or sod, and not published (often not even written down) until long afterward. This was the case with "Home on the Range," now Kansas's official state song, made so by act of the legislature. In 1873, Dr. Brewster Higley, who came originally from Indiana and combined farming with his medical practice, lived alone in a cabin on his claim beside Beaver Creek in Smith County. He is said to have been sitting on a stump on the Beaver's bank one late afternoon, his gun beside him, waiting for a deer to appear, when the words of the song occurred to him. He jotted them down on a long-since-lost piece of paper that he took a little later to a musically talented neighbor of his, Dan Kelley, who had a mill at Gaylord, where the Beaver flows into the Solomon. Kelley promptly set the words to music, the song was given its first public performance at a dance or party in nearby Harlan not long afterward, and in following years the song was presented at every dance, every party, almost every public assemblage of any kind where there was music, all up and down the Solomon valley, whence it spread slowly, and solely from voice-to-ear-to-voice, throughout the Southwest. It was first heard by John A. Lomax in San Antonio, Texas, in 1908, and Lomax, the earliest and perhaps greatest collector of American folk songs, published it in his epoch-making *Cowboy Songs* two years later.

But if the creative ferment of 1870–1895 worked through science and fine arts to no great ends, it worked toward an abundant harvest in the general field of journalism and literature (the two are abnormally closely joined in Kansas) where its energies were concentrated and where, by 1870, a fertile soil had long been plowed and sown.

II

No state in the Union has more relied on the power of the printed word to instigate and guide the public deed than Kansas;

in none other has the press played so active, so decisive a historic role; and in none other has the press been as intensely partisan, violently controversial, and ruthlessly competitive. In this respect the early Kansas press resembled somewhat that of France: a Kansas newspaper was almost invariably the organ of a strictly defined political party or (more often) party faction, or was the crusading spokesman of a cause (this sometimes provided its sole *raison d'etre*), or was the propagandist for some special economic interest, or was a combination of these; and its stand or point of view on these matters was as clearly evident in its news columns, which were shamelessly "slanted" or "colored," as in its frankly labelled editorials. In not a few cases (witness that *Sumner Kansas Gazette* that so beguiled young Ingalls) a newspaper began publication on a townsite as yet almost uninhabited because the very purpose of the paper was to advertise the town, to attract settlers, and thus serve the economic interests of town promoters.

Always and everywhere in Kansas there were many more newspapers than could be adequately supported, economically, by their respective communities. They waged ceaseless war upon one another for circulation and advertising, a war in which the casualty figures were appalling. Far more died than survived. At the close of the Civil War, thirty-seven regular newspapers were published in Kansas—precisely the same number that were published in the Thirteen Colonies when the Declaration of Independence was signed. During the next five years the number increased to eighty. By the mid-1890s the number was well over five hundred, and it continued to increase through the first decade and a half of the present century. But by that time literally thousands of papers had been born of high hopes, had fought feverishly for their particular public purposes as well as for their own survival, and had died into an oblivion that would be total were it not for the bound copies of them preserved in the newspaper and census division of the Kansas State Historical Society in Topeka.

This society, certainly one of the very best historical organizations in the nation, is itself a product of the creative ferment of the 1870s working through the field of journalism, for it was founded in 1875 by the state association of newspapermen.

Newspaper men and women have ever since been prominent if not dominant in the determination of society policy and executive direction. In consequence, the society has from the first placed heavy emphasis on the collection and preservation of Kansas newspapers and other periodicals. It has tried to obtain complete runs of *every* paper and magazine, however ephemeral, published in the state, along with what the society's executive secretary termed, in 1915, "some foreign papers—that is, papers published in the leading cities of the country. . . ."[1] And it had acquired by the early part of this century what was believed to be the largest newspaper collection in the world, more than fifty thousand bound volumes. In 1937, the Bibliographical Society of America published the *Union List of Newspapers,* surveying newspaper publishing in the United States from 1821 to 1936. Kansas was then found to have published more newspapers during its then eighty-three years of existence than any other state had from 1821 until then. (The Kansas total was 4,368; New York, in second place, totalled 3,309.) Moreover, the Kansas State Historical Society had more separate listings of newspapers than the Library of Congress had—4,813 compared with 4,588.

For every newspaper that survived the nineteenth century, at least seven died. In the older larger towns the mortality rate was considerably higher. In Leavenworth, for instance, when the historical society issued its *History of Kansas Newspapers* in 1916, two daily newspapers and one weekly (a German-language paper) were being published. Twenty-nine Leavenworth papers had died, seven of them dailies. In Lawrence, six newspapers were being regularly published, exclusive of university publications—two dailies, four weeklies. Eleven dailies had died, and twenty-three weeklies. Similarly in Kansas City, Topeka, Emporia, Atchison, Manhattan. The figures suggest what the newspapers themselves did much to promote, namely, a remarkably high literacy rate among Kansas from the earliest days: in every statistical report of U.S. literacy from the 1860s onward Kansas stood at or near the top of all states.

1. William E. Connelley, *History of Kansas Newspapers* (Topeka, Kan.: Kansas State Historical Society, 1916), p. 7.

The newspapers' intense competition with one another, their extreme partisanship, their ceaseless embroilment in controversy, these things had, on the whole, a salutary effect upon the quality of Kansas's journalistic prose. The editor who daily or weekly shaped barbed spears of language and hurled them with all his might at his opponents, while simultaneously raising verbal shields for his own protection, could not afford much sloppy workmanship; and his competitive situation demanded that his paper be as interesting as he could make it. His wit was sharpened by the constant friction. He was stimulated to explore and exploit every linguistic device for the achievement of pungency, color, and incisiveness.

As was natural in the circumstances, the Kansas editor was commonly strongly inclined toward hyperbolic vituperation, some of it intended humorously but much of it in deadly earnest and all of it designed to wound. But he was also commonly (or, in another sense, uncommonly) concerned with cultural matters—was quick and eager to encourage creative writing in his community and to print in his paper the resultant verse, sketches, essays, short fiction, or even, on occasion, long fiction in serial form. Most of this writing had little merit, of course, but the publication of it, the experience of being read and reacted to by a "public," was highly educative of those who contributed; and most Kansans who later made names for themselves as authors were first published in their local papers and thereby encouraged toward literary pursuits. In not a few instances the editor himself was a "literary." This was true, certainly, of John J. Ingalls, who as a young man edited the *Atchison Freedom's Champion* and remained actively interested in Kansas newspapers all his life, contributing to them numerous "pieces." It was true of Capt. Henry King, a Civil War veteran who came in 1869 from Illinois to Topeka where, until he moved to Saint Louis, he successively edited the *State Record* and the *Daily Capital* and carved for himself a permanent niche in Kansas cultural history by founding and editing the *Kansas Magazine* in the early 1870s. It was true also of Daniel Webster ("Web") Wilder, a graduate of the Boston Latin School and Harvard who had been a member of the Boston bar before he came to Kansas, in 1857, to edit the *Elwood Free Press*. He subsequently served as state auditor, became editor-publisher of the *Hiawatha World,* served as state commissioner of insurance, and produced, in his *Annals of Kansas* (Topeka, 1875; reissued and brought up to date, 1886), an immense compilation of historical facts and documents chronologically arranged, beginning with the year 1542. It remains an indispensable historical reference work whose entries are often fascinating reading. (It must be used with some caution, however, for it is highly idiosyncratic in its inclusions, exclusions, and emphases, and is not without occasional factual error.)

Thus journalism fed into literature in much the same way as applied science fed into pure science in Kansas, though with more important results. Much of the literature thereby produced was in a style that became academically respectable only after Mark Twain, who employed it, was recognized as a major American writer, but which has always had popular appeal—a style plain, loose and open, making much use of the vernacular; a style reflective and expressive of the western frontier experience, owing little to classical models.

So it was with the prose of Eugene F. Ware, whose chief fame, however, came from his verse, which he often signed "Ironquill." His *Rhymes of Ironquill,* published in 1885, achieved a great and national popularity. Coming to Kansas after having served with Iowa regiments through the whole of the Civil War, and after having been an Iowa newspaperman, Ware edited the *Fort Scott Monitor* in support of Horace Greeley in 1872, subsequently became a highly successful lawyer, and originally published most of his fairly voluminous writings in Kansas newspapers.

One authentic and historically important literary work, E. W. Howe's novel, *The Story of a Country Town* (1883), was written at nights, after full days of work, in the office of the *Atchison Globe,* the newspaper Howe founded in 1877. When he was unable to find a commercial publisher for it, he issued the book himself, setting the type for it in the *Globe*'s back shop. He sent out review copies, one of which came into the hands of the most prestigious literary figure in America at that time, William Dean

Howells, who greatly praised it in the *Atlantic Monthly*. Other reviewers followed suit. The novel was then regularly published and, over the years, became one of the most widely read in the country. A grim tale of midwestern village life told in hard lean prose, it remains famous in literary history as the earliest major work of what became known as the naturalistic school—a precursor of the books of Theodore Dreiser, Hamlin Garland, and Edgar Lee Masters (Masters was born in Garnett, Kansas). Howe himself, pessimistic, sour, and cranky, addicted to that "hard common sense" that conservative minds generally wear as an armor against truly penetrating criticisms of the status quo, wrote several other books, none of which came anywhere near achieving the fame of his first one. He later produced a magazine, *E. W. Howe's Monthly*, whose brief, harsh comments on the foibles of mankind were much quoted nationwide; and became everywhere known by the ironic title he bestowed upon himself, "The Sage of Potato Hill."

Captain King's monthly *Kansas Magazine* issued its first number in January 1872, backed by a stock subscription of $10,000, with most of the stock purchased by Kansas newspapermen, few of whom expected a cash profit from their investment. In the circumstances, this magazine was an amazing production. Relying almost exclusively upon Kansas writers for its material, yet boldly challenging comparison with the *Atlantic Monthly*, upon which it was frankly modelled, it bore such comparison remarkably well, number for number, as was proudly realized at the time by some thousands of Kansas subscribers. These subscribers were never numerous enough, however, to pay production costs; the subscription list shrank as the depression of 1873 came on and most Kansans were hard put to obtain the bare necessities of life; so that, after less than two years of publication, the magazine suspended—a fact far less surprising than that of its appearance in the first place. "[T]he light of it [the magazine] still lingers on the western sky," said, long afterward, University of Kansas Professor William Henry Carruth, whose own verse, "Each In His Own Tongue" (1895), with its "Some call it Evolution/And others call it God," is still much quoted by religionists. William Allen White, in his contribution to the revived (as an annual) *Kansas Magazine* for 1934, used Captain King's magazine as his standard of comparison, his point of departure, as he deplored certain changes that had come over Kansas in the twentieth century. "Reading the old *Kansas Magazine* today, one is thrilled anew . . . with its freshness and virility, its charm, its authentic literary flavor. . . . Never have we been able to approach it since in Kansas."

The *Kansas Magazine* became an important event in Kansas's political as well as cultural history when, in January 1873, Ingalls was elected U.S. senator. The *Kansas City Times* and the *Lawrence World* both editorially attributed his political elevation to his literary fame, recently acquired through his contributions to the *Kansas Magazine*. The *Topeka Daily Commonwealth,* from whose office the magazine was issued, said flatly, "Mr. Ingalls owes his success more to his connection to that publication [the magazine] than to any other one thing. . . ." And years later, in his introduction to *The Writings of John J. Ingalls,* William Elsey Connelley was more specific. "John J. Ingalls . . . became United States senator because he wrote 'Catfish Aristocracy' and 'Blue Grass,' " said he, citing the two most famous of the essays Ingalls had published in the magazine.[2] (In "Blue Grass," Ingalls asserted, only half-facetiously, that what people eat determines their character and achievement, that vegetarians have never been "the kings of men," but that the "races that live on beef have ruled the world." Hence the historical importance of grass, on which beef animals are nourished, and the occasion for the most quoted prose passage that Ingalls ever composed: "Grass is the forgiveness of nature—her constant benediction. Fields trampled with battle, saturated with blood, torn with the ruts of cannon, grow green again with grass, and carnage is forgotten.")

III

Ambiguity and ambivalence were of the essence of Ingalls as politician; they characterized his attitudes toward Kansas and determined to a considerable degree his conception of his sena-

---

2. John J. Ingalls, *A Collection of the Writings of John James Ingalls* (New York: AMS Press, Inc. First published, Kansas City, Mo., 1902), p. 9.

torial role. Similarly ambiguous and ambivalent were the feelings of Kansans about Ingalls. By this reciprocal or complementary double-mindedness is indicated a good part of the *essential* story of the political developments that, in the 1870s and 1880s and early 1890s, accompanied the economic and cultural developments already described.

Ingalls's emotional attachment to the state was strong, but it was by no means one of pure love and enjoyment. He strongly disapproved many of the salient features of the developing consciousness of the state. He had no use for the moralistic passions that were endemic in the New Englandish Kansas of which he himself was a part and that, fed by the religious zeal of immigrants from other states and from Europe, flared into agitation for "uplifting" social reforms following the political scandals (including the one that advanced Ingalls's own career) in the early 1870s. He evinced little empathic understanding of the experience of those who came West without the advantages of education, professional training, and (from his father) economic help that cushioned for him the initial impact of the raw frontier. If his private letters and the tone of much of his published writing are accurate indicators, he actually despised the common run of Kansans as human specimens.

Small wonder that most Kansans, while admiring Ingalls's literary talent and respecting his intellect, had little liking for him as a human being. Small wonder that their great pride in him as their representative, he being widely deemed the "most brilliant ornament of the Senate," was flawed from the first by doubts about the practical value to them of such representation, such "ornamentation," and that these doubts grew toward negative certainties as they were fed by economic misfortune. For though Ingalls may have understood, intellectually, the reasons why his farmer constituents became increasingly alienated from the "system" he represented during his senatorial years, his basic commitments remained unchanged and he showed little personal sympathy for the farmers themselves as they struggled to assuage their grievances.

These grievances, though many and various, had a common root. They stemmed from the fact that the farmer as an unorganized individual, spatially isolated on his farm and operating of

necessity on borrowed money, was increasingly at the mercy of
large and powerful combines of finance, transportation, manufacturing, marketing. These combines steadily shrank in number
and increased in size, approaching monopoly, in every segment
of the economy with which the farmer had to deal as he bought
the new and improved agricultural machinery that was being
rapidly introduced in the 1870s, borrowed the money he needed
for this, paid the shipping costs of his produce as it went to
market, and sold it there to large dealers. He perforce disposed
of the fruits of his labor in an intensely competitive market, had
no control whatever over the price he obtained for what he sold;
but he bought his tools and credit and necessary services in an
increasingly managed market, its prices co-operatively or mo-
nopolistically set to obtain a maximum profit for great corporations. Hence the farmer was, in his own view, underpaid and
overcharged, mired ever-deeper in debt, ground steadily down
into economic bondage to the industrial East—and his lone
voice, raised to its highest pitch of outrage, was far too feeble
even to be heard, much less heeded, in the far-distant corridors
of supreme power. Down those corridors strolled at their fat
ease the *real* rulers of the land, the multimillionaire financiers,
railroad magnates, and manufacturers whose slightest whisper
was enough to send scurrying in their service their bought-and-
paid-for minions in the executive, legislative, and judicial
branches of government. These wealthy few, who were very far
from being the best human material in the land—who were,
indeed, notably shoddy of mind and morality—were dominant
over the national Republican party, and they dictated the fiscal
and economic policies of the national government.

In support of this view, the informed farmer (and he became
increasingly informed as he was radicalized by the written and
spoken arguments of agitators) could point to the fate, after the
Civil War had ended, of the several devices the national government had employed to finance that war.

Every one of these that favored the creditor class (eastern
capital) was retained; every one that favored the debtor class
(western farmers) was abolished. Thus a war-stimulated national banking system with vast currency-controlling powers

was retained, and the high war tariffs were not only retained but in several instances substantially increased; but the greenbacks with which the currency had been inflated were retired or made redeemable in gold, which meant that he who had borrowed cheap dollars in former years was required to repay the principal plus interest in dollars worth much more.

Simultaneously, the federal government had launched its policy of donating huge chunks of the public domain to private corporations for railroad construction, these in addition to large direct-money grants from the national treasury—gifts that were augmented by money obtained (demanded) from state governments and from the municipalities through which the roads would pass—gifts that were outright, in effect, being unaccompanied by any adequate assurances that their recipients would use them in the public's best interest. Created thereby, in the farmer's fearful view, were steel-girded monsters of greed having literally the power of economic life or death over western agriculture and the businesses wholly dependent on it.

Consider the case in Kansas, as seen by the disaffected.

Here the railroads still held in the 1870s most of the more than ten million acres of public land that had been given them, yet paid taxes on only that portion they had patented: the Kansas Pacific paid taxes on but 20 percent of the land given it, twenty years after the gift was made. When they disposed of their holdings, the railroads, especially the Kansas Pacific, often did so in huge tracts to speculators rather than in farm-sized tracts to individuals. In three outstanding cases, much resented by Kansas farmers, these large-scale purchasers were not even American citizens: scores of thousands of contiguous Kansas acres were acquired by Alexander McDonald of Scotland, George Grant of Scotland and England, and an Irish landlord named William Scully. Every railroad watered its stock to some extent—a form of thievery indulged by some more than others, of course—while paying taxes on but a fraction of the actual assessed valuation. In 1877, state taxes were paid on only 11.4 percent of this valuation. "The [Kansas] railroads never paid taxes on a valuation higher than $7,263 per mile [1885], but they were capitalized at over $50,000 per mile," writes William F. Zornow; [3] and the capital inflation of course increased freight and passenger rates, insofar as the railroad must (or tried) to pay dividends on the water in its stocks. Nor were freight rates set as flat charges per pound shipped per mile, as one might have thought, in simple justice, they should have been. Rates varied according to *what* was shipped, and where, and according to the amount shipped (large shippers received rebates) and the length of haul, among other things, making for schedules so complicated no ordinary mind could comprehend them but that certainly discriminated, overall, *against* the farmer, *for* the eastern industrialist. And as if all this were not enough, the railroads also controlled elevators, warehouses, and other storage facilities for the use of which, the embittered farmer was convinced, exorbitant charges were made. Finally, and worst of all by Kansas moral standards, the railroads clogged with corruption the channels of democratic government: they used free passes, large campaign contributions, and indeed every form of bribery to ensure actions favorable to them by legislators, elected executives, bureaucrats, judges, newspapermen, lecturers, and those professional, civic, and commercial organizations most influential of public opinion.

The grievances sparked a third-party movement.

In early 1872, the first Kansas Grange (local unit of the national Patrons of Husbandry) was formed, at Hiawatha. Within two years there was a Grange, actively expressing farmer discontents, in every rural school district in the state, each feeding membership and ideas into a newly created Independent Reform party. This party proved the second strongest in the state in the election of 1874, polling thirty-five thousand votes, compared with fifty thousand for the Republicans. And the left-wing third-party agitation continued in the immediately following years, though the Grange itself lost influence because it was, as a national organization, not radical and militant enough to express the discontented Kansas farmer's views. In 1878 the Independents became a state branch of the national Greenback-Labor

3. William F. Zornow, *Kansas, A History of the Jayhawk State* (Norman, Okla.: University of Oklahoma Press, 1957), p. 146.

party, adopting substantially the platform on which the third-party movement operated into the 1890s. It called for repeal of "the national banking law," and "increase instead of contraction of the currency;" a tax on government bonds and "all incomes exceeding $1,000 per year;" the issuance of money by the government "directly to the people" rather than through national banks; and a total halt to "subsidies of money or public credit," and of grants of "our public lands," to private corporations. All these specifics, save the tax proposals and the flat demand for currency inflation, were soon approved by state conventions of the two major political parties—a clear indication of the radical temper of the time. Indeed, the Republicans had tacitly accepted them as early as January 1877, when five men presented themselves to the Republican legislature as candidates for the U.S. Senate. Each of the five publicly pledged himself to the specifics his party would formally adopt a half-year later, whereupon Preston B. Plumb of Emporia was elected as Ingalls's colleague. At that time and later Plumb proved much more closely attuned to farmer-feeling, and responsive to farmer demands, than Ingalls.

Not that Ingalls was *wholly* unresponsive. He must ride the wind rising out of the west if he were to return to Washington through re-election in 1878; and on February 15 of that election year, in a Senate floor speech on the monetary question, he gave remarkably forceful expression to the prevailing Kansas mood, boldly proclaiming the hostile arrayal of class against economic class in this nation of alleged freedom and equality. "On the one side," said he, "is capital, formidably entrenched in privilege, arrogant . . . , On the other hand is labor, asking for employment, striving to develop domestic industries, battling the forces of nature, and subduing the wilderness; labor, striving and sullen in the cities, resolutely determined to overthrow a system in which the rich are growing richer and the poor are growing poorer; a system which has given Vanderbilt the possession of wealth beyond the dreams of avarice, and condemns the poor to poverty which has no refuge from starvation except the prison or the grave." Gold was the villain. This "most cowardly and treacherous of all metals," this betrayer of friends and breaker of treaties, must be dethroned as sole monarch of the monetary system. Silver was the heroine. She was an "American idea," the "money of the people;" she must be permitted to exercise her queenly virtue by means of free coinage.

And this rhetorical flight into radicalism involved no departure from a Republican partisanship that, in Ingalls's case, was always total and extreme. The Kansas Republican platform in 1878 was an even more flat endorsement of the Greenback articles of faith than that of 1876 had been. Its ambiguous language at crucial points raised, in analytical minds, some doubt about the sincerity of the endorsers; but of the campaign effectiveness of this platform, and Ingalls's stand upon it, there could be no doubt whatever. Eighteen seventy-eight marked the high tide of the Greenback-Labor party in Kansas. Yet Republican candidate for governor John P. St. John won by a majority of almost ten thousand over the combined vote of his Democratic and Greenback-Labor opponents, the Republicans elected all the congressional delegation, and they retained firm control of the legislature. In January of 1879, Ingalls was returned to the Senate.

IV

There followed the years of abundant crops and deceptively easy money—the years of the great real estate boom—during which the formerly flaming discontents of the Kansas farmer, though they were never for a moment extinguished, died down into smoldering coals. Not again did the coals flame until they were fanned by bitter winds of disillusionment and dismay following the collapse of the boom, the initiation of prolonged drouth, and a terrifying multiplication of mortgage foreclosures all across the state in the late 1880s and early 1890s. The interim was chiefly characterized politically by a diversion of attention from economic objects to an essentially moral one, namely, liquor prohibition.

Was this diversion effected deliberately by the "interests" through their control of politicians and the organs of public opinion? Some there were who believed so, at the time and later. They said that Governor St. John, whose name occasioned much malicious mirth, was a pious fraud secretly "in league with the railroads." [4] His commitment of the Republican party to the utmost extreme of the temperance cause was consciously designed, in their view, to erect a kind of sponge-wall across the political landscape, one that would be far more absorptive of reformist energies than of alcohol (it could never "dry up" the state), behind which the exploiters of the people could hide their nefarious activities from the exploited. This view, I think, perceived a principal historical effect of prohibition upon Kansas politics. From well before its adoption as a state constitutional amendment in 1880 until well after its repeal in 1948, or so it seems to me, prohibition bred in the state a disgusting hypocrisy and debilitating cynicism among the most influential portions of the body politic, perennially obtruded an idiot sound and fury upon political campaigns, and in general distracted popular attention from matters of much greater public import. To some extent, vestiges of this disastrous experiment continue so to operate today.

But to say this is *not* to answer affirmatively the question asked above.

Actually, prohibition's roots ran deep into Kansas historical soil. A goodly number of free-staters in Bleeding Kansas, including virtually all the women, were but slightly less strongly opposed to liquor than they were to slavery, not only by reason of a Puritan bias against bodily appetitive pleasures but also in reaction, socially justified, against the alcoholism that had been then pandemic in America since colonial days. Indeed, free-staters had reason to identify proslavery violence with alcoholism: the ruffians who descended upon Lawrence and other free-state communities were always well-liquored. At the Wyandotte Convention an effort was made to confer upon the legislators specific constitutional authority "to prohibit the introduction, manufacture, or sale of spiritous liquor within the State"—a proposal withdrawn only after heated debate during which it was argued that such "special Legislation" had no

4. Zornow, *Kansas*, p. 194.

place in any state's organic document, that its inclusion would give proslavers "a handle . . . to employ against us," and that its purpose could be accomplished without it, as in Maine, "where there is no constitutional provision" but where Neal Dow's stringent 1851 prohibitory law had been declared constitutional.[5]

When admitted to the Union, Kansas retained upon its statute books a territorial dramshop law originally borrowed intact from Missouri by the Bogus Legislature. It was a local option law. By means of it, most communities in the state had rendered themselves nominally "dry" by the late 1870s. But only nominally: saloons ran wide open, their owners having obtained "protection" from politicians in one way or another. Clearly there was need for stricter control of the liquor traffic; and temperance organizations, allied with Protestant churches, rose to the challenge by advocating a total abolition of such traffic by statewide law.

Then, in 1873, was founded the national Women's Christian Temperance Union. Through chapters of it immediately established in Kansas was launched a so-called "Women's Crusade" wherein the crusaders, among other demonstrative acts, invaded saloons to pray with barkeepers and patrons (these, taken by surprise, were invariably embarrassed, often shamed, sometimes even repentant), and also operated as political activists, joined in this by their spouses, their ministers, and other dedicated men including, notably, John St. John. They were concentratedly single-minded, unremittingly persistent, inexhaustibly energetic, and capable of utter ruthlessness, despite a common gentleness of manner, when the success of their cause seemed to demand it. They therefore soon constituted the most powerful special interest lobby openly working in the state. And their movement steadily, swiftly grew through a half-dozen years toward the moment when a newly inaugurated governor, addressing the legislators, could call upon these "to absolutely and forever prohibit the manufacture, importation, and sale of intoxicating liquors as a beverage" in the state.

5. Clara Francis, "Prohibition in Kansas," in William E. Connelley, *Kansas and Kansans*, 5 vols. (Chicago: Lewis Publishing Co., 1918), 2: 797.

This was in January 1879. The legislature was then presented with an administration-sponsored "bone-dry" prohibition amendment to the state constitution, a measure provoking more popular furor than any other single political proposal had done in Kansas since slavery's defeat. A People's Grand Protective Union, assembled in Topeka in January of 1880, resolved that the measure went so "far beyond the public sentiment" that it would be "inoperative," thereby teaching men "not to respect . . . the law" in general. Ex-Governor Charles Robinson (his coldly logical mind, uncompromising temper, and distaste for the prevailing brand of special interest politics had by this time led him into Greenback-Labor ranks), raised a more profound objection. In Robinson's view, prohibition attacked the very foundations of a free society by implicitly repudiating those concepts of inalienable individual right and conjoined personal responsibility that are necessarily assumed by democratic institutions. "[T]he purpose," said Robinson, "is to deprive the citizen of the power of choice, or free agency, in regard to personal habits . . . and to place him under the guardianship of the Legislature." [6]

But prohibition's opponents failed to mount a truly all-out campaign against it, being convinced the proposed amendment was too extreme a measure to recommend itself to a popular majority. They were mistaken. Having barely passed the legislature, the amendment was approved, 92,302 to 83,304, in the same election that, in November of 1880, gave St. John a second gubernatorial term by a large majority. (His Democratic opponent that year was Edmund G. Ross.) Kansas thus became the first state in the Union to adopt constitutional prohibition.

Thereafter, until 1906, resubmission of the amendment was a perennial major party issue in Kansas, the Democrats favoring repeal, the Republicans opposing—an issue militating against decisiveness by the electorate on other matters of partisan dispute—and always, to the extent of its beclouding effectiveness, this perennial issue helped Republicans at the expense of Democrats at the polls. It is true that St. John, running for a third term

6. Charles Robinson, *The Kansas Conflict* (New York: Harper's, 1892), pp. 467–468.

in 1882, was beaten by Democrat George W. Glick, the first of his party ever to win the governorship—but this was in spite, not because, of the Democratic stand on prohibition. St. John was by then personally unpopular with other Republican politicians; a third term was unprecedented; the charge that he was a secret railroad agent, though never substantiated, was widely believed; and because of this charge he may have lost more votes than Glick did to the Greenback-Laborite candidate who, that year, was none other than Charles Robinson. In 1884, when resubmission was a more decisive issue, Glick lost his bid for re-election, though his administration had pursued with success several goals popularized by the third-party movement—had placed on the tax rolls huge acreages of formerly exempt railroad lands, forced reductions in railroad freight and passenger fares, reclaimed for the state and opened for settlement some two and a quarter million acres of formerly closed land.

Yet Kansas was no "drier" than in former years. While drugstores dispensed whiskey for "medicinal purposes," as the law (until revised in 1909) permitted them to, "joints" by the hundreds continued openly to operate. There were five of them in typical Emporia in 1897, according to an *Emporia Gazette* editorial giving the location of each for the benefit of town officials who denied any "personal knowledge" of them. By actual count there were 250 saloons in Kansas City, Kansas, in 1905, a full quarter-century after prohibition's adoption.

By that time, however, a new "women's crusade" of unprecedented militancy was underway, led by Mrs. Carry Nation, wife of the Reverend David Nation, a meek and mild pastor of the Christian church in Medicine Lodge. She was a host unto herself, was hatchet-wielding Carry. She was indubitably fanatical in her hatred of booze (her first husband had died a drunkard), but she was also a woman of utter integrity, far from stupid, superbly courageous—and she was effective as no prohibitionist before her had been. When she was jailed for smashing windows, mirrors, and furniture in places where liquor was sold in defiance of the law, while the owners of those places were unmolested by public officials, the blatant hypocrisy was more than decent, fair-minded Kansans could stomach. Increasingly, thereafter, was prohibition enforced. The sale of alcoholic beverages became considerably more difficult in the state, their purchase more expensive, more bothersome.

By the second decade of the present century, the "joints" had virtually disappeared; so had the possibility of prohibition's repeal in the forseeable future; and the Kansas Democracy no longer called perennially for resubmission. Indeed, Kansas by then prided itself upon being at the head of a parade of states that had followed its example and now marched toward adoption, in the near future, of a prohibition amendment to the Constitution of the United States—an amendment first proposed in 1881 by Kansas's Senator Plumb.

V

Meanwhile, and far more importantly, the long-smoldering discontents of Kansas farmers, blown upon by bitter winds of adversity, had flared into the greatest political upheaval in Kansas history, one having several of the characteristics of a genuine social revolution, with effects that were national.

Even at the height of the boom, as they accepted the loans pressed upon them (at 9 or 10 percent interest), Kansas farmers in significant number continued to nurse grievances while anticipating with dread an inevitable day of reckoning. In their view, they continued to pay too much for the things they bought, to receive too little for the things they sold; continued to bear a disproportionate share of the tax burden; continued to be denied adequate, honest representation in government; continued to be mercilessly exploited by the railroads; and they continued to fuel with their grievances a third-party movement that, in the sum of its various splinters, continued to poll some 10 percent of the total vote in every election.

Then, as the boom collapsed and the drouth began—as a floodtide of mortgage foreclosures forced an ebbtide of migration that drained population from the state in terrifying volume— there swept over Kansas a new farmer movement, the Farmers' Alliance, whose membership grew by leaps and bounds as it proceeded to "Agitate, Educate, Organize!" with a fervor and conflagration-breeding effectiveness never seen before upon the prairie.

Hundreds of meetings in country schools and village halls heard dozens of public speakers whose arguments, bolstered by an abundance of economic statistics, informed the minds as they fired the emotions of myriads of the distressed. Into Kansas homes went literally hundreds of thousands of newspapers, pamphlets, magazines, books (notably Bellamy's *Looking Backward,* George's *Progress and Poverty*) that called for fundamental social change—for the overthrow of the money power and corporate tyranny, for nationalization of the railroads, for an ingenious "subtreasury plan" to relieve agricultural distress, for the single tax, for (in general) the establishment of a true political democracy based on a co-operative economy whose primary motive for production would be the general human welfare, not individual private greed. And as common folk pondered these matters, they prepared to implement through organized political action the conclusions they reached. Alliance candidates were entered in several local political contests in the fall of 1889; in Cowley County a slate nominated at a so-called "People's Convention" won almost every county and township office.

That year 1889 saw a break in the drouth that had blasted crops during the two preceding growing seasons and would do so again in following years. Indeed, the 1889 Kansas corn crop was the largest ever. But this meant no break in the agricultural depression, for the price paid Kansans for their corn fell far below the cost of producing it—well below the cost of shipping it to market in many localities—so that corn was used as heating fuel all over rural Kansas in the winter of 1889–1890 and became fuel, too, for a now already blazing political radicalism. In June 1890, alliance members assembled in Topeka to form a Kansas People's [Populist] party which, a few weeks later, nominated a full slate of candidates for state office and the lower house of Congress.

There followed what was not so much a political campaign as "a religious revival, a crusade, a pentecost . . . in which a tongue of flame sat upon every man, and each spake as the spirit gave him utterance," as Elizabeth N. Barr writes in her highly partisan history of Kansas populism.[7]

The most effective of the "revivalists" was Mrs. Mary Elizabeth (often miscalled Mary Ellen) Lease, star of the Populist speakers bureau, who achieved national fame by the fall of 1890 as the "Lady Orator of the West." Wife of a Wichita druggist, mother of four children, a lawyer (she was among the earliest women to be admitted to the Kansas bar), she possessed a deep, rich contralto voice with which, in 160 speeches during that single campaign, she wrung sardonic laughter, angry tears, and loud cheers of affirmation from uncounted thousands of the dispossessed. "It is no longer a government of the people, by the people, and for the people, but a government of Wall Street, by Wall Street, and for Wall Street," she cried. "The great common people of this country are slaves, and monopoly is the master. . . . Our laws are the output of a system which clothes rascals in robes and honesty in rags. . . . We were told two years ago to go to work and raise a big crop. . . . We went to work and plowed and planted; the rains fell, the sun shone, nature smiled, and we raised the big crop that they told us to; and what came of it? Eight-cent corn, ten-cent oats, two-cent beef and no price at all for butter and eggs—that's what came of it. Then the politicians said we suffered from over-production. Over-production, when 10,000 little children, so statistics tell us, starve to death every year in the United States, and over 100,000 shop-girls in New York are forced to sell their virtue for the bread their niggardly wages deny them." [8] Over and over again, in widely quoted effect if not in actual words, she advised her farmer audiences "to raise less corn and more HELL!"

Far different in personality and oratorical style, but only somewhat less effective in immediate audience impact, was Mrs. Annie Laporte Diggs, wife of A. S. Diggs of Lawrence and the mother of their three children. She was a tiny, intensely "feminine" woman, less than five feet tall, weighing less than

7. Elizabeth N. Barr, "The Populist Uprising," *Kansas and Kansans,* 2:1148.
8. Quoted by Barr, *Kansas,* p. 1150.

one hundred pounds, whose wide sympathies and quick intellect had led her to embrace since 1881 a number of reform causes— she had been a temperance speaker, a supporter of socialist experiments, a Free Religionist, above all, an ardent suffragette, which she yet and ever after remained (she is now chiefly remembered as a leader of the national woman's suffrage movement)—and she depended far less upon ringing war cries than "Mary Yellin" Lease did to move her listeners, far more upon a mingling of blandishments with mild-mannered, quietly reasoned argument.

Among the men who led Kansas populism, the most effective speaker as he became the most famous was a self- but well-educated ex-sailor of the Great Lakes, Jerry Simpson, upon whom was bestowed the cognomen "Sockless Jerry" when Republican Victor Murdock sneered in the *Wichita Eagle* that he, running as Populist for Congress from Kansas's Fifth District, was so poverty-stricken he wore no socks. Simpson gloried in the title. He confessed he was "busted"—he had lost his small fortune (some ten thousand dollars) when his Barber County cattle enterprise was wiped out by the Blizzard of '86; he certainly could not afford the silk stockings that, he said, were worn by his Republican opponent (one J. R. Hallowell). But was not his the common plight? And was not the reason for it obvious? A tiny minority of cheats and thieves dominated the economy. For instance, some two hundred and forty million of the two hundred and seventy million bushels of corn that had been raised in 1889 had been acquired by government-protected "grain gamblers" in Chicago who sold it at forty-five cents a bushel—four times what the farmer received—thereby cheating the Kansas farmer out of sixty million dollars with which he could not only have paid off his mortgage but also improved his land and bought home comforts. Simpson charged that the real seat of Kansas government had long been the Topeka headquarters of the Santa Fe railroad, and cited statistics in support of his contention that the railroads in general, having been paid for several times over in public money and land grants, were in simple justice public property and should be so administered. He also proclaimed, on every occasion, his single tax faith. "Man must have access to the land or he is a slave," cried he. "The man who owns the earth, owns the people, for they must buy the privilege of living on his earth." [9]

The state Republican leaders belatedly realized that the opposition they now faced could not be laughed away, sneered away, nor defeated by any of the usual devices for diverting popular attention from fundamental issues. What they faced was a people's revolt. And so, belatedly, they resorted to the tactic that had served them well in the 1870s: they wrote a platform that incorporated, if in rather fuzzy language, several of the radical alliance planks, and then released their candidates from acknowledged party allegiance, so they might identify more closely with the disaffected, the dispossessed. But this time the tactic was at once exposed to howls of derision by "Sockless Jerry," Annie Diggs, and "Mary Yellin," among others, and so it failed to work as before. On election day, allegedly aided by much fraudulent voting and counting, the Republicans managed to win the governorship and every other state office save attorney general, which went to a man nominated by both Democrats and Populists; but they did so by very narrow margins. And in the voting for the legislature they were buried under an avalanche of Populist victories in contests for the lower house. So huge was the Populist majority there (ninety-one Populists and eight Democrats faced twenty-six Republicans in January 1891) that it more than overcame the majority the Republicans retained, because of holdovers, in the Senate when the time came to elect a U.S. senator.

And this meant the end of the line for John J. Ingalls.

He had been the main target of alliance wrath, especially women's wrath, ever since the alliance invaded Kansas—and for good and sufficient reasons. The gap between his dominant moods and those of the average Kansas farmer was now so wide that his glittering, rolling rhetoric, once a source of political potency, had now become per se a liability. It was deemed both sophistical and pretentious. Unlike Plumb, Ingalls had no personal commitment to prohibition, and it became known he had

9. Quoted by Barr, *Kansas*, p. 1152.

none. Unlike Plumb, he gave an impression of indifference to
the farmer's plight: a Kansas newspaper once reported in an utterly blank column the "remarks" he had "recently" made
about the agricultural discontents of his state. Unlike Plumb, he
strongly opposed woman suffrage (Plumb as strongly favored
it) on the ground that all government is ultimately force, that
only those strong enough to enforce the law should be permitted
to make it, and that women, too weak to compel masculine
obedience, must by that token be denied the "privilege" of
legislating over men. On the same ground of confused and con-
fusing Social Darwinism he condemned, as fatuous and futile,
reform and reformers. In the spring of 1890, when he had been
for three years president pro tem of the U.S. Senate, he granted
an interview to the *New York World,* a featured photographic interview, in which he declared flatly that "the purification of politics is an iridescent dream." Why so? Because government
"is force," politics is a "battle" for power, political parties are
"the armies," and any "commander who lost the battle through
the activity of his moral nature would be the . . . jest of history." The "modern cant" about political corruption proceeded, he sneered, from "tea-custard and ayllabub dilettantism
and frivolous sentimentalism." [10]

This aggressively "he-mannish" declaration could not have
been worse-timed by one who sought victory for himself and
party in the upcoming "battle" and who had himself been repeatedly and plausibly charged with corruption. Six months
later (September 1890), in a front page exposé article, the *New
York Times* charged him with secretly buying up Dickinson
County farmers' paper that had been discounted 18 percent by
an Abilene bank in which he had invested about ten thousand
dollars and which was under state investigation. The bank's
president was quoted. The *Times* suggested that Ingalls may
have engaged in similar operations through the other banks
(there were four or five) of which he was a director, thereby
"robbing the hard-working citizens" he was supposed to represent in the nation's highest legislative body. Ingalls promptly
denied the charge, of course. He also attempted, after the No-

10. *New York World,* April 13, 1890.

vember election, to explain away his "iridescent dream" statement, claiming now that he had meant merely to describe the
prevailing condition and not to say that politics *could* not be
purified. He did this as part of a desperate last-minute effort to
save his Senate seat—a floor speech (January 14, 1891), obviously designed for Populist consumption, whose main substance was a reiteration of his advocacy of "free silver."
American society, said he, "is becoming rapidly stratified . . .
into a condition of superfluously rich and hopelessly poor. We
are accustomed to speak of this as the land of the free and the
home of the brave. It will soon be the home of the rich and the
land of the slave." [11]

But by then there was no way in which he could have been
re-elected.

The Populist candidate for U.S. senator was the lawyer-edi-
tor of the *Kansas Farmer,* William A. Peffer, who had been at
least nominally a Republican until 1888 but was now wholly
dedicated to alliance principles. Though eccentric (for one
thing, he wore the longest chin-whiskers ever seen in American
politics; they reached to his waist) he was an able man, dry but
forceful in speech and writing, remarkably well-informed, and
absolutely incorruptible. On January 27, 1891, in balloting notable for its honesty (there were, unprecedentedly for an Ingalls
contest, no following charges of vote-buying), the Kansas legislature elected Peffer. The final vote was 101 for Peffer to 58 for
Ingalls, whose defeat occasioned a more widely demonstrated
popular joy than that of any other politician I can think of in
Kansas history.

Soon thereafter, Eugene F. Ware penned Ingalls's political
epitaph: [12]

> Up was he stuck,
> And in the upness of his stucktitude
> He fell.

---

11. John J. Ingalls, speech to U.S. Senate, Jan. 14, 1891, printed in full in *Atchison
Globe,* January 17, 1891.

12. Eugene F. Ware, "The Kansas Bandit, or The Fall of Ingalls," in Kirke Mechem, ed., Jennie Small Owens, annalist, 2 vols. *Annals of Kansas, 1886–1925* (Topeka, Kan.: Kansas State Historical Society, 1954), 1:116.

VI

And this was but the beginning of the Populist revolt.

By the end of 1891, the Kansas example and Kansas Populist leaders had spurred the formation of a national People's party which purported to be, and whose top leadership tried hard to make, a labor as well as farmer organization. Strong efforts were made to enlist urban workers, organized and unorganized. "Wealth belongs to him who creates it," declared a key convention resolution. "The interests of rural and urban labor are the same; the enemies are identical." (Alas, labor leaders had lurking doubts that this declaration was pragmatically true, however true idealistically—doubts shared by farmers who could not really regard themselves as "rural labor" so long as they were or tried to be individual entrepreneurs. The attempted fusion never really obtained. This was a grave misfortune for American democracy, in my opinion. It contributed to the failure of our society to effect the transition from a predominantly rural-agrarian economy to a predominantly urban-industrial one in a way that did not utterly destroy the former, with its distinctive moral and aesthetic values, but instead preserved it as an effective partner in the overall American enterprise of making men and women truly whole, truly free. Such fusion could certainly have helped us to humanize what was not yet, in the 1890s, a humanly overwhelming technological "progress.") A year later, in 1892, the new national party proclaimed the platform on which it would run candidates for national and state offices—a platform at once attacked by the conservative press, especially in the East, as a compendium of the mouth-frothings of failure-maddened fanatics. It called, among other things, for a graduated income tax, a postal savings bank, an eight-hour work day, the Australian (secret) ballot, the direct election of U.S. senators, the initiative and referendum, woman suffrage, expansion of paper currency, direct issue of such currency from government to people (i.e., abolition of the national bank system), "free silver" in a ratio of sixteen to one, implementation of the subtreasury plan, and government ownership of railroads, telegraph, and telephone.

Nominated for president on this platform was the man who had been Greenback-Labor's candidate in 1880, Gen. James B. Weaver of Iowa; and his showing in November 1892, if disappointing to overly optimistic rank-and-file Populists, was encouraging to most Populist leaders. It was proportionately, portentously dismaying to conservatives of the two major parties. Weaver won more than a million popular votes: he sufficiently reduced Republican strength in the North to enable Democrat Grover Cleveland, with five and a half million votes, to achieve the second term that the popular vote of four years before would have given him had there been no electoral college. Moreover, Weaver became the first third-party candidate since the Civil War to win an electoral vote: he had twenty-two of them, having carried five western states.

Of these last, Kansas was emphatically one.

Here, where there was a virtual fusion of the Populist and Democratic parties, Weaver's popular vote nearly equalled that of the two major party candidates combined. Here, his party made a clean sweep of the state executive offices (Lorenzo D. Lewelling became governor), elected five of the eight congressmen ("Sockless Jerry" won a second term), and gained decisive control of the state senate. The Populists failed, however, by a narrow margin, to win clear control of the house—and from this fact proceeded an event unique in the history of American states, namely, the "legislative war" of 1893. It riveted upon Topeka such excited national attention as Kansas had not received since territorial days.

The Populists claimed that the house was rightfully theirs to organize, if only the ballots were honestly counted. But the Republicans indubitably held sixty-five of the house's 125 election certificates, including three from districts where balloting irregularities were so gross as to more than suggest deliberate fraud; and they refused to concede that any of these certifications could be legitimately questioned. Here, then, was the stuff of dangerous quarrel. If Populists controlled the house they would enact their program. If Republicans did so, the Populist program was vulnerable to what, in that year, was assuredly a minority (conservative) veto. And the difference between majority and minority status consisted of the three highly questionable certifications. So the Populists attempted to force a recount of the original ballots and were frustrated by a state supreme court ruling in early January 1893, only a few days before the legislature convened, that the house must be sole judge of its own elections. But *how,* in the circumstances, could a fair, disinterested judgment be rendered by the house? If those who held disputed certificates were permitted to vote during organization proceedings, as the Republicans insisted they must (certification was prima facie evidence of election, said they, citing precedents)—if they did this they would be prejudging their own case and would, of course, be permanently seated in a Republican house. If they stood aside until the house was organized, as the Populists demanded, they would as certainly *never* be seated: the Populists would then be in full command of both the legislative and executive branches of government.

What followed was as near an approach as has ever been made in this country to social revolution in the classic sense—that is, a violent seizure of the apparatus of government accompanied by class warfare in the streets.

Revolutionary portents were very much in the Topeka air on inauguration day, January 9, 1893. The capital's streets were thronged by thousands of wildly jubilant common folk for whom "the occasion meant the wresting of the government from the tools of corporate greed and turning it over to the people," as Elizabeth Barr puts it in her aforementioned history. They listened to an inaugural address by Governor Lewelling in which "Government" was defined as "a voluntary union for the common good," a "social compact" which "guarantees to the individual [person] life, liberty and pursuit of happiness. If the Government fails [to fulfill this guarantee] . . . it ceases to be of advantage to the citizen" who is thereby "absolved from his allegiance, and is no longer bound by the social compact. . . . The people are greater than the law. . . ." A few hours later, in the capitol's Representative Hall, Populist orators addressed hundreds of the party faithful. Among the orators was Jerry Simpson who, fearful that the fruits of honest party victory were about to be snatched away by legalistic chicanery, was grimly belligerent. The *essential* "struggle in this state was not

between the People's Party and the Republican Party," he asserted, "but between the People's Party and the railway corporations. You have beaten the Santa Fe railroad and you must
take charge of the government. You must organize the Legislature in this Hall tomorrow, and I wouldn't let the technicalities
of the law stand in the way. Call this revolution if you will." [13]

But such organization, on the morrow, proved impossible: the
Republicans adamantly refused to give up the advantage they
derived from legal "technicalities" and the Populists as adamantly refused to give up what they conceived to be their rights.
The upshot was that *two* houses were organized—a Populist
house, which was promptly recognized as the legitimate one by
governor and senate; a Republican house, which the three Democratic representatives, for various complicated reasons, found
it expedient to join. After a long day and night during which
both houses occupied the hall simultaneously, an arrangement
was worked out whereby the rival houses met alternately, each
doing its own speechifying and passing its own laws—a wholly
untenable situation that nevertheless persisted into mid-
February.

Then the Republicans, determined to force the issue into the
Republican-dominated courts, announced that at the end of one
week hence they would no longer permit in Representative Hall
any legislator who refused to recognize the Republican house
organization. Whereupon Populist house members, with armed
guards, took possession of the house chamber, camping there
for the night, after the Republicans had made the mistake of ad-
journing. Next morning, Republican representatives, accompanied by some fifty armed deputy sergeants-at-arms, came in a
body to the chamber's door, where the Populists refused entry
to all who were not, in their view, duly elected legislators. The
Republicans, having somehow diverted the attention of the Populist guards, then smashed in the hall doors with a sledgeham-
mer, and, amid much scuffling and some fist-fighting, drove out
the Populists, occupying the hall. No shot was fired: each side
quailed at the prospect of fatal violence.

But the situation was now dangerous in the extreme. It re-

13. Barr, *Kansas*, pp. 1169–1171.

mained so for the next forty-eight hours, during which armed Republicans in the house chamber were closely besieged by armed Populists and both sides mobilized for possible street battles. The Republicans reportedly called upon the Santa Fe to furnish two thousand employees for this purpose, and it is certain that they assembled a force of much more than a thousand armed men. The governor called out the local state militia, some two hundred fifty men, whose Republican commandant promptly refused to obey orders and was relieved. Into Topeka from elsewhere in the state came grim armed men of both political parties as a literally dreadful excitement mounted to unbearable heights and a frantic governor, his conscience tortured by the responsibility he would bear for the bloodshed his opponents appeared willing to accept, his nerves frazzled by sleeplessness, strove for a negotiated settlement.

The denouement was reminiscent of the bloodless Wakarusa War of 1855.

The National Guard was summoned. Eight companies of infantry and a battery of light artillery, armed with carbines and a gatling gun, arrived on the capitol grounds simultaneously with a blizzard whose ten inches of snow and bitter winds had a decidedly chilling effect upon hotly belligerent tempers. A truce was arranged—a truce that amounted to a Populist surrender. It was agreed that the state supreme court should decide which of the rival houses was the legal body. Meanwhile the arrangement of alternate meetings was resumed. On February 25, the inevitable court decision in favor of the Republicans was rendered.

Nor was the loss of the house, with its disastrous consequences for Populist proposals, the whole measure of the Populist's defeat. They lost also, and badly, in the court of popular opinion as the Republican press reiterated the conclusion that they, a party of red rebellion and anarchy, were solely responsible for the "legislative war." Worse still, the Populist administration, frustrated and angry, began now to present to the public a sorry spectacle of ineptitude, internal dissension and, in the highest post, possible personal dishonesty. The inexperienced Lewelling badly mishandled patronage matters. Moreover, astonishingly, he and his private secretary, Fred Close, became personally involved in land-leasing and railroad corporation schemes that made him a target for charges of corruption hurled not only by the Republican press (with glee) but also by much of the Populist press (with fury, out of a bitter sense of betrayal).

Small wonder that, in the local elections of 1893, the Populists fared badly. In 1894, when the Populists and Democrats went their separate ways, with the Populists laying heavy stress on woman suffrage and the Democrats flatly opposing it, the Republicans surged back into power.

The times, however, continued propitious for political radicalism in state and nation—more so, in fact, than ever before, now that there was no longer a western frontier to serve as a cushion (a psychological cushion, at least) for economic shocks to long-settled areas. A financial panic, begun in the spring and climaxed by a stock market crash in late June of 1893, ushered in a national depression as severe as the agricultural depression had long been in the plains states; and in the latter, distress was augmented by the disastrous efforts of the continuing drouth. Out of the East into the coal fields of southeastern Kansas, into the railroad yards of the Santa Fe and Missouri Pacific, rolled a wave of strikes as wages were cut and men laid off. Violence flared around Pittsburg and at railroad switching points throughout the state, some of it provoked when employers imported strikebreakers and, by means of court injunction, implemented their private advantage with public police power. Nor was the employing class itself exempt from the general calamity. Financial institutions and employing businesses by the score were swept into bankruptcy, an early victim being the Kansas Trust and Mortgage Co., in Atchison, of which John J. Ingalls was president. Between mid-June and late July 1893, bank closings in Kansas averaged one a day. Forty-four had failed by year's end; 114 failed in the year that followed. The Union Pacific abandoned its Leavenworth Division—went finally into receivership nationally, as did seventy-three other railroads in 1893, including the Santa Fe, though the latter managed to survive without significant change in ownership or control.

Meanwhile, the Democrat in the White House, Grover Cleveland, pursued economic policies indistinguishable from those of a right-wing eastern Republican.

So in 1896, the Kansas Populists again won sweeping victories at the polls—greater victories than in 1892. They elected their entire state ticket, headed by gubernatorial candidate John W. Leedy; won clear majorities of both houses of the legislature; and elected all five congressional representatives, including "Sockless Jerry" for a third term. But they won on terms of party realignment that spelled the early death of their party, state and national. Eighteen ninety-six was the year when William Jennings Bryan of Nebraska stampeded the Democratic National Convention with his "Cross of Gold" speech on behalf of "free silver" and won for himself the party's presidential nomination, thereby persuading many Populists that their movement had actually captured the national Democracy—that there was no longer need for an independent People's party on the national scene. When the People's National Convention met, it put up no presidential candidate of its own but merely seconded Bryan's nomination. Nor did the Kansas Democracy put up candidates of *its* own in the state election that year. Leedy's was a triumph of fusionism. And it was overshadowed, its effectiveness reduced, by Bryan's loss to Republican William McKinley in a national contest in which Populist proposals were at issue.

Thereafter, the Populists floundered, in Kansas as in the nation.

Most of the leading as well as the rank-and-file Populists were common folk, more heavily burdened by the tasks of daily living than their opponents were. They were economically insecure. They were also psychologically insecure, accustomed to placing very modest estimates upon their personal rights, their personal abilities—and this deficiency of self-assertiveness or even self-confidence was certainly not supplied by their view of their party's performance in legislature and state house: the Leedy administration placed no more uniquely Populist legislation upon the statute books than the Lewelling administration had done. They were therefore highly vulnerable to psychological assaults by their "betters." They shrank more and more under the relentless fire of ridicule directed at them and their cause by the makers of "respectable" public opinion—a fire whose effectiveness increased in proportion to the return of more prosperous times in the latter half of the 1890s. For as the effects of the panic of 1893 were absorbed gradually by the pain and suffering of millions, new goldfields were opened up over the world and the cyanide process for extracting gold from crude ore was perfected. The resultant cheapening of gold boosted wages and prices and made "free silver" no longer a viable political issue: agricultural prices doubled, or more, as national and world purchasing power increased. Simultaneously the prolonged series of drouth years was followed in Kansas by a series of excellent crop years.

In 1898, as Manifest Destiny reached out to seize the Philippines from Spain and martial patrotism overwhelmed for the time being other public concerns, the Republicans again swept the Kansas election, winning every state office, both legislative houses, and all but one of the congressional seats. They continued this renewed absolute domination of state government for the next dozen years.

7

Twentieth-Century Kansas:
Phase-Change and Aftermath

I

*Y*ET much of what Kansas populism had failed to accomplish in its own name by 1900 was accomplished in the name of progressivism by 1912, and accomplished in part because of populism's gathering together of great energies of protest and reform, focusing these upon clearly defined evils.

Everywhere in America, the new century as it opened was seen as a shining new canvas-tablet of Time, whereon mighty events would be penned and an ever-brighter glow of human happiness painted by the arts of triumphant, indefatigable progress. Nowhere was this more evident than in Kansas. The nation, having fought its "splendid little war" with Spain, was newly and acutely aware of itself as a world power, complete with overseas colonial possessions; and though many Kansans questioned the economic and moral wisdom of our adventure in imperialism far across the Pacific (how would the white man's burden effect farm markets? Were bullets and bayonets truly civilizing agencies?), virtually every Kansan gloried in the battle record of the 20th Kansas Volunteers and its regimental commander, Col. Frederick Funston of Iola, as they fought Emilio Aguinaldo and his Filipino insurrectionists in a campaign that began when the Spanish-American War ended. If the United States was a world power, Kansas was literally at the heart of it. And it was in the conviction that no specific unit of national force had affected world history more importantly than the "Fighting 20th" that Topeka, on November 2, 1899, welcomed this regiment home from the Philippines "with a 13-gun salute, a nine-band parade, a reception and banquet staged by 75,000 persons." [1] Had not Maj. Gen. Arthur MacArthur himself informed Washington and the nation that these Kansans, who suffered more casualties than any other regiment, were "the backbone of my division"? Had he not nominated ten of them for congressional Medals of Honor? (At the top of this list were Privates William B. Trembly and Edward White of Kansas City who, in April 1899, became national heroes when they swam across the Rio Grande de la Pampanga under heavy fire, dragging a rope behind them, thereby enabling Americans to effect a crossing in force and rout the Filipino enemy in an engagement of strategic importance.)

But this glory in martial exploits was only one element of a mighty resurgence of state pride (creative pride). The more important elements of it were of a socio-political nature. There was an immense sense of release and relief, everywhere in the state, as prosperity returned after feverish years of boom-and-bust and prolonged depression—a prosperity at once higher and more soundly based than any the state had experienced before. Tens of thousands of people who in former years had identified with the dispossessed, the exploited at the bottom of the economic heap, began now to identify with the middle class and to feed into its augmented ranks (augmented by their own entry), and into its overall mind and mood, a vital remnant of the Populist passion for social justice, along with a relatively ineffectual vestige of the advanced Populist's reasoned commitment to structural change. These became fused, in the towns, the cities, with the concerns of business and professional people over the costs to them in money and depleted social environment of a

1. Kirke Mechem, ed., Jennie Small Owen, annalist, 2 vols. *Annals of Kansas, 1886–1925* (Topeka, Kan.: Kansas State Historical Society, 1954), 1:295.

continued corrupt alliance of big business, other special interests, "boss-run" political organizations, and government officials. "Boss busting" was joined with "trust busting" in an
unprecedentedly powerful movement toward that "purification
of politics" that Ingalls had cynically dismissed, only a few
years before, as an "iridescent dream."

II

Catalytic agent of the process was Theodore Roosevelt. A
chief Kansas actor in it was William Allen White. The first
meeting of White and TR, in early 1897, may therefore be
viewed as an event of importance in Kansas's political and cultural history—an event not lacking in ironic overtones with
regard to both its cause and its effect.

Some twenty-odd months before, young White (he was then
twenty-seven; he was on the staff of the *Kansas City Star*) had
bought the *Emporia Gazette* with a borrowed three thousand
dollars. The paper had been launched as a Populist organ during
the "crusade" of 1890. White pleased his creditors by making
it into a Republican organ of the most rock-ribbed conservatism.
By his own later admission he was in those days a bit of a snob,
overly impressed by wealth and power and overly eager to become himself one of the ruling elite. And because his editorial
excursions into political economy were as brash and smug (if
flamboyantly so) as they were poorly reasoned and ill-informed,
he quickly brought down upon his somewhat swollen head the
mingled wrath and contempt of his Populist-farmer readers. He
sneered at them as raggedy ne'er-do-wells. They dubbed him
"Silly Willy." Yet they invariably sought to educate him ("Agitate, Educate, Organize!") whenever they encountered him on
Emporia's streets, despite his scared reluctance to engage in
face-to-face debate with them.

They did so with a special forcefulness one fervidly hot Saturday afternoon in mid-August, 1896. White had just published
two particularly obnoxious editorials. One, entitled "Patriotism
or Anarchy?" equated Republicanism with the former, Populism with the latter. The other, entitled "The Sweep of It," as-

serted that the Republican party spoke "for old-fashioned, sturdy Americanism," saying "to the man who asks that the state shall step in and relieve him of his burden: 'You had equal opportunity with your fellows. You had . . . as fair a start; if you are behind and the other man is ahead, the thing for you to do is catch up. . . . He is running his own race; if he is violating no law we shall let him go ahead—the faster he goes the better.' " [2] Small wonder that a shabbily clothed crowd of fifteen or twenty men surrounded him as he tried to make his way from post office to *Gazette* office. They would not let him go until they had provoked from him a spluttering defence of his editorials. Whereupon with fact and logic they easily demolished his argument, mercilessly shredded his pretence that he had earned his opinions through serious thought, and exposed naked to the broiling sun his ignorance, his assertive bias. He carried this bias fuming into his office, sat himself down at his rolltop desk, and there poured out as easily as sweat (the thermometer registered 107 in Emporia that afternoon) an editorial that gave him national fame and had some influence, indeterminate but real, on national history. "What's the Matter With Kansas?" he asked, and answered in luridly vitriolic prose that populism was the matter.

Because of populism, Kansas had deservedly become an object of universal contempt:

"Go east and you hear them laugh at Kansas, go west and they sneer at her, go south and they 'cuss' her, go north and they have forgotten her. Go into any crowd of intelligent people gathered anywhere on the globe, and you will find the Kansas man on the defensive. . . .

"What's the matter with Kansas?

"We all know; yet here we are at it again. We have an old moss-back Jacksonian who snorts and howls because there is a bathtub in the statehouse; we are running that old jay for governor. We have another shabby, wild-eyed, rattle-brained fanatic who has said openly in a dozen speeches that 'the rights of the user are paramount to the rights of the owner'; we are running

2. *Emporia Gazette,* August 11, 1896.

him for chief justice, so that capital will come tumbling over itself to get into the state. We have raked the old ash heap of failure in the state and found an old human hoop skirt who has
failed as a business man, who has failed as an editor, who has
failed as a preacher, and we are going to run him for con-
gressman-at-large. He will help the looks of the Kansas delegation in Washington. Then we have discovered a kid without a
law practice and have decided to run him for attorney-general.
Then for fear some hint that the state had become respectable
might percolate through to the civilized portions of the nation,
we have decided to send three of four harpies out lecturing,
telling the people that Kansas is raising hell and letting the corn
go to weeds. . . .

"That's the stuff! Give the prosperous man the dickens!
Legislate the thriftless man into ease, whack the stuffing out of
the creditors and tell the debtors who borrowed the money five
years ago when money 'per capita' was greater than it is now
that the contraction of the currency gives him a right to repudi-
ate.

"Whoop it up for the ragged trousers; put the lazy, greasy
fizzle who can't pay his debts on the altar, and bow down and
worship him. . . ." [3]

Thus, in part, White's tirade against the men who had just
discomfited and humiliated him (there was much more of it, all
equally hyperbolic, all equally colorful)—a tirade that within a
few weeks had been read by virtually every literate citizen in the
nation. For Republican newspapers all across the land reprinted
it in full. Mark Hanna used it as McKinley Republican campaign literature, distributing millions of copies of it in broadside
or pamphlet form. And if it had no perceptible effect upon the
election in White's hometown or state that year (Emporia and
Lyon County went Populist by a considerable majority), Hanna
was convinced it influenced in some degree the national outcome and was duly grateful. It was because of Hanna's gratitude, or the train of circumstances initiated thereby, that White
found himself in Washington shortly after McKinley's inaugura-

3. *Emporia Gazette,* August 15, 1896.

tion and there was introduced to McKinley's assistant secretary of the navy.

For White, this meeting was a life-transforming experience, somewhat on the order of Paul's vision on the road to Damascus.

TR was a young man, only ten years older than White— "hard-muscled, hard-voiced even when the voice cracked in falsetto." He was indubitably of the American elite, his social and financial position so solidly assured by inheritance that it need never enter, and did not consciously enter, into career calculations. He was obviously highly intelligent, intellectually sophisticated, amazingly well-informed in a wide variety of fields, possessed of a literally overwhelming personality. Yet he inveighed "with vocal eloquence and ironic rage" against everything Mark Hanna stood for in public life, "the reign of privilege . . . the deep and damnable alliance between business and government for the good of business"—in sum, the plutocracy that White had been so vociferously and ignorantly defending against opposing forces, "the order . . . to which," as he later wrote, "I had commended my soul." White did not even protest. Within an hour he had "accepted his [TR's] dictum as my creed." And the conversion was as total and permanent as it was abrupt. TR had "sounded in my heart the first trumpet call of the new time that was to be." Thereafter, "I was his man." [4]

Returned to Kansas, White remained in frequent and voluminous correspondence with his hero, who became a shining hero to all the nation as well when his Rough Riders charged up San Juan Hill, then became boss-fighting governor of New York, and finally, in 1900, with initial reluctance but subsequent awesome energy, candidate for vice-president of the United States. He bore the brunt of the battle against William Jennings Bryan that year and was given, in the popular mind, a lion's share of the credit for McKinley's re-election. By that time a number of Kansas Republicans (Victor Murdock, Joseph L. Bristow,

4. William Allen White, *Autobiography of William Allen White* (New York: Macmillan Co., 1946), p. 298.

Henry Allen, Edward Hoch, Walter R. Stubbs, et al) were joining White as "Roosevelt men," TR having made two tre-
mendously effective speaking tours of Kansas, in July and
September of the election year. There were enough of these men
to constitute, with former Populists who had returned to the
party's rank and file, a powerful faction. And during Stanley's
second term they began to coalesce into a definite faction, began
to prepare for war upon the Old Guard machine politicians for
party control.

They were yet too weak to nominate their top candidates, but
became a dominant force in the state senate, in 1903, after TR,
as a result of McKinley's assassination, had become president.
The governorship went to an orthodox conservative Republican,
Willis J. Bailey, whose chief prior claim to popular attention
had been an expressed hostility to populism as virulent as
White's "What's the Matter . . . ?" (White now attacked him
for timidity and indecisiveness in the face of a palpable corruption of the legislature, asserting that "Kansas needs a man with
. . . a firm jaw who can set it by time lock and go after the
petty larcenists . . . ." [5]) But in 1904, when TR was elected
president (he got 66 percent of the Kansas vote), an antimachine
Republican, Edward R. Hoch of the *Marion Record*, was
elected governor, and there began eight years of effective reformist, progressive government such as Kansas had never
known before and has not known since. For Hoch was re-
elected in 1906 and succeeded in 1908 by Stubbs who, as an
unusually forceful speaker of the house during the Hoch administration, had been responsible for much of that administration's legislative success. Hoch was an excellent governor.
Stubbs was an even better one, quite possibly the best Kansas
ever had, measured in terms of the legal and institutional in-
novations of permanent value to the general welfare that were
made in his administration. He had acquired a fortune as a
railroad contractor before entering politics, hence understood
business and businessmen, and was thoroughly knowledgeable
about the ways in which corporations, especially the railroads,

5. *Emporia Gazette*, July 13, 1903.

made state government the servant of their special interests. With his powerful physique, booming voice, rock-hard integrity, and a personal force approximately as overwhelming as TR's, he was a born leader of men—and he led with an unswerving commitment to government that was truly democratic in its roots, efficient in its executive operation, boldly progressive in its purpose. He was a superb political tactician. He knew how to mix force with persuasion in effective doses, and was willing to spend his personal popularity in amounts sufficient to buy specific program items—items whose relative values he shrewdly assessed. During his four years in the governor's chair (he won re-election in 1910, though he ran well behind his ticket), Kansas's peculiar brand of New England-western Puritanism, Kansas's distinctive blend of idealism and practicality—the representative Kansan's view of the government as (in Carl Becker's phrase) "the individual writ large"—all this achieved its happiest political expression.

During the Hoch-Stubbs years, the power of the railroads was curbed by replacement of the old board of railroad assessors with a three-man commission to assess railroad property realistically, for taxation purposes; by arming the board of railroad commissioners with some control over railroad stock issuance, then transferring this authority to the Public Utilities Commission when it was created to regulate *all* public service corporations in the state; and by adoption of an antipass law, the free pass having been a principal means by which railroads influenced public officials and the molders of popular opinion. There was also a forced reduction in passenger fares, and a maximum freight-rate law that cut grain shipment costs 15 percent. The submission of a woman suffrage amendment to the voters; a workman's compensation law; a strengthened child labor law; the direct primary; the direct election of U.S. senators; a pioneering law providing for state review and approval of all stocks offered for sale in Kansas; a pioneer bank guarantee law; laws granting unique powers of regulation and prohibition to the state board of health—all these were written into the statute books between 1904 and 1912.

There was also attracted into the state's executive bureaus a remarkably competent and dedicated group of public servants. Outstanding among them was Samuel J. Crumbine, M.D., executive secretary of the board of health. Actually, Crumbine had already accepted this position when Hoch won his first election—but when he took over in July 1904, the board's annual appropriation was precisely $3,080 for all purposes and his position with it was a part-time one (he continued his private medical practice). It was the Hoch administration that granted his requests for vast increases in the board's appropriations, making the executive secretary's job full-time, whereupon he gave up his private practice and launched a series of public health crusades that made Kansas a model in this field and himself nationally famous. His 1905 "Swat the Fly" slogan-and-campaign made not only the state but the nation acutely conscious of the house fly as a disease-spreader and stimulated a fellow Kansan, a young high school teacher of Wier City named Frank H. Rose, to nail squares of screening wire to pieces of yardstock, thereby inventing what he called a "fly bat" and Crumbine a "fly swatter." The doctor's campaign against the common drinking cup stimulated native Kansan Hugh Moore, who had recently moved to Boston, to make, in 1909, the first paper drinking cup. Moore went on to invent a cup-making machine and a penny machine for vending them, and to become chairman of the board of the Dixie Paper Cup Company. Crumbine was both inspiration and draftsman of Kansas's food and drug act of 1907, which became a model for other states, and for national legislation.

It was this Kansas of the Hoch-Stubbs years that Carl Becker came to know and love, and sought lovingly to interpret in his "Kansas," published in the year of Stubbs's re-election. It was this Kansas, too, that William White wrote of in a 1922 editorial. "Kansas," he then proclaimed, "is the Mother Shipton, the Madame Thebes, the Witch of Endor, and the low barometer of the nation. When anything is going to happen in this country, it happens first in Kansas. Abolition, Prohibition, Populism, the Bull Moose, the exit of the roller towel, the appearance of the bank guarantee, the blue sky law, the adjudication of industrial dispute as distinguished from the arbitration of industrial differences—these things come popping out of Kansas like bats out of hell. Sooner or later other states take up these things, and then Kansas goes on breeding other troubles. . . . Kansas, fair, fat, and sixty-one last month, is the nation's tenth muse, the muse of prophecy.'' He averred that the only way to ''stop progress in America'' would be ''to hire some hungry earthquake to come along and gobble up Kansas,'' but that this earthquake ''would have an awful case of indigestion for two or three epochs afterward.'' [6]

III

Brave words! Gaudy words! They have delighted many a citizen of White's native state over the years. . . .

But by the time White wrote them, alas, the Kansas he spoke of in present tense, as if it were a continuing reality, had undergone a drastic change of phase.

There had been a great war, the First World War, during which the government, as the alleged price of martial victory, halted virtually every movement toward a democratic control of growing technological-economic power and, indeed, vastly increased the control of this, and of its political effects, by corporation executives whom Populists and Progressives had deemed the principal enemies of individual liberties, of genuine human freedom.

Kansas's experience of the war was not markedly different, in most respects, from that of other states. A huge troop training camp rose on the old Pawnee Flats, adjacent to the first territorial capitol (then in ruin, now restored) at the eastern edge of the Fort Riley military reservation, and was named after Kansas's chief martial hero up till then, Frederick Funston. At Camp Funston was organized and trained the 89th Division, one of the three divisions in which served most of the Kansans who saw combat overseas. The other two were the 35th, made up of Kansas and Missouri National Guard units, and the 42nd (Rainbow), made up of National Guard units from twenty-six states.

6. *Emporia Gazette*, April 25, 1922.

The 35th spearheaded the Meuse-Argonne attack in October
1918 and suffered there heavy casualties. Altogether, some
eighty-three thousand Kansans donned army, navy, or marine
uniforms during the war. Of these, 816 died of battle wounds,
1,453 of disease, and some two thousand others were wounded.
Two Kansans were awarded the congressional Medal of
Honor—George S. Robb of Salina (he later served twelve terms
as state auditor) and Erwin R. Bleckley of Wichita, the latter
posthumously. Over two hundred won the Distinguished Service
Cross for "extraordinary heroism in action." Three Kansans
served as general officers, the highest ranking and most distinguished being Maj. Gen. James G. Harbord of Americus, who
was chief of staff to Gen. Pershing, then commanded the marine
brigade that fought in Belleau Wood, and finally commanded
the services of supply for the whole American Expeditionary
Force. On the home front, the war's most distinctively Kansan
impact, fraught with significance for the state's future economy,
was the plowing of huge acreages of High Plains grassland and
planting them to wheat in 1917 and 1918, this in response to
high wheat prices and the government's chant that "Food Will
Win the War." In Kansas, as elsewhere, were ugly instances of
"superpatriotism," stirred up in generally conservative tempera-
ments by fervid war propaganda; they inflicted their usual inju-
ries to civil liberty and human decency, especially in the case of
the pacifistic Mennonites (German Mennonites!) in the central
part of the state. By Armistice Day, Kansas, like the rest of the
nation, was in the grip of an unprecedented and, fortunately,
unsucceeded pandemic of so-called "Spanish" influenza—a
particularly virulent fever, often fatal. Literally hundreds of
thousands of Kansans were stricken by it (whole families went
down simultaneously), and some fifty-five hundred died of it in
this state before it ceased to rage.

All of which added up, as I've said, to an experience not
unlike that of other states, and one which had, of itself alone,
no unique character-transforming effect. Yet the Kansas that
emerged from the war was very different in essential ways from
that of 1912. White's "hungry earthquake," swallowing Kansas
in 1922 or after, might well have suffered indigestion, but it
would not have been the indigestion of a substance overly rich,

tumultuously and creatively fermentive, but rather of a fodder dry and hard, almost impervious to the juices of change, leaving a sour taste of decayed Puritanism in the mouth.

What had happened? How had it happened? And what was the inward nature of the Kansas that resulted?

My own several attempts to answer these questions have often had as starting point and central theme a consideration of salty, humorous, lovable, exasperating William Allen White himself. For White was not only a remarkably symptomatic Kansas character, he was also in many ways the state's most influential single citizen. His conception of himself and of his proper role on the public stage, his personal acts and editorial stands in the political arena, were of determinative importance in the Kansas community.

By 1912, White had been for years among the most prominent of those who, in state and nation, fought for control of the Republican party against the Old Guard of William Howard Taft. A personal interview in the White House, not long after the 1909 inauguration, convinced him of the invincible conservatism of TR's hand-picked successor; he was not surprised when Taft repudiated in official acts almost every article of the progressive faith and revealed himself a pliant tool of big businessmen when he dealt with public lands and the tariff. White *was* outraged, however. He early joined other leaders in efforts to replace Taft with a progressive at the head of the Republican ticket in 1912, his first candidate being progressive Republican Sen. Robert M. LaFollette of Wisconsin. But when TR declared for the Republican nomination and then, robbed of the nomination by Old Guard control of the convention machinery, led his followers into an independent Progressive party, White promptly took his stand "at Armageddon" and there did "battle for the Lord." (It is significant that Louis Brandeis, who joined with White in initial efforts to promote the LaFollette candidacy, flatly refused on firm grounds of principle to support TR: he shifted instead to the Democracy of Woodrow Wilson, as did virtually all other leaders of the original LaFollette movement.) Few men thereafter devoted more energy and talent to the Bull Moose than did William Allen White.

In Kansas, the Progressives of 1912 did not put up a separate

state ticket. They ran their candidates for state office and the
U.S. Senate as Republicans, and managed to win the primaries
in a factional fight of surpassing bitterness. But the party was effectively split, all the same, between Taft and Roosevelt forces,
with the result that Wilson carried the state, though with a
minority of the total vote; Democrat George H. Hodges defeated
progressive Republican Arthur Capper for the governorship,
though by just twenty-nine votes [!]; and Democrat William H.
Thompson resoundingly defeated progressive Republican Stubbs
for the U.S. Senate, Stubbs having devoted much more of his
campaign to the promotion of TR than to his own election. The
Democrats also won control of the legislature, enabling Hodges
who was committed to progressive principles, to continue for
another two years the reign of progressivism in Kansas politics.
And if White had not before been aware of the fate awaiting
Kansas Progressives who remained in, or returned to, a Republican party whose organization was now firmly controlled by the
Old Guard, he was surely made so by the Old Guard's reaction
to the election returns. Typical was the editorial comment of the
Kansas City (Mo.) *Journal* on the morrow of election day.
"Kansas has redeemed herself. . . . She has by one firm stroke
of patriotism killed off the Bull Moose dictators, and the Republican party in Kansas stands today cleansed and rejuvenated. . . ."

Hence White, insofar as he continued to crave behind-the-
scenes political power and influence, had good reason to struggle
mightily to keep the national Progressive party alive, hoping
that it would grow into one of the two major American parties.
And he did so struggle. In Kansas, in the 1914 election, a
"cleansed and rejuvenated" Republican party swept back into
power. The successful gubernatorial candidate, Arthur Capper,
then in process of creating a publishing empire (the *Topeka
Daily Capital,* a string of farm magazines, a national woman's
magazine), bore a Progressive tag, but the legislature was predominantly conservative, and Progressive Bristow was replaced
by archconservative Charles Curtis in the U.S. Senate. Nevertheless, White continued to hope and work for national progressivism, and for a recapture of Kansas Republicanism by

progressives. He had no love of combat. Yet he engaged in harsh intra-Progressive battles with ex-Morgan partner George W. Perkins and his eastern wing of wealthy financiers and industrialists, men whose clear design was to destroy the party from within, effecting fusion, in 1916, with Republicans who nominated a supposedly (dubiously) progressive Charles Evans Hughes for president. None was more dismayed than White when TR himself, out of personal hatred for Woodrow Wilson and an eagerness to involve the United States on the Allied side in the then-raging war, joined the Perkins wreckers: the Bull Moose was stabbed to the heart by TR's refusal to accept the Progressive nomination for president in 1916, his announcement that he would support Hughes. When the Progressive national committee met to give Hughes its endorsement, White, a committee member, refused to vote; and even after thirty years had passed he looked back upon that bitter moment and upon the dream which then died, with poignant sadness and regret. "It was the end of a great adventure," he wrote in his autobiography, "politically and emotionally probably the greatest adventure of my life." [7]

It was also effectively the end, for decades to come, of liberalism as a predominant element (or even an important one) in the Kansas body politic—the end of Kansas as a uniquely valuable laboratory of social experimentation, motivated by that "insurgency" that had seemed to Becker, in his essay, "native" to the state.

The national Democratic administration of 1913–1917 had written much of the 1912 Progressive platform onto the federal statute books. The party of Bryan and Wilson seemed clearly to have a greater liberal potential than the party that had barely tolerated Theodore Roosevelt, had finally utterly repudiated him, and was now more than ever in the tight control of giant business interests. Yet White never seriously considered following Brandeis and other liberals into the Wilsonian Democracy. Neither did he consider withdrawing altogether from party politics, declaring his political independence and devoting himself

7. White, *Autobiography*, p. 527.

primarily to his literary career, which, by then, was well-launched (he had published several highly successful books, including a best-selling novel, *A Certain Rich Man*). Instead he returned, hat in hand, to the Republican fold. In 1918, when the Republican party leadership was ostentatiously engaged in "harmonizing" with former party dissidents, and several former Bull Moosers won elective office as Republicans, White tried to convince himself and the public that the GOP was being progressivized, liberalized. He worked hard for a Kansas Republican ticket that successfully ran Henry Allen for governor and Arthur Capper for U.S. Senate, Capper having served two gubernatorial terms. But in his heart, as his autobiography makes clear, he knew that what was really happening was a blunting, a neutralization of the liberal thrust within his party. Allen's election symbolized "the rise of a chastened, weary, and disillusioned liberalism in the Republican party" but did little or nothing to "curb . . . the activities of the greedy, egoistic forces . . . which controlled" the Republican "organization," wrote White, in retrospect. "They treated us liberals who were getting the offices to liberal helpings of veal from the fatted calf; but, like the elder brother, they kept right on running the farm." [8]

IV

And White kept right on supporting with all his talent and influence the straight Republican ticket in every election save one, through the twenties, the thirties, the early forties.

The single exception was in 1924 when White himself ran for governor as an independent. His doing so was of a piece with the one strand of consistency that ran straight and true through all his public life, namely, his commitment to civil liberties in general and the First Amendment in particular. He was outraged by the rise to dangerous power and influence of the postwar Ku Klux Klan, and by the evident willingness of the state Republican leadership to accept Klan support. (The Democrats were

8. White, *Autobiography,* p. 546.

more restrained in this regard; most Roman Catholics voted Democratic, and the Klan was virulently anti-Catholic.) Beginning in 1921 he inveighed in his strongest language, editorially, against the Klan as "an organization of cowards . . . [and] traitors to American institutions" that, nevertheless, elected a mayor of Emporia in 1924 and bade fair to capture control of the state's Republican organization. It was with the avowed purpose of laughing the Klan out of existence in his state that White ran his independent campaign, and there is no doubt that his campaign speeches and writings, provoking loud and national laughter, contributed to the KKK's subsequent swift fading from the Kansas scene. Republican Ben Paulen won the election, but evidently despite and not because the Klan supported him—for White, who didn't announce until September 20, had no organization, and spent only $474.60 on his campaign, gained almost as many votes as the Democratic candidate, and the two together outpolled Paulen by ten thousand.

But this, to repeat, was White's sole departure from Republican regularity through the last quarter century of his life—and even in that year his "independence" was a strictly local phenomenon of brief duration.

He had generally approved of Woodrow Wilson's domestic policies and conduct of the war. He strongly favored the League of Nations. He had been disgusted by the cynical "smoke-filled-room" convention in which Warren G. Harding received the 1920 Republican presidential nomination. Yet he editorially supported Harding's candidacy in the *Gazette,* repeatedly asserted that the League was not at issue in the campaign (though it obviously was), and, after Harding in office had repudiated U.S. participation in the League and abundantly demonstrated what "normalcy" meant in practice, along with his own personal flabbiness, found it possible to declare in a mass-circulation magazine that Harding had gathered around him "the best minds" in America and was "doing a better than fair job" as president! [9] In 1924, U.S. entrance into the League, which White continued to favor, was the single clear issue dividing

9. White, "The Best Minds, Incorporated," *Collier's,* March 4, 1922.

Democrat John W. Davis from Republican Calvin Coolidge in the presidential campaign. White also deplored the total subservience of Coolidge to big business, and professed profound admiration for Wisconsin's Bob LaFollette, running that year on a revived Progressive party platform, which asserted that the "great issue before the American people today is the control of government and industry by private monopoly." But all this did not keep him from strongly supporting the Coolidge candidacy in his public statements nor from publishing, a year later, a book, *Calvin Coolidge, The Man Who Is President,* showing Silent Cal in the most favorable light.

Of course White supported his personal friend Herbert Hoover against the all-too-urban Al Smith in 1928—though again the Democratic platform (aside from its implicit opposition to prohibition, to which White was always committed) was in far closer accord with White's basic views than was the Republican one. Subsequently, he expressed editorial displeasure over Hoover's support of the Smoot-Hawley tariff, Hoover's veto of the Muscle Shoals bill, Hoover's failure to act on relief problems that grew huge in the depression aftermath of the 1929 stock market crash—three matters on which the Democratic candidate in 1932, Franklin D. Roosevelt, took the stands White favored. But it was Hoover whom White supported that year. (FDR carried Kansas, 424,204 to 349,498.) The same story, with variations, was repeated in 1936. By then there had been added to Kansas's depression woes a prolonged drouth: the topsoil of vast areas of west-central and western Kansas, much of it war-plowed out of virgin sod for a wheat market that collapsed after the war, had begun to ride the sweeping winds of the plains in terrifying dust storms (all southwest Kansas was part of the Dust Bowl) and Kansas farmers everywhere depended on AAA checks and New Deal relief programs. By then, too, White had publicly proclaimed that "by and large, I am for the New Deal." ("Much of it is necessary," he told a college audience in 1934. "All of it is human. And most of it is long past due.") [10] He was hostile to the Liberty League of big

10. White, commencement address, University of Kansas, June, 1934.

businessmen who conducted a virulent campaign against the New Deal and FDR personally. He editorialized for the re-election of Nebraska's Sen. George Norris, who supported FDR that year. He admitted privately that the Republican presidential candidate, Kansas Governor Alf M. Landon, was in his opinion far less well equipped for the White House than its present occupant and that Landon's vaunted state budget-balancing had been accomplished only with New Deal federal aid. Yet his support of Landon's candidacy was not limited to a public endorsement: he contributed propaganda, composed in his own inimitable style, for Landon's campaign use. (FDR again carried Kansas, and by a margin only somewhat less than that of 1932, despite Landon's personal popularity in the state.) It was during this 1936 campaign that Roosevelt publicly embarrassed White by summoning the reluctant editor to the rear platform of the Democratic presidential campaign train when it paused in Emporia and there hailing him, before a great crowd, as "My good friend Bill White—three and a half years out of every four!"

White, of course, had a rationalization for this self-contradictory behavior. It was that his election-year party regularity gave him a decisive leverage within the GOP: it enabled him to exercise, in favor of what he *really* believed in, an influence he would have lost had he operated differently. This rationalization, unconvincing to liberals across the land, was flatly rejected, and with at least as much anger as sorrow, by Kansans of liberal persuasion in the years of my youth. We could not see the slightest evidence that White had a liberalizing influence upon the GOP. We saw abundant evidence of the value to the GOP of what we deemed his sophistry—his talent for making the dull seem interesting, for cloaking with sympathetic attractiveness what was nakedly repulsive, and (in general) making the worse seem the better cause. He was, we thought and said, the kind of "liberal" whose function is to focus upon himself popular energies that might be organized for fundamental change, this in order to dissipate them at the only times and places (notably polling booths in election years) at which they could become truly effective.

V

But though we thus blamed White for his service to men and forces we saw as inimical to the well-being of our home state, we were well aware that the forces themselves were not of his making. In large part, they were generated outside our state, in that increasing portion of the national economy that was hugely industrialized, in that increasing portion of the national society that was hugely urbanized while Kansas, for various reasons (one was a freight-rate structure that continued highly discriminatory against our manufacturers) was being industrialized and urbanized much more slowly, much less hugely. In this respect, Kansas lagged, drifting back toward the tail end of the parade. It yet remained predominantly rural in outlook, continued in fact to *be* (if less so than Kansans generally believed) a land of farms and communities economically dependent on farming—continued to be the neighborly small-town middle-class America that White himself epitomized, the America of Norman Rockwell's *Saturday Evening Post* covers. And this America was increasingly vestigial. Wrapped in nostalgia by those who had grown up in it, it was alien to the direct experience of a postwar urbanized generation.

Hence Kansas, which only a few short years before had been in the vanguard of social progress, began to be viewed as a backward state. Indeed, a subtle but powerfully effective shift in emphasis and priorities among the choices presented to a new set of Kansas leaders had already occurred, and the change in state personality this shift made or reflected was already well underway by the time the world war ended, with the result that Kansas began to *act* as a backward state, fighting rearguard actions against social change instead of (as formerly) trying to mold the economic dynamic of such change in ways that would serve genuine individual human freedom. The image of the state spread abroad began to bear a closer resemblance to the one White had presented in "What's the Matter . . . ?" than the one presented in his above-quoted 1922 editorial.

For instance, when coal-mining and petroleum-producing southeast Kansas, the one portion of the state that was quite highly industrialized and consequently unionized, was swept by the great United Mine Workers strike of 1919, ex-Progressive Henry Allen, state governor, responded by denouncing labor leaders as "radical and disloyal," thereby helping along the Mitchell Palmer "Red Scare" which the employing classes found so useful as a union-breaking device. Calling a special session of the Kansas legislature (January 1920), Allen presented it with a bill that was in essential respects an anticipation of Mussolini's corporate state. It provided for the abolition of the public utilities commission and the creation of a court of industrial relations. This last was a three-man appointive body having jurisdiction over labor disputes affecting public health or safety or the "flow of absolute necessities" (in effect, it outlawed mine and railroad strikes)—having also an ill-defined authority to prevent public discussion of cases it must deal with until such cases had been decided. The legislature quickly, by a huge majority, passed the bill. Whereupon Alexander Howat, the fiery and able president of District 14, UMW, Pittsburg (Kansas), announced that he and the twelve thousand miners he represented would defy the law while testing it in the courts (Howat was soon arrested, was jailed for a time). Nor could White obey that portion of it that was in clear violation of the First Amendment, though he was originally in favor of this experiment of "adjudicating" rather than "arbitrating" labor disputes. When his friend the governor ordered removed from store windows signs declaring "We are for the Strikers 100 Percent"—signs distributed by Santa Fe workers in Emporia during the nationwide railroad strike of 1922—White promptly put one in the *Gazette* window (though not before he had, typically, crossed out "100" and lettered in its place "49") and publicized the fact that he was doing so, forcing the governor to order his arrest (he was never jailed, of course; the attorney general successfully moved for dismissal of the case a few months later). It was at this time that White wrote his eloquent defense of free speech, "To an Anxious Friend," which was awarded the Pulitzer Prize as "best editorial" in the following spring.

Ultimately, the industrial court, having proved almost totally ineffective of its stated purposes, was ruled unconstitutional by the federal courts.

And the nation that was treated to this spectacle of "barren social experimentation'' (the phrase is from Becker's 1910 essay) was simultaneously entertained by the crusading pieties of one Lizzie Wooster (Lorraine E. Wooster, Salina), the remarkably aptly named state superintendent of public instruction, elected to that post in the Republican landslide of 1918 and re-elected, with the Allen administration, in 1920. In late May of 1919, Lizzie, author of a successful arithmetic textbook, announced that she would revoke the certificates of school teachers who used tobacco and that "schools and colleges that permit the use of tobacco in any form by administrative heads, instructors or pupils cannot remain on the accredited list." Seven months later she refused to permit a KU professor of psychology to lecture at teachers' institutes because he smoked and because his lectures dealt with "elemental subjects." In May of 1922 she attempted to oust the school superintendent of Cimarron because he smoked, and several Cimarron women teachers because they danced, an ouster order the Cimarron school board defied. A month later, the state attorney general ruled that Lizzie's antitobacco decrees were illegal.[11] But he had to engage in a good deal of legal tortuosity to arrive at this decision. Lizzie's disputed acts were in accord with at least the "spirit" of a recently enacted law banning the sale of cigarettes in Kansas. (This last was a typical piece of "moral" legislation: it effected no perceptible reduction in cigarette smoking but *did* reduce state revenues; no state tax could be collected on the cigarettes sold, in undiminished volume, "under the counter.") Which is to say that Lizzie, like Carry Nation before her, became an acute embarrassment to Kansas officialdom, and she was not renominated in the primary of August 1, 1922. Her name then disappeared from the public prints.

But Kansas did not cease to make her kind of news.

Sporadic efforts to enforce the anticigarette law, which remained on the books for several years, continued intermittently to produce publicity of a kind that made rural Kansas appear ridiculous abroad. In 1923, when a Republican legislature was at war with Democratic Governor Jonathan Davis (he won election

11. Mechem, and Owen, *Annals of Kansas,* 2:238, 248, 323.

in 1922 as a result of factional fighting within the Kansas GOP), it made headlines by yielding to the demand of pious prudes that a pioneering division of venereal disease control, established by Dr. Crumbine within the state board of health, be abolished. This division, in the course of waging one of the most effective campaigns against the spread of "social diseases" ever seen up till then, had necessarily exposed the fact that some high school students engaged in sexual intercourse; so the legislature knocked out its appropriation without giving Crumbine a chance to be heard in its defence. The good doctor was so "shocked and grieved" by this (the words are his) that he promptly accepted the offer to a key staff position in the American Child Health Association and, in June of 1923, left Topeka for New York, never to return. In 1927, a dean of women at Kansas State in Manhattan aroused national hilarity with her order that no co-ed in her college could attend a dance unless attired in bloomers that met the tops of stockings. (When comedian Will Rogers entertained at that college a few months later he advised an amendment to the dean's edict: the bloomers, said he, should be purple, for that was the school color.) A year or two after that, Sherwood Eddy of the YMCA provoked a furor at Kansas State and elsewhere when he spoke on "Sex and Youth" and offered for sale copies of his book bearing the same title.

All through the 1920s a quack doctor named John R. Brinkley publicized Kansas in ways not conducive of respect abroad. Having moved to the state in 1916 and found it fertile ground for his brand of quackery, he announced in 1919 his perfection of an operation that restored male sexual virility by means of goat-gland transplants. Soon he moved to Milford, established there a private hospital where he treated all manner of ailments (not just sexual debilities), and established there, too, in 1922, the second commercial radio station in Kansas, KFKB ("Kansas First, Kansas Best"), with a transmitter powerful enough to reach from its central location into far corners of the nation. Over this station, Brinkley personally solicited and answered medical questions in an unctuous voice that dripped of piety, charity, and human kindness (I've seldom heard a voice so perfectly Pecksniffian), flavoring his broadcasts with Christian patriotism and framing them with wholesome country entertainment. Regularly featured was a guitar-playing folk singer billed as "The Lonesome Cowboy." Brinkley greatly prospered for a number of years while arousing the ire of the American Medical Association, the Kansas board of medical examination and registration, and the *Kansas City* (Mo.) *Star,* which set out to destroy him with a series of articles exposing his dubious past (he had obtained his medical degree from no properly accredited institution) and fraudulent present.

In 1930, after his license to practice medicine in the state had been revoked and his license to broadcast was being threatened, Brinkley abruptly decided to run for governor as an independent, write-in candidate (he filed too late to have his name printed on the ballot). His platform called for free textbooks, tax equalization, free community health clinics, vast highway improvements, a "lake in every county" and no increase in taxes. He campaigned with great vigor, mingling religion with politics in ways that convinced thousands of his close kinship with Jesus Christ. And he came within an ace of winning. As a matter of fact, most students of that election are agreed he *did* win and was robbed of his victory by ballot-counters who threw out not only every write-in that varied in the slightest from the prescribed "J. R. Brinkley" but also a considerable number that were correctly inscribed. (At least fifty thousand Brinkley votes were thrown out. Democrat Harry Woodring, whose basic political views were not perceptibly different from those of the Republican right wing, won the governorship by just 215 votes over his Republican opponent, who dared not demand a recount because the inevitable gain in the recorded Brinkley totals would have elected Brinkley.)

The "goat-gland specialist" ran again in 1932, this time with his name printed on the ballot, and garnered 244,607 votes despite the intense and unremitting "bad publicity" that had by then been given him for nearly three years by the press. Clearly, much of Brinkley's vote was not really *for* him but, confusedly, *against* the powers that be, especially the *Kansas City Star,* which was widely unloved. (For such protest, Republican Alf M. Landon, who won the governorship that year, had reason to be grateful. Only narrowly, 278,581 to 272,944, did he defeat Woodring. He probably could not have done so in the face of that year's New Deal Democratic landslide, thereby opening the way toward his Republican presidential nomination four years later, if Brinkley had not taken more votes away from the Democratic candidate that he did from the Republican.)

In the mid-1930s, after Hitler had come to power in Germany, there rose up a Kansas figure much nastier and more sinister than "Goat-gland" Brinkley. His name was Gerald B. Winrod. He was a Protestant fundamentalist radio preacher in Wichita, whence he broadcast virulent Jew-baiting, Catholic-hating, pro-Nazi propaganda over the air and in a magazine of unrelieved viciousness called *The Defender*. With ample funds whose source was highly secret (he had been warmly received in Hitler's Germany when he visited there) he flooded the mails with antidemocratic, hate-mongering, pro-totalitarian propaganda, attracting as he did so a Kansas following sufficiently large to frighten the state's GOP leadership when he announced his candidacy for the U. S. Senate in 1938. It was their fear of Winrod that caused the businessmen-managers of Kansas Republicanism to unite that year behind the senatorial candidacy of Clyde M. Reed, editor-publisher of the *Parsons Sun,* a man whom they had earlier sternly opposed because, though properly conservative, he was too forceful and independent a character to be easily handled. They believed Reed was the only available candidate who could defeat Winrod. (Having won the nomination, Reed went on to win election by a large majority, ousting a Democrat, George McGill, who had ridden into office on the Roosevelt landslide in 1932.)

The year that saw Winrod running for the U. S. Senate also saw the administration and faculty of Kansas University under intense fire because of "Red activities" on that campus. An intense, idealistic young student, Donald Henry of Dodge City, having come to the university as a "Boy Scout interested in patriotic and religious activities," was soon led by his commitments, his sense of consistency, into campus activities dominated by members of the Young Communist League (KU had a chapter; every large university then did). He enlisted in the International Brigade of the Spanish Loyalist army, and on September 2, 1937, his first day under fire, was killed on the Aragon front. The university was charged by his parents with responsibility for his death. He had been corrupted, said they, by the faculty's Communistic teachings. And so a special regents committee conducted an immensely publicized investigation that, in the process of absolving the university of all responsibility for the boy's heroism, did considerable damage to free speech and academic freedom on the campus. "Since the appointment of this Committee some changes have been made at the University, eliminating certain of the personnel, which we believe will minimize un-American activities," said the final report.[12]

VI

All this, from Lizzie's pieties to Winrod's fascism (and there was, simultaneously, much more of the same unedifying character)—all this not only injured Kansas's image in the eyes of the nation, it also did great injury to the state's overall mental health. It was as if the body politic, having in its cultural soul a broad streak of Puritan masochism, now gave full sway to that imp of perversity, a kind of sullenly assertive egoism, which causes a man to stress in emphatic repetitive behavior precisely those traits he knows to be most obnoxious to others, inviting blows and ridicule—traits he also knows to be intrinsically harmful, to himself as well as others, when freely expressed. Kansans as individuals continued to have a remarkably strong emotional attachment to their state; but the *nature* of this attachment, by the 1930s, was very different from what it had formerly been. Gone, as a dominant mood, was the old delight and happy pride in a congeries of distinctive vivid personalities elevated to posts of prominence and importance, and in a bold venturesomeness and creativity by the body politic in general. Gone was the old delight in the state's landscapes and weathers, a

12. Findings of the Regents Committee, quoted by William Allen White, "The Kansas Red Scare," *Kansas Magazine* (1939): 130.

delight often expressed through the perverse boastfulness of "tall tale" exaggeration. Into their places crept now a species of shame, a pervasive sense of inferiority.

Symptomatic William Allen White deplored the change, though without revealing any slightest sense of his own partial responsibility for it, in a 1934 magazine piece entitled "Just Wondering"—a piece contrasting sharply in tone with his earlier-quoted 1922 editorial.

The White of 1934 took note of the fact that no Kansan "preserves anecdotes of our politicians today" as Kansans did of the political heroes and rascals of yesteryear. "Is it because they [the politicians] are dull and say or do nothing worth embalming in memory?" he asked, evidently rhetorically. "Are they dull leaders of a dull multitude? . . . Was it because the early Kansan was near the danger line . . . . [that] he kept his wits about him and demanded leaders who would also be nimble, gay or tragic?" He further noted that Kansas writers no longer had a distinctively Kansas audience, that Kansas painters and composers were no longer the objects of a prideful state-wide admiration. "What has happened?" he wondered. "Where has the old delight in Kansas gone, the old state pride . . . ?" He ended his piece with a summing-up of his questionings: "What has passed over the conscious dream that is our changing destiny to make us so different from our fathers only a generation or two before us? . . . Times change and men change with them, but where in our hearts is the blood that begot us?" [13]

Five years later, another famous citizen of the state, psychiatrist Karl A. Menninger of the Menninger Clinic in Topeka, published a magazine article entitled "Bleeding Kansans" in which he pondered the inferiority complex that was, by 1939, everywhere evident in the state. He told how, having just returned from a holiday in the mountains or on the seashore, he was sometimes accosted on Topeka streets by friends who spoke sympathetically about how "hard" it must be for him to return from "such beautiful places" to the "drab monotony" of

13. William Allen White, *Kansas Magazine* (1934): 87–88.

Kansas scenery, though in Menninger's view "our Kansas scenery is beautiful"; he pointed out how Kansans habitually maligned a climate he found more pleasant and healthful than most; and he deplored the fact that this denigrating falsification of the state's physical self was not offset by any expressed pride in its spiritual or cultural self. Indeed, some of the brightest, most promising young Kansans seemed inclined to deny that the state *had* any valuable culture. *Why,* this persistent "self-depreciation"? asked Menninger. He would like to have deemed it an expression of good taste—a "revulsion against the flamboyant egotism of California" and certain other states—but it was too extreme, too insistent for that. There must be "a far deeper psychological origin," namely, an actual profound feeling of inferiority. Menninger thought this might spring from "over-conscientiousness"—from the Kansan's "wish to identify . . . with the most idealistic and fruitful ways of life" joined to a realization of his inability to live at so high a pitch. What the Kansan failed to realize is that others can't live at so high a pitch either; he imagined they did live there, and so felt inadequate, inferior to these others. At any rate, concluded Menninger, the consequence was a "humility and self-distrust so great as to be crippling to our [Kansas] energies." [14]

Yet these energies continued undiminished, in quantity *or* intrinsic quality. There was no lack of ability and creative fire in the state.

Consider, for example, White and Menninger themselves. Each was a man of outstanding ability and sharply distinctive personality. Their membership of any community would be justifiable ground for community pride. Or consider a very different but equally sharply distinctive personality, E. Haldeman-Julius of Girard. In 1912 he had taken over the famous Socialist organ, *Appeal to Reason,* which J. A. Wayland had founded in Girard in 1897, and had continued the publication under various names (*Haldeman-Julius Weekly,* then *New Appeal,* finally the *American Freeman*) ever since. With his wife Marcet he had co-authored two grimly realistic novels (*Dust,* and *Violence*) in the

14. Karl A. Menninger, *Kansas Magazine* (1939): 3–6.

1920s, and had launched in his little Kansas town a remarkable book-publishing enterprise. Most of his published hard-cover titles were of iconoclastic works—they dealt with women's liberation, agnosticism or atheism, and political radicalism—but the famous E. Haldeman-Julius Little Blue Books (five cents apiece), a pioneering and highly successful paperback venture, ranged over the whole field of literature and introduced countless millions of disadvantaged readers to the greatest writers, and to the infinite variety of the world of ideas. It was at E. Haldeman-Julius's money-backed urgings, and as a series of Little Blue Books, that Will Durant originally composed the chapters of his *Story of Philosophy*.

Or, again, consider the magazine in which White and Menninger published their above-quoted views—the *Kansas Magazine* that young Russell I. Thackrey of Kansas State's journalism department had revived as an annual publication in 1933. Its pages contained abundant evidence of the state's continuing cultural vitality. Thus the 1934 and 1939 issues that carried White's and Menninger's pieces carried also fiction, nonfiction, and verse of high quality by T. A. McNeal, Ed Howe, W. G. Clugston, Marco Morrow, Vance Randolph, John P. Harris, Marion Ellet, Kirke Mechem, Nelson Antrim Crawford, Eunice Wallace, Paul Jones, and a dozen others who continued to make their homes in the state; along with the work of former citizens who had moved elsewhere but whose subject matter, and often their style, remained emphatically Kansan. Paul I. Wellman, for instance, then a staff member of the *Kansas City Star*. Or poet Kenneth Porter of Sterling, author of *The High Plains* (1938) and, later (1946), *No Rain From These Clouds*. The contributors often celebrated their state—they evinced much of that delight in its scenes and people that White mourned as a departed phenomenon—but they were by no means uncritical. Several actually attacked the prevailing Kansas mores. There were articles that satirized the smug hypocrisy that so generally streaked the official Puritanism of the state; there was a short story in which political "radicalism" was equated with honor, political "conservatism" with dishonor; there was a long poem (by Kenneth Porter), "To the Jayhawkers of the International

Brigade," extolling, as a continuation of the great Kansas tradition, the heroism of Don Henry and other Kansans who fought for Loyalist Spain ("John Brown of Kansas . . . goes marching on," sang Porter; "his tread is on the plains of Aragon!")

Equally if not more impressive were the magazine's reproductions of oil paintings, etchings, water colors, lithographs and woodcuts by a dozen and more artists who currently lived in the state, plus the work of departed natives whose reputations had been largely made with distinctive Kansas subject matter. Outstanding among them was Birger Sandzen of Lindsborg, who had made Bethany College's art department (which he headed) nationally known and whose canvases and lithographs, done in a style uniquely his own (if influenced by French impressionism), generally of Kansas landscapes empty of people, were a major element of every Kansan's cultural environment when I was growing up. There were Kenneth M. Adams, formerly of Topeka, who had soaked up the *feel* of the Southwest during his years of growing up in Kansas and had become one of the finest painters of Indians after his move to Taos; Ed L. Davison, a successful Wichita banker who did outstanding work, including portraits, in oils; C. A. Seward, also of Wichita, one of the founders of the Prairie Printmakers (1930) and the Kansas Federation of Art (1932); John F. Helm, Jr., professor of painting at Kansas State, whose lyrical evocations, in etchings and water colors, of landscape moods around my hometown of Manhattan have always had for me a special appeal; and the internationally famous Henry Varnum Poor, a Chapman native and close friend of Sandzen who not only painted but also sculpted, designed furniture and houses, and became generally recognized as America's leading craftsman in ceramics. There was the even more famous John Steuart Curry. Born on a farm near Dunavant in Jefferson County, in 1897, and reared to manhood in this state, he had studied at the Chicago Art Institute and then in Paris for a time before returning to his native soil in 1927. He then and there eschewed all fashionable modernity in order to paint the country, the life he had most intimately known since infancy. With such canvases as *Baptism in Kansas, The Tornado* (reproduced in the 1934 *Kansas Magazine*), *Sun Dogs, Line Storm, Hogs Killing a Snake* (also reproduced in the 1934

Kansas Magazine), he had become "the Homer of Kansas," one of the triumvirate of regional painters (the other two were Thomas Hart Benton of Missouri and Grant Wood of Iowa) who loomed over the American art scene in the 1930s.

And John Steuart Curry (the case of Curry) may perhaps be used as point example of how, if not why, the undiminished creative energies of the state, the undiminished number of Kansas through whose "hearts" surged in full flood "the blood that begot us," were now rendered so little effective of overall state personality.

In the early 1930s a new library building was completed on the campus of Kansas State College at Manhattan. Money was appropriated for the painting of murals in the high-vaulted main reading room of that building. John Helm, Russell Thackrey, and others at Kansas State interested in the arts (there were a good many) begged the college administration to employ Curry as the mural painter—indeed, to establish him permanently on campus as "artist in residence." Curry had let it be known that he longed for such a post and had mentioned a salary (twenty-five hundred dollars, I believe) that was modest for so famous an artist, even by depression standards. Thackrey, as a journalist concerned with public relations, pointed out that the college would gain immeasurably in prestigious publicity, as well as in cultural excitement, from Curry's working presence. But Kansas State's top administration, representative of the system of values and priorities that operated in virtually every major post of decision in the Kansas of those years, operated in this case, as it so often did, to drive outstanding talent out of the state, or deny it entrance. The administration could see no justification for hiring even so famous a Kansas artist at two hundred dollars a month when long-time faculty members, teaching useful subjects, were taking drastic salary cuts. So Curry, perforce, accepted an offer from the University of Wisconsin to become that institution's "artist in residence," for a salary of thirty-six hundred dollars and provision of a campus studio. K-State's magnificent mural space was ultimately filled with conventional art (men and women in classical robes, cornucopias, etc.) by an artist paid out of WPA funds.

There was backlash.

William Allen White declared editorially that "Kansas would be able to hold her head a little higher if she . . . [had] taken John Curry under her wing." [15] There began a selective but statewide newspaper campaign to raise private money (twenty thousand dollars, ultimately), and to achieve the necessary legislative sanction, to bring Curry back into the state to paint murals in the state capitol. In 1937, Curry accepted the commission. His execution of it, however, provoked conservative outrage and controversial storm. Curry's John Brown, central figure of the mural, was a gigantic figure reminiscent of Michelangelo's Moses, wild-eyed and bloody-handed, clutching a Bible in one hand and a rifle in the other, towering against a background of tornado- and fire-swept prairie. A saint was being desecrated! Kansas was being portrayed as a land of raw violence! Moreover, Curry was fundamentally ignorant of the subjects on which he made such vividly outrageous comment: the tail of the pig which he tastelessly included (along with snakes) curled the wrong way! Curry, who was rather more thin-skinned than I would (on the basis of his work) have expected him to be, flinched under these sneering criticisms. He left Topeka with his project not quite completed—and it remained incomplete when he died in 1946.

This, to repeat, is a point example of a generally prevailing condition—a condition almost maddening to those of the state's liberal intelligentsia who were not yet wholly alienated, who continued to care deeply about Kansas as a human community, and who were still able to look about them with a vision undimmed or undistorted by mists arising from inward swamps. Everywhere could be seen clear evidence that Kansas yet possessed rather more, not less, than its fair share of native intelligence and talent, of idealistic commitment, of colorful and highly individual characters, and even of people who continued the old Kansas tradition of radical political protest. But almost nowhere of state-determining importance was all this given fair, honest, adequate, practical expression. The disparity between

15. William Allen White editorial quoted in Federal Writers' Project, Works Progress Administration, *Kansas, A Guide to the Sunflower State* (New York, 1939), p. 142.

what was possible and what was actually achieved was tragic, the former being so immensely greater in every respect than the latter.

Thus, in politics, Alf Landon came to represent an extreme conservatism—became in the national public mind a personification of the backwardness of what Jim Farley dismissed as a mere "prairie state." Two of the most distinctive acts of his gubernatorial administration were the forming with other states of an oil and gas compact to hold up prices for independent producers (he was one himself), and the calling out of the National Guard to maintain "law and order" in strike-swept lead and zinc mining areas of southeast Kansas—these in addition to a budget-balancing act that involved drastic cutbacks in essential state services (some college faculty salaries were cut one-fourth) in the face of increasingly desperate needs. The human costs of this would have been unbearable, but for New Deal relief programs. As presidential candidate, the governor vehemently attacked as "socialistic" the federal deposit insurance program! (It should perhaps be mentioned, as an interesting if not particularly significant juxtaposition, that the Communist candidate for president in the year of Landon's candidacy was another native Kansan, Earl R. Browder, born in Wichita. Browder ran on a popular front platform whose slogan ultimately became, "Communism is Twentieth Century Americanism.") Yet Landon personally was a man of wit and urbane intelligence, well-informed in current affairs. An original Bull Mooser, he had bolted the state Republican party over the KKK issue in 1924, was an ardent conservationist and (partially but not altogether for private business reasons) a battling foe of giant oil and gas combines. He was considerably more strongly committed to free speech and civil liberties in general than FDR personally was. (I vividly remember an occasion in a Topeka auditorium when he, governor of the state, introduced with a gracious personal tribute, and a ringing statement of the principle of free speech, that evening's featured speaker, Socialist Norman Thomas.)

Perhaps even wider was the gap between potential and performance in the administration of the governor who succeeded Landon. Democrat Walter Huxman, a Hutchinson lawyer and farmer who was carried into office by the FDR landslide of 1936, had humane commitments, a carefully thought-out political philosophy, and personal leadership qualities of a high order. Making full use of New Deal patronage, he managed to get through the legislature more of his program than most governors have been able to do, though the legislature was, of course, controlled by the opposition party. On crucial items, however, he was frustrated by a sullen, partisan opposition. The need for more state money forced his recommendation of a 1 percent sales tax, though he was opposed to sales taxes as regressive, plus a levy on oil production. It was upon the latter that he counted most heavily for increased revenue. But the legislature, against his strong protests, doubled the sales tax to 2 percent, applied it to food as well as other necessities, and flatly refused to enact any oil levy at all. Moreover, the sales tax revenue was then used, not for the expanded welfare and relief purposes that Huxman intended, but largely to reduce local property taxes. An administration-sponsored bill to establish conservancy districts in order to obtain federal flood control, soil conservation, and irrigation funds was defeated out of pure reaction against Roosevelt, New Deal "socialism," and the governor himself as allegedly an emulator of FDR's dictatorial methods and aspirations. When Huxman called a special session of the legislature to deal with now loudly crying relief needs, his recommendations were for the most part rejected in a session that was stubbornly prolonged for some three weeks beyond the five days or so that Huxman had deemed necessary. When he ran for re-election in 1938 he was resoundingly defeated.

Such "crippling of energies," seen in fields educational and cultural, political and journalistic, was doubtless due in part to the inferiority feelings Menninger had descried. These feelings constituted a morbid kernel of the soul whence sprang psychic insecurities that did, certainly, sour and twist decision-making processes among the multitude. Encouraged was that "tendency to conform," which Carl Becker in his essay had seen as "a fundamental characteristic of Kansas individualism." Consequent, to a far greater degree than Becker could have measured in 1910, was what he had then called "the deification of the average" or "the dogmatism of the general level."

But there was a more important cause of the calamity, in my opinion—one from which the generalized sense of inferiority itself mostly stemmed. This cause was the fact that the powers of ultimate decision over the allocation of resources, in every department of state life, had become more and more concentrated in the hands of those "greedy, egoistic" men whom White had seen take control of the Republican organization; men whose minds had been long ago made up in terms of their private economic interest, then tightly closed against every doubt, every challenging idea; men inclined to equate imaginative wit and gaiety with frivolity of character, and to dismiss the possessors of such qualities as "lightweights" who, lacking sound sober "mature" judgment, must be barred from controlling positions; men who, on the other hand, found useful those rural pieties that could be so easily provoked into passionate "moral" crusades, diverting popular attention from matters whose consideration might lead to major shifts of power foci—men, in fine, who kept their values in cash registers and summed them up on adding machines. The dominance of the press by such men was especially calamitous. Among the state's departed glories were the old vivid, biting arguments the newspapers had once carried on with one another in their editorial columns. With a couple of exceptions, the major papers now had precisely the same point of view, were committed to precisely the same doctrines, and they generated in chorus a standardized mental environment that, presenting to the public no important alternative choices, was empty of stimuli of popular thought.

Seldom has a community with so much vibrant idealism in its soul, so much creative potential in its mind, become so thickly incrusted with petty bourgeois mediocrity.

8

Twentieth-Century Kansas:
A Second Phase-Change

I

*O*F a community so incrusted, and isolated from the main-stream of national domestic affairs, an extreme of isolationism with regard to foreign affairs could be expected—and no state's leadership was more blindly isolationist than Kansas's during the great foreign policy debate that began with FDR's "quarantine-the-aggressors" speech of 1937, intensified with Hitler's seizure of Czechoslovakia in March of 1939, and became the dominant theme of American politics with the fall of France in the spring of 1940.

In 1939, a bill appropriating three hundred and seventy-six million dollars to build 3,050 war planes sailed through the lower house of Congress on a vote of 367 to 15—but of the negative votes, five were cast by Kansas representatives! (A sixth Kansas congressman was absent.) In 1940, a major draftsman of the antiwar (isolationist) plank in the national Republican platform, on which ran Wendell Willkie in self- and policy-distorting ways, was Alf Landon. Shortly thereafter, ex-Governor Harry Woodring, who had become secretary of war in the Roosevelt cabinet, was forced to resign because his obstructionist isolationism seriously impeded, in the face of an increasingly "clear and present danger," the development of an adequate na-

196

tional defense—a defense that obviously depended upon Britain's survival. Senators Capper and Reed both fought tooth and nail against the lend-lease bill, without whose passage Britain could *not* have survived and of which Willkie became a major, and decisive, supporter. Landon fought the bill, too. And Kansas's governor, Payne Ratner, Huxman's successor, who had been re-elected in 1940, was so exercised by the proposal that he felt called upon to attack it in an address to the Kansas legislature! "Only a matter of gravest concern" would cause him to speak on such a subject in such a forum, said he (Ratner aspired to become the elderly Capper's successor in the U.S. Senate), but it was obvious to him that lend-lease, if passed, would give the president "the same power over material supplies now exercised by Hitler, Mussolini, and Stalin" and "bring dictatorship to the United States." [1]

A different view was taken by William Allen White. He was acutely aware that U.S. survival as a free society was at stake in the war (". . . a free country and a free people . . . [cannot] live beside Hitler's world enslaved," he editorialized). [2] Immediately after Hitler's attack on Poland, he accepted the chairmanship of a national Non-Partisan Committee for Peace through Revision of the Neutrality Law (Frank Knox, Landon's 1936 runningmate, was a leading member), which did much to persuade the country that the arms embargo, preventing aid to Hitler's enemies (our protectors), must be repealed. It was notably unsuccessful with the politicians of White's own party, however: when the repeal bill passed the House, only twenty Republicans voted for it while 140, including the Kansas delegation, voted against. In the spring of 1940, a national Committee to Defend America by Aiding the Allies was formed. Again White accepted the chairmanship. He was no mere figurehead. He worked hard on this assignment. And his identification with the committee, which became everywhere known as the White Committee, greatly increased its prestige and power as it fought

1. Quoted in William F. Zornow, *Kansas, A History of the Jayhawk State* (Norman, Okla.: University of Oklahoma Press, 1957), p. 343.

2. *Emporia Gazette,* November 1, 1940.

for public opinion against the organized isolationism of America First. But his effort produced no perceptible crack in the isolationism of the upper crust in his own state.

One reason for this is that White's contribution to freedom's cause, though substantial, was in this instance, as in so many others, sadly flawed—and flawed in ways that perpetrated the evils he publicly deplored. Obviously of first importance to the committee's aims was the defeat of those incumbent isolationist senators and congressmen running for re-election in 1940. Most committee members took it for granted, therefore, that the organization would publicize the voting records of these men and work actively against them in the campaign in favor of candidates supporting the committee's cause. But White refused to permit this. Doing so would destroy the nonpartisan character of the committee, he argued; it would mean that the committee opposed re-election of virtually every Republican up for re-election! Nor did White stop there. He actually worked *for* the re-election of these men! He editorially urged Kansas independents to vote the straight Republican ticket "because, taken by and large, man for man, from top to bottom, the men running for office on the Republican ticket in the nation, in this state and this county are men of high character and superior ability." He even sent a letter to the archreactionary, Roosevelt-hating, Nazi-sympathizing Rep. Hamilton Fish of New York, expressly for Fish's campaign use, saying: "However you and I may disagree about some issues of the campaign, I hope as Republicans we are united in our support of the Republican ticket from top to bottom in every district and every state." [3] He was soon forced by committee outrage virtually to retract this endorsement, but the harm was by then done: Fish was re-elected, along with other isolationists whom active committee opposition might have defeated, and these continued dangerously to obstruct the administration's aid-to-the-allies program until Pearl Harbor.

In December of 1940, informed that the Scripps-Howard newspapers were about to attack him and the committee as warmongers, White dashed off a typical epistle to Roy Howard, then gave Howard permission to publish it. Wrote White: ''Look now Roy, you and I have been buddies. . . . The only reason in God's world I am in this organization is to keep this country out of war. . . . The story is floating around that I and our outfit are in favor of sending convoys with British ships or our own ships, a silly thing, for convoys unless you shoot are confetti and it's not time to shoot now or ever. . . . If I were making a motto for the Committee . . . it would be 'The Yanks Are Not Coming'.'' [4] A violent storm at once descended upon White's weary head, for by then leading members of the committee were convinced that even furnishing armed convoys for ships bearing aid to Britain would not be enough—that the crushing of the Axis and the survival of the free world required full active participation by the U.S. in the war.

White, then nearing his seventy-third birthday, and in failing health, resigned the committee chairmanship on January 1, 1941. Three years later, on the morning of Kansas Day, January 29, 1944, he died. . . .

II

In general, as in the case of World War I, Kansas's World War II experience, after Pearl Harbor, was not significantly different from the experience that other states had.

Some two hundred and fifteen thousand Kansans served in the armed forces. Of these, 3,879 were officially listed as killed in action or dead of wounds. Fort Leavenworth became a draftee-processing center as well as a major ground-troop training post. Camp Funston was reactivated and Camp Phillips established at Salina as major infantry training posts. Fort Riley, long the army's major cavalry center, became (horses having disappeared from the battlefield) a center for training for mechanized troops. The Kansas topography and cloud-free sky make the state unusually well-suited to flight training, and aviation train-

---

4. White to Roy Howard, December 20, 1940. Quoted in Johnson, *White's America,* pp. 543–545.

ing fields were established at Salina, Topeka, Pratt, Olathe, Hutchinson, Walker, Herington, Great Bend, Liberal, Independence, Dodge City, Coffeyville, Garden City, and Winfield. Fairfax Air Base became a principal station of the Army Air Force ferry command. A 2,200-bed army hospital, Winter General, was opened in Topeka. The state had three giant munitions plants: the Sunflower Ordnance Works near De Soto, which manufactured gunpowder; the Jayhawk Ordnance Works near Baxter Springs, which produced anhydrous ammonia; and the Kansas Ordnance Works near Parsons, which loaded artillery shells. There were also an alcohol plant at Atchison, a helium refining plant at Otis, and a plant at Hugoton producing carbon black. Wichita, one of the earliest centers of aircraft manufacture, became now a major center of war-plane manufacture. B-17s (Flying Fortresses) were produced there, as were the first and nearly half of the total number of the B-29s (Super Fortresses) that were so important in the final stages of the war with Japan. Kansans of course grew "Victory Gardens," conducted scrap drives, bought war bonds, contributed to service funds, and did all the other things that were done everywhere else as part of the war effort.

But though the Kansas war experience was thus part and parcel of the national experience, indistinguishable overall from that of other states, two elements of it were distinctive. And these initiated another change of phase in the life, the personality of the state—one not abrupt, as the earlier one had been (the Kansas that emerged from World War II was not as different from the Kansas that entered it as was the Kansas of 1919 different from that of 1912), but slow and gradual. Ultimately, however, it was quite as profound, and far more salubrious.

One of these two elements was economic.

All through the depression, Kansas's per capita income had lagged well behind the national average. This meant that the war's elevation of Kansas incomes to near the average was a greater percentage improvement in the economy than most other states experienced. There was, of course, an insatiable demand for farm products, whose prices shot to the uppermost limit permitted by the administration's remarkably effective price controls. And this period of unprecedented demand, which continued undiminished after the war, fortunately coincided with a series of excellent crop years. Record crops of wheat, corn, and other grains were successively grown; livestock production boomed; and a valuable new cash crop, the soybean, which remains of major importance, was added to those previously grown. Simultaneously came an immense expansion of Kansas's industrial plant and output of manufactures, and a dispersal of these over the state, laying foundations for what would be by the 1960s a vast and rich "agribusiness," as it came to be called, and a mix of agricultural, industrial, and commercial activity, and of urban and rural ways of life, that was better balanced and healthier overall, economically and sociologically, than had formerly prevailed. There began, too, a process of revising the railroad freight rate structure to reduce what had formerly been an insurmountable obstacle to any large-scale industrialization in the state.

The other distinctive element of the Kansas war experience was psychological, and centered on one man.

The name "Eisenhower" was not unknown in the state, was indeed quite widely known, when America entered the war. David Eisenhower, who had come as a boy with the large colony of Pennsylvania River Brethren that settled in Dickinson County in 1878, married Ida Elizabeth Stover (she, too, was of German Mennonite stock) and became the father of six sons who grew to maturity in Abilene. These six sons made careers in six different fields of endeavor, each of them succeeding beyond the average. Especially well-known by 1941 were the eldest son, Arthur, executive vice-president of one of the largest banks in Kansas City, and the youngest, Milton, a Kansas State journalism graduate who, aged twenty-six, had become information director of the U.S. Department of Agriculture and then, during the New Deal, an outstandingly effective "trouble-shooting" administrator of large governmental programs and agencies. Within a few months after Japanese bombs fell upon Pearl Harbor the Kansas press announced that Milton Eisenhower had become associate director of the Office of War Information; in the spring of 1943, that same press announced under large head-

lines that Milton had resigned his O.W.I. post in order to return
to his native state as president of Kansas State College, his alma
mater.

But by that time the Eisenhower name was not just "well-
known;" it had become one of the most famous in the world.
On June 25, 1942, a War Department communiqué had announced "the formal establishment of a European theater of
operations for the United States forces" with the theretofore unknown Maj. Gen. Dwight D. Eisenhower, already headquartered in London, as theater commander. Ever since, General
Eisenhower had been continuously at the top of the world's
most important news. By his command were conquered North
Africa and Sicily. He accepted Italy's surrender after the fall of
Mussolini. He ordered the landing at Salerno. He directed the
initial slow drive up the Italian boot toward Rome. Then, on
Christmas Eve, 1943, came the beginning of his climactic fame.
In London, in Washington, the announcement was made that a
Supreme Headquarters of the Allied Expeditionary Force
(SHAEF) was being established, obviously to prepare and
launch the long-awaited cross-channel assault upon Hitler's
fortress Europe. The supreme commander of this unprecedentedly huge and complicated allied operation, headquartered
in London, was Dwight D. Eisenhower.

A *Kansan* had become the supreme soldier of the greatest war
in history! The subsequent crushing of Hitler was rendered,
thereby, a peculiarly Kansan triumph!

For certainly many of the qualities that enabled Eisenhower to
make SHAEF the uniquely integrated and effective allied command that it became were distinctively *Kansas* qualities, as he
himself appeared to be, in several respects, the archetypical
twentieth-century Kansan. The wide and sunny skies of his
state, and the width and openness of the Dickinson County landscape, might be seen in his wide sunny grin, in his seemingly
invincibly sunny and open disposition. Similarly with his basic
mind-set and attitudes. He had grown up in a small town that
was notorious historically for wild western violence and wicked-
ness, Wild Bill Hickok its most famous citizen until Ike Eisenhower came along, but a town also remarkable for the
number of its churches, the general piety of its citizenry. He had

been raised in a family of the strictest Bible-reading religiosity, his parents being Puritans in the most literal meaning of that word, with extreme pacifism a cardinal article of their faith (both ultimately became members of the sect now known as Jehovah's Witnesses); yet these same parents had trained their sons to the hardest kind of physical self-reliance and had done nothing to discourage the development of a combative tough-ness, a physical self-assertiveness and self-defensiveness, which involved frequent savage fist-fighting. His family had certainly not been well-to-do, even by Abilene standards, had in fact been on the lower side of the town's income median, as the plain frame house in which they lived was on the "wrong" side of the railroad tracks; but on the other hand, the family had not been accounted actually poor in a community inclined to regard property as a sign and consequence of virtue. And within one hundred miles of the family home was the exact geographical center of the United States, which is to say that the physical en-vironment of the boy's growth to manhood was balanced pre-cisely halfway between every pair of national geographical ex-tremes. All this seemed designed to develop in him a balanced tension between frontier pragmatism and religious idealism, with the balance tipped toward the former by a revulsion against the rigid pieties imposed upon his boyhood—seemed designed in general to promote a psychology of "middleness" or "togetherness" that worked *against* unequivocal either-or choices and *for* coalitions, amalgamations, homogenizations on the basis of perceived common denominators among diverse people and things and forces. Such twentieth-century "Kansas" qualities had not theretofore been deemed heroic by the multi-tude. They were the essentially conservative attributes of a suc-cessful "chairman-of-the-board," which is what Eisenhower frankly said he was. A hostile critic might even see them as per-nicious insofar as they encouraged halfway measures—measures that were, in effect, affirmations of the status quo—in situations demanding bold decision on the side of change, of novelty. Yet the possessor of these qualities had become, and *by virtue of his exercise of them,* the greatest hero of the Western world!

From this heroism Kansans could and did draw a spiritual

sustenance that went far toward overcoming the formerly prevailing sense of state inferiority. Instead of being backward and "out of things," contemptuously ignored by current history, Kansas was, or could feel itself to be, again in the thick of things, a focus of national and even world attention. Ike himself encouraged this resurgence of state pride. He seemed in his own person proof positive of the truth of Ingalls's assertion that "no genuine Kansan can emigrate," however far he roams, for Ike repeatedly and emphatically identified himself with Abilene, a town of five thousand souls near the center of the most central state of the Union, and did so on occasions of the greatest possible publicity. Thus, in his famous Guildhall speech during his London triumph in June of 1945 he spoke of a "kinship" between London and Abilene that consisted of a shared commitment to free speech, religious freedom, and mutual respect. When he returned to America later that month and received the greatest triumph New York City has ever given any man he said that "New York simply cannot do this to a Kansas farmer boy and keep its reputation for sophistication." And it was in Abilene, a few days afterward, that his triumphal return achieved what he himself stressed as its supreme moment. To the largest, most joyous throng in the town's history (it was four times greater than Abilene's resident population) he said, and almost tearfully, ". . . the proudest thing I can claim is that I'm from Abilene." [5]

Nor was it only through this kind of radiational elevation of the psychological temperature, promoting a renewed glow of state pride (a "positive" rather than "negative" mood) conducive of fresh, self-confident initiatives—it was not only in this way that General Eisenhower contributed to his home state's salubrious change of phase. He made also an explicit direct contribution. Widespread among the historically minded had been a fear that the American people, and especially those at the center of the nation, would again draw back into an isolationist

---

5. London and New York speeches quoted in Kenneth S. Davis, *Soldier of Democracy* (New York, 1945, 1952), pp. 543, 547. Abilene quotes from newspaper accounts of his homecoming, June 22, 1945.

shell once the war was over and certain inevitable disillusion-
ments concerning it had occurred. The returned hero deliberately employed his heroism to prevent this happening. Thus, in
his speech at Kansas City on the eve of his Abilene homecoming in late June 1945, he said to thousands gathered before him
and millions listening over the radio: "This country here, this
section, has been called the heart of isolationism. I do not believe it. No intelligent man can be an isolationist. . . . The
world today needs two things: moral leadership and food." And
of both, he indicated, the Midwest (especially Kansas) had
abundant supplies, of which it would surely freely give. He
elaborated on this theme in Abilene next day, saying: "No
longer are we here independent of the rest of the world. . . .
Our part is most important. There is nothing so important in the
world today as food, in a material way. Food is needed all over
Europe and must be sent to preserve the peace. In that way you
see immediately your connection with the problems of Europe.
. . . In a more definite way, since I am now a citizen of New
York City, that city is a part of you—one of your larger sub-
urbs. . . ." [6] There can be no doubt that his words, in his circumstances, were unusually effective of their purpose.

Even more effective in this regard, in part because of the general's fame, were the words and deeds of his youngest brother,
Milton, the president of Kansas State. Milton Eisenhower as
college president became chairman of the U. S. National Commission for UNESCO (the United Nations Educational, Scientific, and Cultural Organization). He performed brilliantly in
this capacity, evoking the enthusiasm and concerting the talented efforts of some hundred leaders of America's educational, scientific, and art organizations (among them were three
or four Nobel laureates in science) in national and international
conferences having as their stated purpose the laying of the
foundations of world peace "in the minds of men" where, according to the UNESCO charter, "wars begin." He dreamed of
initiating, under UNESCO auspices, a kind of "grassroots"
movement toward an international community based on com-

6. Davis, *Soldier*, p. 548.

mon cultural interests and able, on that basis, to moderate the
political differences and reduce the war-breeding aspects of national sovereignty. He conceived the idea of organizing, all over
Kansas, local and county "UNESCO councils"—groups of
people committed to UNESCO purposes and willing to work actively toward them in their home communities—his hope being
that other states would follow the Kansas example and that other
nations would, too. He allocated a portion of Kansas State's extension (adult education) resources to this effort. He dedicated
to it his own prestige and major talent for public speech. And
though his larger dream never came close to realization, of
course, the effort he stimulated uncovered and mobilized in a
truly worthy cause, especially in central and western Kansas,
idealistic energies and talents that had long been hidden, frustrated, dissipated. The U. S. Department of State was so impressed that it took the unprecedented step of issuing a special
bulletin, handsomely printed and illustrated, for national and international distribution, entitled "The Kansas Story on
UNESCO."

Only a vestigial isolationism—struggling desperately, and for
the most part vainly, to capitalize on the fact that hated Communist Russia was a member of the United Nations—remained active in Kansas by the end of the 1940s.

Less vestigial, but clearly waning through these earliest postwar years, was the kind of Puritanism that passionately dedicated itself to petty personal prohibitions. (Milton Eisenhower
made passing comment on the latter phenomenon in a notable
address to the Native Sons and Daughters of Kansas, in Topeka,
on the eve of Kansas Day, 1949: ". . . the State's . . . remarkable energies have been spent too often upon issues which
are no longer of crucial importance in a world struggling to organize itself for the atomic age," said he. "It is as though a
huge tractor, badly needed for plowing acres of wheatland, were
being used to plow and replow a kitchen garden.") [7] There was
a flare-up of the prohibition issue. Indeed, from 1946 through

7. Milton S. Eisenhower, "The Strength of Kansas," address, Native Sons and
Daughters, Topeka, January 28, 1949.

1948, decades after the Eighteenth Amendment had been repealed and social drinking had become an established fact of the Kansas social life, prohibition was *the* dominant political issue as "wet" forces made a truly determined effort to repeal the state constitutional prohibition amendment. Harry Woodring won the Democratic gubernatorial nomination in 1946 by calling for an end to the hypocrisy of statutory "dryness" in a state obviously "dripping wet" (the U. S. Treasury Department reported in 1946 that 570 Kansans held federal retail liquor licenses). Republican Frank Carlson, who won the governorship, was forced to promise to submit a repeal proposal to the legislature, which in turn voted to submit it to the people in 1948. And there ensued a sound and fury reminiscent of that in St. John's day. A propaganda war was waged between an organization called the Kansas Legal Control Council (it fought for repeal) and another called United Dry Forces (it vehemently reaffirmed the traditional identification of liquor with the Devil, drinking with sin). A western Kansas rancher and newspaper publisher organized what he called a "Temperance Tornado"—a caravan of cars bearing some scores of earnest church folk, mostly of high school and college age, and starring Glenn Cunningham, the western Kansan who in the 1930s had been the greatest mile-runner in the world. The "Tornado" swept across fifteen hundred miles of the state in a dozen days, presenting anti-repeal songs and speeches. But in November 1948, the state at last belied William Allen White's famous dictum ("Kansans will vote dry as long as they can stagger to the polls") by voting for repeal, 422,294 to 358,310. Among the communities voting "wet" was Medicine Lodge, Carry Nation's old hometown.

Repeal did not wholly end the liquor controversy, of course, nor practical hypocrisy in the state's dealings with the liquor question, alas. The 1949 legislature had to decide between a bill providing for a state monopoly of liquor sales (that is, state-owned sales outlets) and a bill permitting privately owned package stores. The former would provide tighter control of the liquor traffic, thus serving a Puritan desire to mitigate the liquor evil to the maximum degree possible in the circumstances. It would also provide more state revenue. But it smacked of "so-

cialism;'' it meant that the government "engaged in business."
And so the Republican legislature rejected it in favor of a law
that provided for private package stores only, liquor sales only
in towns that had voted "wet" the preceding November or did
so in special referenda, and no "public drinking"—that is, no
selling of liquor by the drink in restaurants and bars, though
such sales in "private clubs" were permitted. The latter provision disgusted Kansans having a strong bias toward plain speech
and straightforward honesty, along with a loathing for class legislation. A Wichita police captain angrily averred when the law
was enacted that it would "increase the popularity of the rest
room as the Kansas cocktail bar for the common man." [8] Yet it
remained upon the statute books, arousing political controversy
of the old barren kind whenever an attempt was made to remove
it. Every such attempt has failed. To this day, no liquor can be
served by the drink in a public place in Kansas unless that place
has gone through the legal hypocrisy of defining itself as a
"private club."

But even while the prohibition issue raged in its last major
political flare-up, Kansas as body politic was actively concerned
with much more substantial matters. Topeka became "the psychiatric center of the world" when the state strengthened the
ties between the Topeka State Hospital for the mentally ill and
the Menninger Clinic (the clinic began a great expansion program in 1946), and Winter General became a psychiatric hospital under the U.S. Veterans Administration (Winter General and
the clinic also worked closely together, sharing personnel and
facilities). A dynamic young dean of the University of Kansas
medical school, Franklin Murphy, proposed a rural health plan
that, adopted by the legislature, expanded the medical school
and provided matching state and federal funds to supply doctors
and hospital facilities to country places from which medical services, for lack of adequate economic support, had been withdrawn or had never entered. The plan was adopted, was highly
successful, was emulated by other states. Meanwhile, Milton

8. Quoted, Kenneth S. Davis, "What's the Matter With Kansas?" *New York Times
Magazine,* June 27, 1954, p. 41.

Eisenhower struggled to transform Kansas State from the technical, vocational training institution it had formerly largely been into a true university—attempted to shift emphasis from the applied sciences, from the development of economic skills in general, to the liberal arts as the core of the undergraduate curriculum, thereby developing (as he stressed over and over in his speeches) whole human beings rather than narrow specialists. The importance of this in terms of statewide phase-change derived in good part from the fact that the apportionment of legislative representation in the state continued heavily to favor rural agricultural areas whose young people, if they continued their education beyond high school, were more inclined to enroll in the state's traditional agricultural college than in the university at Lawrence. Milton's effort had done little more than initiate a trend by the time he left Kansas in the early 1950s to assume the presidency of Pennsylvania State University. The trend, however, gathered momentum under Milton's successor at Kansas State, James M. McCain. The University of Kansas was also revitalized during these years, after Franklin Murphy had become the university chancellor. For example (just one, but a typical, example), an outstanding young librarian, Robert Vosper, with Murphy's solid backing, worked hard and effectively, not only to improve the library's collections and services, but also to help make the university an active, leading participant in the life of the state.

III

And from the postwar career of General Eisenhower, Kansas continued to draw a prideful spiritual sustenance. When he launched his campaign for the Republican presidential nomination on June 4, 1952 (he had first publicly declared his allegiance to the Republican party and his willingness to accept its nomination barely five months previously), he did so, on a day of torrential rain, in Abilene. On that same day he participated in the ceremonial laying of the cornerstone of the Eisenhower Museum, which was to rise on what had been the family's garden plot when he was a boy, just east of his boyhood home. This last was dedicated that day as a historical monument, having been purchased for that purpose by leading citizens. His subsequent political conquests—of the nomination, in a contest with Robert Taft; of the presidency in two election victories over Adlai Stevenson—could be deemed and were felt to be a continued national popular approval of Kansas qualities and principles, especially since he as president, and after, continued to identify himself with Abilene, and to return there on hugely publicized occasions.

He made his last, his permanent return in April 1969, when he was buried in Abilene. Today, the Eisenhower home, museum, and chapel are leading Kansas tourist attractions, bringing many thousands of visitors to Abilene from all over the country every year, while to the Presidential Library come hundreds of historians for scholarly research.

A Personal Conclusion

O N January of 1975 I returned to Manhattan, Kansas, my old hometown, to be a visiting professor of history at Kansas State University, my alma mater, during the spring semester. My title was more honorific than descriptive. The university, in an act itself expressive of what I am bound to regard as salubrious change, made it possible for this book to be written amidst the scenes and peoples with which it deals; and for this I am profoundly grateful.

The town and university I returned to are very different physically from those I knew when last I lived there, twenty years ago. They are much larger, for one thing. The university campus, formerly open and parklike, is now far less so, being in fact fairly crowded with buildings, sports facilities, and parking lots for the accommodation of a student enrollment over three times what it was when Milton Eisenhower left and James McCain came to the presidency of the institution. There were some five thousand students then; there are more than seventeen thousand now. The town's permanent population has not grown proportionately, but it has increased by a third, and the new additions sprawl westward for miles from the old town, across hills that were wild and lonely when I was a boy.

Such growth is *not* typical of Kansas towns in general, nor representative of the state as a whole, I hasten to add. For various reasons, the state's population growth has not kept pace with the nation's. Of the 105 Kansas counties, sixty-four actually lost significant percentages of their population between 1950 and 1970, while six others remained about the same in size; which is to say that the state's modest total population increase during these two decades, from a little more than 1.9 million to approximately 2.25 million (the national population shot up from 151 million to 203 million during this same period), was confined to thirty-five counties. Indeed, a single county, Johnson, where grow rich portions of greater Kansas City, provided more than half the total statewide increase as its sixty-three thousand of 1950 became two hundred forty-one thousand in 1970.

More typical and representative of the whole state is the marked improvement in the material standard of living in Manhattan. Here are entire streets of private dwellings whose average grandeur surpasses that of the most pretentious homes in the town of my growing up—and everywhere I went in the state I saw similar evidences that Kansas's per capita personal income, which was only 71.6 percent of the national personal per capita in 1940, climbed above 100 percent of this in the early 1970s. Per capita recreational facilities, too, are immensely greater than they were in former years in almost every Kansas town—greater here now than in most other parts of the country.

For Manhattan, they center on the sixteen-thousand-acre lake formed behind Tuttle Creek Dam across the Blue River just north of town. Twenty-five years ago, the army engineers' proposal to build this dam as part of the so-called Pick-Sloan Plan was strongly opposed by many disinterested students of the Missouri valley's water problems and by nearly all residents of the Blue valley. We were convinced there were valid upstream alternatives to creating, in the name of flood control, permanent floods downstream, drowning rich and lovely valleys behind dams costing, *in toto,* a billion or more tax dollars. We were convinced that any accurate measurement of cost-benefit ratios would greatly favor these alternatives. And we cited, in support of our conviction, evidence supplied by soil and water conservation specialists. Nor were our minds changed by the "100-year-flood" of the summer of 1951—a disaster that killed forty-four people and did more than one billion dollars of damage down the Kaw. In the following year, as a matter of fact, a 73-year-old Hiawatha farmer named Howard D. Miller, a sweet, shrewd, lovable man, ran as a Democrat for Congress on an anti-Tuttle Creek platform in Kansas's First District and, to his own great astonishment, won by some seven thousand over the

Republican incumbent. This was in Eisenhower's first landslide year—and no Democrat had *ever* carried the First District! Perhaps this caused the Corps of Engineers to pay more attention to multipurpose development, especially recreational development, than would otherwise have been paid, when construction began on Tuttle Creek in 1953—but this (if true) was the outermost limit of the effectiveness of our opposition.

The completed project, however, with its picnic and camping areas, marinas, and swimming beaches, does definitely enhance the quality of life in my old hometown. Moreover, it is but one (and only somewhat the larger) of many that do the same thing for their Kansas communities. Twenty completed flood control reservoir-lakes, the least of them covering hundreds of acres, are now scattered across a state whose natives used to drive for hours to recreate themselves in or beside a muddy five-acre pond. Caught and held by twentieth-century engineering, in quiet and deep repose, are streams that flowed turbulently, for all their shallowness, through Bleeding Kansas history. Thus the Delaware has its Perry Reservoir, the Wakarusa its (or soon to be) Clinton, the Marais des Cygnes its Pomona and Melvern, the Neosho its Council Grove and John Redmond. Similarly with streams that flowed out of the West, if often meagerly, intermittently, through a history of buffalo hunts and Indian wars and cowtown violence, in the earliest years of Kansas statehood. There is the Milford Reservoir (in Doc Brinkley country) on the Republican. There are the Glen Elder, the Kirwin, the Wilson on the Solomon with its twin forks. There are the Cedar Bluff and Kanopolis on the Smoky Hill. These latter western lakes startle the vision when first encountered. One sees them initially as contradictions of the drouthy treeless plain. They seem to insist upon their presence in places where they clearly do not belong, and they jar and grate upon the sensibilities as contradictions and artificialities commonly do. Soon, however, the vision becomes accustomed; whereupon each lake acquires a beauty at once strange and natural. Remaining remarkable in a land of little rain, it yet comes to seem perfectly consistent with its surroundings in a country where most of what one sees is sky—as if a portion of that sky, assuming liquid form, had somehow crossed the far horizon and laid itself down upon an earth which, far from resenting it as an alien intrusion, now ardently embraces it in sun-browned arms.

Physically, then, the Kansas I returned to was (is) in better shape, being healthier and more fair to see, than ever before.

But what of the Kansas mind, the Kansas spirit?

A new legislature had just opened its session when I first arrived in Manhattan. The major publicized issues before it concerned "bingo" and liquor. Should "bingo" be legalized for the fund-raising of churches and charity? Should the serving of alcoholic beverages by the drink be permitted in restaurants and bars? These earth-shaking questions, considered by the legislative body of one of the great food-producing areas of the world in a time of increasing world famine, used up much time and energy. I confess to dismay as I contemplated this at the beginning of a labor whose product would be, I hoped, a sympathetic as well as accurate portrait of a state I love. Was there to be forever this spinning of wheels in the same old ruts?

But as time passed and my work proceeded, my initial dismay was more than offset by a justifiable pleasure and pride in other aspects of a changed and changing Kansas.

For one thing, politics in Kansas are now more open, are less a cut-and-dried presentation to an ill-informed electorate, than they were when I last lived in the state. Back in 1956, after a Republican factional battle of unwonted ferocity, the Kansas electorate rose up in wrath and put into the governor's chair a Democrat (albeit a very conservative one), George Docking, a Lawrence banker. Moreover, unprecedentedly, this Democratic governor won re-election in 1958. He was defeated in his bid for a third term by Republican John Anderson, Jr., in 1960; and Anderson served the two terms that had been virtually automatic, historically, for a Republican governor. But his successor, Republican William H. Avery, having successfully fought for a tax increase in aid of the state's needy schools, was limited to a single term. He lost in 1966 to Democrat Robert B. Docking. And Robert Docking, son of George, went on to win not only a second term in 1968 but a third in 1970 and an astonishing fourth in 1972! He did not run in 1974. Republican Robert F. Bennett was elected to the first four-year term in Kansas history, as per a constitutional amendment. But clearly Kansas has not reverted to the monolithic Republicanism that formerly characterized it, with the sad consequences that always flow from prolonged one-party rule. There is now definitely a two-party system in the state; and though far more Republicans than Democrats win office, every aspiring Kansas politician is acutely aware that his election success or failure is likely to turn upon a "swing-vote" of independents who regularly split their tickets.

This, from my point of view, is a hopeful development. So is the resurgence of creative community life—a directing of the new prosperity into culturally productive channels—that is evident in many parts of the state. Kansas towns—Lindsborg and Hays, notably, but many other towns also—are consciously developing communities that stress unique local historical and ethnic traditions, while greatly improving their appearance and their general living facilities. There is an emphasis on cultural events, a sophisticated emphasis, greater than in former years, and a definite improvement in the quality of those newspapers with which I was familiar in the 1950s. Most hopefully significant of all, I think, is the way the state's colleges and universities are being transformed into truly educational institutions and are assuming leadership roles in local and state affairs. It has always seemed to me that a state prospers as a human community to the extent that its colleges and universities actively participate in its decision-making processes, feeding ideas and information and personnel into government; and this seems to be happening increasingly in Kansas.

Even the "wheel-spinning" I spoke of may have some measure of hopeful significance, I suppose, in a time and nation that suffer from too much permissiveness, too much self-indulgence, too cavalier a rejection of traditional standards.

It is my belief—I suppose the descriptive writing in this essay has more than suggested my belief—that the Kansas landscapes, the Kansas weathers, have had a marked psychological effect upon the citizenry of the state. No environment is wholly external to the environed. There is interpenetration. When the environed is a living entity the environment is *actively* internalized, becoming part and parcel of the individual psyche to some indeterminate degree. And I think that the Kansas weather-and-landscape, as an internalized environment, has made the Kansan in general more aware of elemental forces and of being at their mercy, has bred a somewhat more acute sensitivity to the natural world as both scene and agent of the world drama, than is common among people who live in weathers less prone to extremes and in landscapes having shorter views. The Kansan was religious to begin with—and being compelled by circumstances to look constantly into the heavens through *interested* eyes, his religiosity was increased by historical memories of sky-borne catastrophes. He had seen God's wrath expressed in dust-darkened, locust-darkened, blizzard-blanched, storm-blasted skies; he felt he had reason to fear the Lord's chastisement of the whole community if individual members of it succumbed, even in the privacy of their own homes, to the devil's temptations of alcohol and gambling and extramarital sex. He must therefore become, literally, his brother's keeper in matters of moral concern—was obliged to coerce his neighbor as well as himself into paths of righteousness, which he was inclined to define narrowly. But this was and is only the least attractive manifestation of the Kansan's religious concern—of his somewhat greater reverence for eternal verities, his somewhat greater concern for the fundamentals of life and conduct, his somewhat more strict and conscientious regard for right and wrong than is common elsewhere. There have been and are highly attractive manifestations as well—a genuine respect for other people and concern for their welfare, a scrupulous regard for the laws upon which a civilized community depends, a real human warmth and generosity and kindness, a generally prevailing human decency that must strike with particular force anyone coming into the state from eastern urban centers in the bicentennial year.

If there were to be (as I have long believed possible) a political and cultural renaissance in Kansas—if the centrality of the state in the nation were to become again vital and not merely that of a balance-point or wheel-hub—then the very essence of the contribution made by the state to the United States would be, I think, a renewed Puritan emphasis upon moral concerns, a renewed insistence upon individual moral responsibility. And surely such renewals are essential if we as a nation are to reaffirm in action, amidst the long and dreary aftermath of Vietnam and Watergate, the divine and human purposes for which, two hundred years ago, this Republic was founded.

Suggestions for Further Reading

Those desiring to go further into the Kansas story than permitted by the space limitations on this project may find useful the following partial list of books consulted by the author. Most of the titles are shelved in libraries of medium size.

Andreas, A. T. *History of the State of Kansas*. Chicago: A. T. Andreas, 1883.

Barry, Louise. *The Beginnings of the West, Annals of the Kansas Gateway to the American West, 1540–1854*. Topeka, Kan.: Kansas State Historical Society, 1972.

Boyer, Richard O. *The Legend of John Brown*. New York: Alfred A. Knopf, Inc., 1973.

Castel, Albert. *A Frontier State at War: Kansas, 1861–1865*. Ithaca, N.Y.: Cornell University Press, 1958.

———. *William Clarke Quantrill: His Life and Times*. New York: Frederick Fell, 1962.

———. *General Sterling Price and the Civil War in the West*. Baton Rouge, La.: Louisiana State University Press, 1968.

Connelley, William E. *Kansas and Kansans*. 5 vols. Chicago: Lewis Publishing Co., 1918.

———. *Life of Preston B. Plumb*. Chicago: Brown and Howell, 1913.

Cornish, Dudley T. *The Sable Arm: Negro Troops in the Union Army, 1861–1865*. New York: W. W. Norton and Co., 1966.

Crawford, Samuel F. *Kansas in the Sixties*. Chicago: A. C. McClurg, 1911.

Dary, David. *The Buffalo Book: The Full Saga of the American Animal*. Chicago: Swallow Press, 1974.

Davis, Kenneth S. *Soldier of Democracy: A Biography of Dwight Eisenhower*. New York: Doubleday and Co., 1945, 1952.

———. *River on the Rampage*. New York: Doubleday and Co., Inc., 1953.

Hale, Edward E. *Kanzas and Nebraska*. Facsimile of 1854 edition. Black Heritage Library Collection. Freeport, N.Y.: BFL Communications, Inc.

Hicks, John D. *The Populist Revolt*. Minneapolis: University of Minnesota Press, 1931.

Howes, Charles C. *This Place Called Kansas.* Norman, Okla.: University of Oklahoma Press, 1952.

James, Edwin. *An Account of an Expedition From Pittsburgh to the Rocky Mountains Performed in the Years 1819 and 1820.* 2 vols. Facsimile of 1823 edition. Westport, Conn.: Greenwood Press, Inc., 1968.

Johnson, Walter. *William Allen White's America.* New York: H. Holt, 1947.

Lowman, H. E. *Narrative of the Lawrence Massacre.* Lawrence, Kan.: State Journal Steam Press, 1864.

McNeal, T. A. *When Kansas Was Young.* New York: Macmillan Co., 1922.

Malin, James C. *John Brown and the Legend of Fifty-Six.* Negro History and Culture Series No. 100. Reproduction of 1942 edition. New York: Haskell House Publishers, 1970.

Manypenny, George W. *Our Indian Wards.* The American Scene Series, reproduction. New York: Da Capo Press, Inc., 1972.

Mechem, Kirke, editor; and Owen, Jennie Small, annalist. *Annals of Kansas, 1886–1925.* 2 vols. Topeka, Kan.: Kansas State Historical Society, 1954, 1956.

Miller, Nyle H. and Snell, Joseph W. *Why the West Was Wild.* Topeka, Kan.: Kansas State Historical Society, 1963. Paperback, *Great Gunfighters of the Kansas Cowtowns, 1867–1886.* Lincoln, Neb.: University of Nebraska Press, 1967.

Monaghan, Jay. *Civil War on the Western Border, 1854–1865.* Boston: Little, Brown and Co., 1955.

Nevins, Allan. *Ordeal of the Union.* 2 vols. New York: Charles Scribner's Sons, 1947.

————. *The Emergence of Lincoln.* 2 vols. New York: Charles Scribner's Sons, 1950.

Nichols, Alice. *Bleeding Kansas.* New York: Oxford University Press, 1954.

Nugent, Walter T. K. *The Tolerant Populist: Kansas Populism and Nativism.* Chicago: University of Chicago Press, 1963.

Pike, Zebulon M. *The Journals of Zebulon Montgomery Pike With Letters and Related Documents,* edited by Donald Jackson. 2 vols. Norman, Okla.: University of Oklahoma Press, 1966.

Ray, P. O. *Repeal of the Missouri Compromise.* Cleveland: Clark, 1909.

Richmond, Robert W. *Kansas, A Land of Contrasts.* Saint Charles, Mo.: Forum Press, 1974.

Robinson, Charles. *The Kansas Conflict.* Black Heritage Library Collection. BFL Communications, Inc. Facsimile of 1892 edition.

Robinson, Sara T. L. *Kansas: Its Exterior and Interior Life.* Boston: Crosby, Nichols and Co., 1856.

Sageser, A. Bower. *Joseph L. Bristow: Kansas Progressive.* Lawrence, Kan.: University Press of Kansas, 1968.

Sanborn, F. B. *Recollections of Seventy Years.* 2 vols. Reproduction of 1909 edition. Detroit: Gale Research Co., 1967.

Socolofsky, Homer. *Arthur Capper.* Lawrence, Kan.: University Press of Kansas, 1960.

Socolofsky, Homer, and Self, Huber. *Historical Atlas of Kansas.* Norman, Okla.: University of Oklahoma Press, 1972.

Speer, John. *Life of Gen. James H. Lane.* Garden City, Kan.: Speer, 1896.

Spring, Leverett W. *Kansas: The Prelude to the War for the Union.* Reproduction of 1906 edition. New York: AMS Press, Inc.

Stephenson, Wendell Holmes. *The Political Career of General James H. Lane.* Topeka, Kan.: Kansas State Historical Society, 1930.

Streeter, Floyd B. *The Kaw.* New York: Farrar and Rinehart, 1941.

Thayer, Eli. *A History of the Kansas Crusade.* Facsimile of 1889 edition. Freeport, N.Y.: BFL Communications, Inc.

Villard, Oswald Garrison. *John Brown, Eighteen Hundred to Eighteen Fifty-Nine: A Biography Fifty Years After.* New York: Peter Smith Publishers, Inc., 1910.

White, William Allen. *Autobiography of William Allen White.* New York: Macmillan Co., 1946.

―――. *Forty Years on Main Street.* New York: Farrar and Rinehart, 1937.

Williams, Burton J. *Senator John James Ingalls, Kansas' Iridescent Republican.* Lawrence, Kan.: University Press of Kansas, 1972.

Wilson, Don W. *Governor Charles Robinson of Kansas.* Lawrence, Kan.: University Press of Kansas, 1975.

Works Progress Administration, Federal Writers Project. *Kansas, a Guide to the Sunflower State.* New York: The Viking Press, 1939.

Zornow, William Frank. *Kansas, A History of the Jayhawk State.* Norman, Okla.: University of Oklahoma Press, 1957.

Index

Abilene: home of Eisenhowers, 203, 204, 205; of Eisenhower library, 210; mentioned, 110, 112, 116, 121, 152, 209

Agriculture: of Indians, 28–29; of free-soilers *vs.* slaveholders, 42; of frontier, 72–73; in state seal, 94–95; and dislike of farmers for longhorns, 109; attraction of immigrants to, 114–116; promotion by state government, 115; and technology of 1870s, 123–124; affected by financial combines, 138; and relation to 19th-century politics, 140–142, 147–151; growth of in World War II, 200–201; contribution to world order, 205; mentioned, 9. *See also* Farmers, Grasshopper plague, Kansas State Agricultural College, Wheat

Antislavery: suppressed in South, 23; growth of in North, 23; in U.S. Senate, 35–36; of westerners, 53–54; mentioned, 27, 96

Apache Indians, 14

Arapaho Indians, 101, 102, 103

Arikaree Creek, 103–104

Arkansas River, 16, 105, 107, 113

Artists: Kansas natives as, 190–191; and cultivation of art, 127–130

Atchison, Sen. David R.: on slavery in Nebraska Territory, 35–36; on slavery in Kansas, 40; as leader of Border Ruffians, 50; Grand Army of, 61–62

Atchison (city of): home of John J. Ingalls, 97; and overland freight trade, 98; newspapers of, 132, 134; bankruptcy of Kansas Trust and Mortgage Co., 159; site of aviation field, 200

Becker, Carl L. (quoted), 3–4, 169, 194

Beecher Island, battle of, 103–104

Bethany College, 129, 190

Big Springs convention, 52, 54, 56

Black Kettle (Cheyenne chief), 102, 105

Bluemont Central College, 45, 99

Bogus Legislature: passed proslavery laws, 50–51; intimidated governors, 63; ended, 69; and effect on local option laws, 144

Border Ruffians, 50, 53, 56

Brinkley, John R. (quack doctor), 183–184

Brown, John, 53–65 *passim;* at Harper's Ferry, 71; in poetry, 190; in Curry mural, 192

Buffalo: as meat for Indians, 13; scarcity of in 1863, 101; slaughter of, 106–108; collection of bones of, 121

Butterfield Overland Mail Co., 76

Capper, Sen. Arthur, 174, 176, 197

Cattle: trail drives, 108–112; cattlemen *vs.* farmers, 123–124; overgrazing, 126

Cheyenne Indians, 101, 102, 103, 106

Chippewa Indians, 29

Chisholm Trail, 110

Cimarron, 127, 182

Civil War: Kansas mortality rate in, 81–82; participation of Kansans in, 82; and ending of cattle prohibition, 109; mentioned, 83, 84, 86, 87, 88

Coffeyville, 91, 200

Comanche Indians, 14–15, 32–33, 101

Commerce and business: *See* Economics, Kansas

Compromise of 1820, 26–27

Coronado, Francisco Vasquez de, 15–18

Coronado Heights, 17

Council Grove, 32, 33, 99

County-seat wars, 125–126

Crawford, Samuel J.: in Civil War, 81, 83; elected governor, 85–86; appointed Edmund Ross to Senate, 89; quoted, 94; as

221

222   *Index*